The Healing Forces of MUSIC

The Healing Forces
of
MUSIC

HISTORY, THEORY and PRACTICE

by
RANDALL McCLELLAN, Ph.D.

Rockport, Massachusetts • Shaftesbury, Dorset

© Randall McClellan Ph.D.

Published in the U.S.A. in 1991 by
Element, Inc.
42 Broadway, Rockport, MA 01966

Published in Great Britain in 1991 by
Element Books Limited
Longmead, Shaftesbury, Dorset

Cover design by Max Fairbrother
Cover illustration by William D. Donovan
Textual illustrations © Deean Verrelli
Printed and bound in the U.S.A. by
Edwards Brothers, Inc.

Library of Congress Catalog Card Number available

ISBN 1-85230 – 255-0

Feeling the emptiness
at the center of things,

One experiences the
profound silence
Which is the birthplace of sounds,
of planets, of suns, of thoughts and
of life itself.

It is here that we hear the
Celestial Music
and
remember.

CONTENTS

INTRODUCTION

In the dim mists of our past, before the first civilizations, before the earliest agricultural villages, indeed before the concept of recorded time itself, lay the origins of what would be known as music. Born of a sense of communal sharing and our need to be more fully with each other, to understand the inter connectedness of the universe and our place within it, and to mark in a ritualistic way the various events in our life's passage, music gave expression to those thoughts and emotions too expansive and too deeply felt for our rudimentary languages.

It is doubtful that we shall ever know when or under what circumstances the first musical utterance was made, yet every culture developed some form of musical tradition and many of them possessed legends that pertain to the origin of music.[1] Almost all of these legends attribute a divine origin to music; in no case was music said to be invented by humans. In the world's mythologies music was either discovered or was bestowed on us by supernatural beings.

The earliest physical evidence of musical activity that we possess, a clay ocarina with five holes, bespeaks an already flourishing music as early as 10,000 B.C., whereas our emergence as a species has been dated to at least one hundred thousand years ago. So too, our earliest civilizations have been estimated to have been established no more than 8,000 years ago, yet within them we find evidence of an already flourishing culture where music occupied a well-regulated position in the social and religious life of its people.[2] In the approximately 95,000 years between these two points in time, our earliest ancestors began to attribute magical powers to sound — power over the spirit world, the natural world as they perceived it, and power to create and sustain human life.[3] It was this belief in the magic of sound that, in later civilizations, evolved into highly complex concepts of esoteric musical practice understood by an inner circle of the initiated.[4] Such esoteric concepts of music served as a complement to the exoteric musical practices which were practiced by the general public. Encompassing the categories of folk music, art music, and music intended for public religious and state ceremonies, exoteric musical practices are responsible for the incredible wealth of diversity in musical languages and styles that we enjoy today — a diversity, however, that is built on common cross-cultural principles. By contrast, esoteric musical concepts have been less culturally confined and, in fact, are more relatively uniform throughout history — in some cultures surviving almost unchanged to the present day.

Basic to these esoteric concepts is the belief that there are many levels of understanding inherent in each sound and that the listener perceives the meaning of the sound according to his level of spiritual awareness. Echoes of this belief sound throughout almost all successive civilizations and reverberate today in musical cultures where continuity of tradition is intact. In his study of Egypt, musicologist Henry Farmer concludes that music "had a two-fold influence on man in ancient Egypt: one brought about by purely physical sensation, and another created or sustained by a power known as *heka* or *hike*, which was something like, and yet different from, what we understand by 'spell'."[5] He then quotes an observation made by the Greek historian, Plutarch, that "All through the history of music in ancient Egypt, modulated sound itself was an arcanum. The name for sound was *herw* (lit. voice;), and the word had an esoteric import in the Cults."[6] Likewise, musicologist Lawrence Picken states that within the ancient Chinese concepts of music, "The belief in the power of music to sustain (or if improperly used, to destroy) Universal Harmony was but a further extension of the belief in the magic power of sounds. As a manifestation of a state of the soul, a single sound had the power of influencing other souls for good or ill. By extension, it could influence objects and all the phenomena of Nature."[7] Presumably, it was the level of understanding of the musician producing the sound that determined whether the music was properly or improperly used.

In the later Islamic cultures the same concepts are in evidence. Ibn Zaila (d. 1048) stated that "sound produces an influence in the soul in two ways: one on account of its musical structure (i.e., its aesthetic beauty), and the other because of its similarity to the soul (i.e., its spiritual meaning)."[8] According to Henry Farmer, "Sufi disciples, such as the Persian Al-Hujwiri (11th century) and Al-Ghazali (d. 1111), divided people influenced by music into two classes — those who hear material sound, and those who apprehend its spiritual meaning."[9]

At the core of all esoteric musical philosophy, examined later in greater detail, is the conviction that all of manifested creation is organized with and governed by one "root" sound that permeates the entire universe and everything within it. All of the energy of the universe is created from that one root sound and is in a continual state of transformation. At each succeeding moment, therefore, the manifested universe continues to be created anew in response to the continuous root sound that is the vehicle by which the manifested universe evolves from the unmanifested. Thus all of the manifested creation is in constant motion and the energy involved is never depleted.[10]

"Everything is in flux," the ancient Greek philosopher, Heraclitus, is reported to have said,[11] and in Indian philosophy, "everything is in motion — all matter is moving and changing its forms, and manifesting the energy within it. Suns and worlds rush through space, their particles constantly changing and moving."[12] The universe may be seen as an inseparable web where the inter connections are dynamic. Any change occurring in one area ripples in waves throughout the world, whether it be the explosion of a star, the disappearance of a galaxy, a sound sent forth from a musical instrument, or a thought from a human mind. Unmanifested creation, the source from which all manifested creation emanates, is the state of absolute perfection within which there is no movement. Absolute perfection means total immersion in the source of all things; it is the state of perfect balance, perfect unity and perfect repose. Therefore, everything in the perceived universe exists as the result of having moved away from perfect equilibrium and is continuously seeking to regain its state of perfect repose. The tension produced by these two forces creates a back-and-forth movement within all things. This movement is known as vibration, a state of constant unrest that seeks its own point of stillness within its center.

> All energy, all forces of the universe, are movements which emanate from one point — their own center — and radiate in circular waves in all directions, manifesting themselves as vibrations or oscillations. The manifestations cease only when the forces that have got out of balance regain their primordial state of equilibrium, the divine unity. Hence when we speak of the primordial state we mean the state in which all material phenomenon have ceased to exist. In its true essence matter, too, is motion, and if this motion comes to a stop, matter must necessarily cease to exist.[13]

All that exists in the manifested state does so because it has a complementary unmanifested state that is its source. We perceive light, therefore, in the manifested state only because there exists an unmanifested state which is total darkness. We perceive sound only because there is an unmanifested state of absolute silence, the state from which all sound originates. We hear sound only because there is silence; we experience silence only because there is sound. Therefore sound is the source of silence and silence is the source of sound. All sound dissolves into silence; silence tends to manifest into sound.[14] It is because of this principle of sound and silence that esoteric musical philosophy recognized two complementary components which in Sanskrit writings are referred to as "struck sound" — which we can hear — and "unstruck sound" — which we cannot hear. Unstruck sound is the center from which all struck sound emanates. Through the practice of music one may experience the state of absolute equilibrium, absolute balance, perfect unity and harmony which exists both at its center and our own, for both are identical to and inseparable from the unmanifested creative state of the entire universe. At the center lies the perfected emptiness of total union to which we, music, and all manifested things aspire.[15] "Things", in essence, are not "things" but processes in a state of continual becoming. Therefore music, as a manifestation of energy, is a force that interacts with the physical world for music influences our thoughts, our emotions, our dense physical bodies and the electro-magnetic field that surrounds us. Because all of the physical universe is in continual movement, Lama Govinda concludes...

> all things or beings produce sounds according to their own nature and to the particular state in which they find themselves. This is because these beings and things are aggregates of atoms that dance and by their movements produce sounds. When the rhythm of the dance changes, the sound it produces also changes... Each atom perpetually sings its songs and the sound creates each moment dense and subtle sound forms. Just as there exist creative sounds, there exist destructive sounds. He who is able to produce both can, at will, create or destroy.[16]

These philosophical concepts became the foundation upon which all musical practice of the ancient world was formed. The musicians, shamans, priests, prophets and philosophers held one philosophical concept in common — that music represents a microcosm of the order of the universe and follows cosmological laws, and that through the practice of music one could better understand these laws as well as the intelligence behind them. The ethereal quality of music was regarded as a miniature of the ethereal substance that filled the vast spaces of the cosmos within which the celestial bodies moved. The rhythm of music, for example, reflected the movement of galaxies, stars and planets, of the sun and moon, the cycle of seasons, days and nights, the tides of the seas and the birth and death of our own cells. Music was regarded as the force that could bring about harmony within the mind and body of Man, within the human community and ultimately with the heavenly bodies themselves — the fluidity of energy changing and merging with energy, the primordial force of the universe.

These concepts formed the basis of the practice of music as a healing force and gave birth to the many legends that recognized the power of music to effect change. Thus, among many of the world's cosmologies the universe began with a Sound.[17] For the Hopi people this sound was a creating song;[18] for the native peoples of Australia the sound was caused by beating the original seas with a reed.[19] The Ethiopians speak of a time when the first humans could only sing but eventually forgot the melodies and had to revert to the speaking of words,[20] while "in the language of the Ewe the word *lo* means both 'to sing' and 'to weave'."[21] For the people of India the whole universe "hangs on sound"[22] upon which all of human activity is dependent:

> By Sound the letter is formed, by letters the syllable, by syllables the word, by words this daily life. Hence this human world is dependent on sound.[23]

In the temples of Egypt, Greece and Rome residing priests chanted incantations as they administered medicine to the sick, while among the Ojibwa of North America the "jessakid," practitioners, sat near their patients and sang songs to the accompaniment of gourd rattles.[24] On the Aleutian Islands one may hear a story of the girl who raised a man from the dead by singing,[25] The Greek god of healing and music, Apollo, produced harmony in the heavens through his rhythmic movement through the heavens,[26] and his servant, Orpheus, applied remedies to body and soul through poetry, music, and medicine, and returned his beloved Eurydice to life with his song.[27] In Hindu mythology music was originally reserved for the Gods alone, but they took pity on the struggles of human beings and so brought music to them in order to relieve their suffering.[28]

In ancient China the new emperor called together his musicians the astrologers, both of whom were members of the Imperial Bureau of Weights and Measurers, and commanded them to determine the exact length of the Imperial Pipes in order to insure that the music played during his reign would be in accord with the heavenly bodies and therefore insure peace throughout the empire.[29] In the Greek epic, *The Odyssey*, the flow of blood from the wounds of Ulysses was stopped by the singing of Autolycus. Similarly, among the Winnebago and Lakota, shamans who obtained their power from the Bear Spirits were able to heal wounds with their songs.[30] The ancient Greek scientist, Pythagoras, freed the minds of his disciples from the cares of the day by playing music which would calm their minds and produce deep sleep and prophetic dreams. In the morning he banished the lingering effects of sleep by playing stimulating melodies and rhythms.[31] The legendary Orpheus, son of Apollo, could soothe the beasts of the forest and influence the Gods by the power of song alone.

Among the ancient Hebrews all prophets foretold the future through chanting, and Miriam, the sister of Moses, is said to have had immense visionary powers which were conveyed through chanting.[32] The young American Indian of the plains and Northwest fasted and meditated for four days and nights hoping for a vision of an animal spirit who would teach him a song of protection from harm for the duration of his life. Shamans cured disease and mental anguish by coaxing the evil spirits into leaving their victims through the power of chanting.[32] In Bali, in Africa, in the South Sea Islands and in the Arctic, entire villages would sing and dance themselves into a state of ecstasy and obtain visions while in Japan mendicant monks traversed the islands on foot, and played the shakuhachi in the belief that they could reach enlightenment through music,[33]

In the ancient kingdoms of Assyria, Babylonia, Sumeria and Egypt, musicians were priests who calculated the calendar and astrological measurements of the heavenly bodies, supervised all ceremonies and cured the sick.[34] To the ancient Hebrews and early Christians the singing of psalms was believed to have healing power.[35] The Talmud mentions a song which when sung is reported to protect one from epidemics,[36] and in the Old Testament King Saul's insanity was cured overnight by the power of David's harp.[37]

These stories — some mythological, some historical — represent but a handful of the many examples of the belief in the power of sound to sustain life and effect change that were held by our ancestors. Although, in most cases, they may not be regarded as evidence, they do provide clues to an understanding of the essential purpose of music as a means of healing. From them we may surmise that throughout those cultures which recognized the therapeutic value of music — and these may be in the majority — there have been two distinct approaches. One has combined rhythm and melody into songs created for specific healing purposes; its roots lie in the many shamanistic traditions of pre-history. The other has employed specific tones and mantric formula for their vibrational properties which were applied to specific parts of the body, melodies, to the extent that they are used, are generally incidental and of secondary importance.

The difference between these approaches is of great importance for they represent two distinctive but equally valid philosophies and methods. The former, which for the sake of convenience may be referred to as "music healing," begins the healing process through its influence on the emotions and mind first and the physical body second. The latter, which may be referred to as "sound healing," treats the body through resonance first and affects the emotions and mind second.

The esoteric philosophy and practice of music is our legacy and heritage — perhaps the oldest and most sacred of our musical traditions. Born of an awareness that in some way music-making helped us to feel bolder and less afraid, music was a vehicle through which we expressed the inter connectedness of our pulsing universe and the unity of its rhythmic cycles long before we were able to give verbal expression to the concepts that were beginning to take shape in our minds. And in that experience of union is music's primary value as a healing force. Overcoming the anxiety of separateness in a world so often perceived as hostile, music is the reassurance of the harmony and purposefulness, the essential order and beneficence of our universe.

PART ONE

Basic Concepts: Sound, Hearing and the Vibratory Nature of the Human Body

CHAPTER ONE

The Physical Manifestation of Sound

Sound is a form of energy which is caused by vibration. When sound is combined with rhythm the result is music. Therefore it is basic to an understanding of music's healing potential that we examine these two components in some detail not so much with the scientist's approach, for the scientific study of sound (acoustics) is highly complex,[1] but from the more immediately applicable approach of the musician.[2]

To begin, three conditions must be met before a sound can be produced. There must be:

1. A material that has the quality of elasticity.

2. An energy force which, when coming in contact with material, sets it in motion.

3. A medium through which the resulting sound will be carried.

By elasticity is meant the tendency of a body to return to its original state of rest after it has been displaced by a force that has been applied to it. The motion can best be illustrated by a pendulum in the following manner: (fig. 1)

When undisturbed the force of gravity keeps the pendulum in a state of rest. When the pendulum is pushed it moves in the direction of the applied force until it reaches its maximum point of deflection, whereupon it pauses briefly as the force of gravity overcomes the force which set it into motion. The pendulum now returns to its original point of rest, but because of momentum, a product of its mass × velocity, it passes its rest point until it reaches an equal distance in the opposite direction. Upon reaching this point the pendulum again pauses before returning to its point of rest. When it has returned to its point of rest we have one complete cycle, or one vibration, and the amount of time it has taken to complete this one cycle is its periodicity or natural rate of vibration. In truth, however, the pen-

FIGURE 1
Cyclic Motion of Pendulum

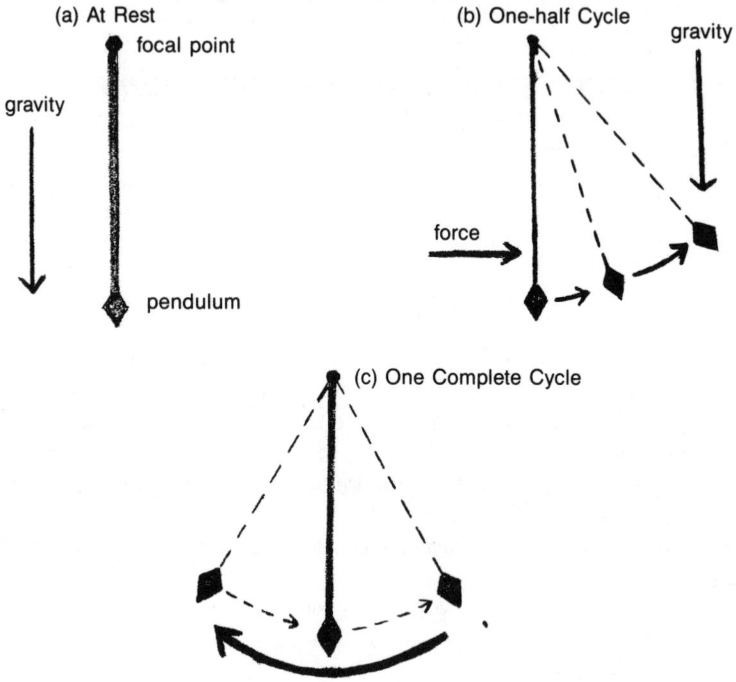

(a) At Rest

focal point

gravity

pendulum

(b) One-half Cycle

gravity

force

(c) One Complete Cycle

Cyclic Motion of String

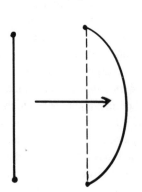

FIGURE 2
One-half cycle

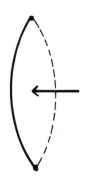

FIGURE 3
Complete cycle

dulum does not stop when it has reached its point of rest but will continue past the resting point to begin its second cycle. It will continue to swing back and forth, its arc becoming smaller each time, until the momentum of the force which originally set it into motion is overcome by the gravitational pull on its mass. The rate of time in which one cycle occurs depends upon the distance of the pendulum from the focal point while the distance of the arc made by the pendulum depends on the amount of force used to set it in motion. The farther the pendulum is from its focal point, the slower is its rate; the greater the force used to set it in motion, the wider is its arc. The two are independent of each other. Therefore, pushing the pendulum with more force does not result in a faster vibration rate but rather a wider arc which, if the pendulum was producing a sound, would determine its amplitude or loudness level. In other words, the greater the area of the arc the louder is its amplitude. A pendulum does not produce a perceivable sound, however, since its vibration rate is slower than the minimum required for us to hear. We will therefore consider the motion of a string, as found on a violin.

In contrast to a pendulum, a string is stationary on both ends. Because its weight is less and is under tension, its rate of vibration will be much faster. The natural frequency of the string is determined by three conditions:

1. Its length — the longer the string the lower its vibration rate and the longer its tone will last.

2. Its mass — the thicker the string, the slower will be its vibration rate.

3. Its tension — the greater its tension, the faster will be its vibration rate and the shorter will be its duration.

In other words, a long, thick string under little tension will vibrate at a slower rate than a short, thin string under great tension. However, there are many variables here: for example, a thin long string under little tension may vibrate at a slower rate than a thick short string under great tension. The point of greatest movement of the string will be its middle.

When a string is set into motion either by plucking it or by drawing a bow across it, the string will first move in the direction of the force which has been applied. Once again, the amount of force determines the amount of movement and therefore its loudness level. (fig. 2) When the string has reached its maximum point of deflection, determined by the amount of tension it is under, it pauses very briefly before returning to its original point of rest. However, its momentum carries it past this point until it reaches the point of maximum deflection in the opposite direction. (fig. 3 here) Again it pauses, then returns to its position of rest, which it passes again. One vibration has occurred. If left to vibrate freely it will continue this motion, each time covering less area (and therefore becoming gradually less loud) until its momentum is overcome by its tension and by friction with the air molecules around it.

FIGURE 4
Change in rate of Vibration by shortening string length

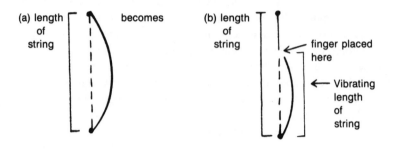

Frequency of "b" is higher than that of "a".

FIGURE 5
Segmented Motion of Vibrating String

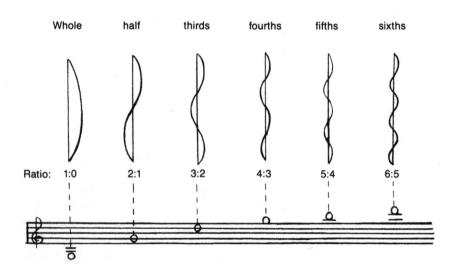

In order to change its rate of vibration we can shorten the vibrating length of the string by placing our finger on the string and pressing it against the fingerboard beneath it.[3] (fig. 4) What has been described, i.e., the vibration of the whole string as one unit, is called **simple harmonic motion**. But in actual fact strings vibrate in segments as well. When the string vibrates in segments it is known as **complex harmonic motion.**

Before we examine this fact of physical sound, it might be appropriate to pause for the purpose of clarifying some acoustical terms used thus far.

Rate of Vibration — the number of complete cycles of the vibrating body within a given time, usually seconds, expressed mathematically.

Frequency — the acoustical and objective term used to express the rate of vibration. For example, if the frequency is 440 cycles per second (C.P.S.), what we are saying is that the string completes 440 complete cycles each second.

Pitch — the subjective (or musician's) term to express the frequency of a tone by pitch names (a b c d e f g). Pitch is subjective because it is relative and arbitrary (i.e., depending on the culture and tuning system) and also because under certain conditions we might hear a pitch as lower or higher than its actual frequency.

Amplitude — the acoustical and therefore objective term for the amount of energy used to produce a tone. Amplitude is measured in "decibles" on a scale of 0 (silence) to 120 (maximum). A sound heard at 120 decibels would be physically painful.

Loudness — the subjective music term for amplitude. It is subjective because some tones require more energy than others to be heard at the same loudness level, the amount of which is determined by several factors.

Complex Harmonic Motion

A string, as mentioned earlier, does not just vibrate as a whole unit, but also in uniformly calculative segments as well. In Western culture this fact was first discovered and investigated by the Greek musician-mathematician-astronomer-mystic and found of the science of acoustics, Pythagoras[4] (c. 700 B.C.) although the Chinese and Hindus knew about it some time earlier. Pythagoras determined that a string vibrates not only as a whole but also in segments of halves, thirds, fourths, fifths, sixths, sevenths, eighths, and so on up to sixteenths. In order to get an accurate picture of a string in motion, each of these diagrams would have to be laid on top of each other for a composite image.[5] (fig. 5) Pythagoras further discovered that each segment vibrated in exactly the same manner as the whole string — with a back-and-forth motion — as the whole string but at a faster rate than the fundamental pitch. How much faster could be calculated by multiplying the fundamental frequency by the number of segments. This he expressed mathematically in the following way:

FIGURE 6
The Harmonic Series

segments:

1	2	3	4	5	6	7	8	9	10	11	12	13	14	15	16
	half	3rd	4th	5th	6th	7th	8th	9th	10th	11th	12th	13th	14th	15th	16th

harmonic:

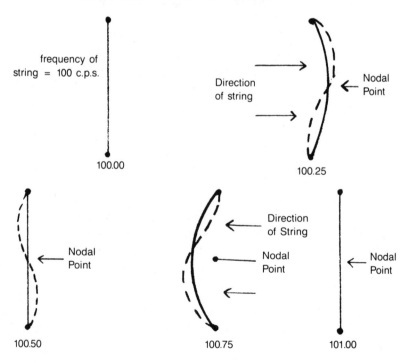

sounding
pitch

1*	2	3	4	5	6	7	8	9	10	11	12	13	14	15	16

(*not actual frequencies)

FIGURE 7
First Nodal Point of a Vibrating String
Time Period = 1/100th of 1 second

frequency of
string = 100 c.p.s.

100.00

Direction
of string

Nodal
Point

100.25

Nodal
Point

100.50

Direction
of String

Nodal
Point

100.75

Nodal
Point

101.00

$$X \times 1 = X$$
$$X \times 2 = 2X$$
$$X \times 3 = 3X$$
$$X \times 4 = 4X$$
$$X \times 5 = 5X; \text{ and so forth}$$

For example, if the fundamental frequency of the string is vibrating at 100 cycles per second then the frequencies produced by the segments are:

$$100 \times 2 = 200$$
$$100 \times 3 = 300$$
$$100 \times 4 = 400$$
$$\text{up to } 100 \times 16 = 1600 \text{ c.p.s.}$$

The principle (fundamental) tone plus its **"harmonics"** results in a sound of incredible richness. (fig. 6) This phenomenon, known as the **Harmonic Series**, is present in every tone used in music[6] whether it be the human voice, a stringed instrument or a wind instrument and is the reason why sound has the quality of aliveness to it. It is an unalterable fact of nature, and is the governing factor behind all musical practice and development.[7] There are several important observations to be made with regard to this harmonic series which are critical for an understanding of music and sound. First, it must be stressed that most of the time we are unaware of the existence of the upper harmonics unless we listen very carefully; they do not exist separately from the fundamental tone. Yet if we were to divide a string in half and touch the string lightly with our finger at the division point, we would hear the second harmonic. (Remember that each segment of the string is vibrating faster than the fundamental vibration!) Let us illustrate this point as it would occur in one complete cycle. (fig. 7) The string vibrating as a whole has completed one cycle, whereas the two segments have completed two cycles, vibrating, therefore, twice as fast. What has been referred to as the "cross-over" or "node" and is a place where, at the juncture of the two halves, there is no movement. It is the place where the violinist — or any other string player — would place his or her finger to produce a natural harmonic.

Second, not all of the harmonics are equally strong in loudness. Rather, they tend to diminish in strength the farther away from the fundamental pitch they are found. Thus harmonics two through eight are more prominent than harmonics nine through sixteen because the upper harmonics do not last as long as the lower harmonics. In most cultures the lower harmonics have had a greater influence on the development of music than the upper harmonics since the lower harmonics have greater force and energy. Because they have greater force, we are more greatly affected by them; the lower harmonics have more stability, the upper harmonics less so.

Third, the distance between each adjacent harmonic becomes progressively smaller as their distance from the fundamental tone increases. Between any two adjacent harmonics an interval is formed (an interval being the distance between two tones). Thus the distance between the fundamental tone (1) and the harmonic (2) is one octave; between two and three is a fifth; between three and four is a fourth; between four and five is a major third; between five and six is a minor third; between six and seven is another minor third (but smaller than the previous minor third); between seven and eight is a major second (but larger than the major second we now use); and between eight and nine another major second, smaller than the first and the one which was adopted as our major second for many centuries. It was through the harmonic series that Pythagoras was able to calculate the intervals which were used throughout the Western world until a different, more artificial tuning system was adopted — namely the predecessor of our present equal temperment scale.

PYTHAGORAS' CALCULATIONS

Harmonic	Interval	Ratio
1-2	octave	2:1
2-3	fifth	3:2
3-4	fourth	4:3
4-5	major 3rd	5:4
5-6	minor 3rd	6:5
8-9	major 2nd	9:8
15-16	minor 2nd	16:15

From Pythagoras' calculations it is possible to determine the frequencies of all the intervals if the frequency of one pitch is known. For example, if the first tone has a frequency of 100 cps and you wish to determine the frequency of the major second above it (i.e., from "Do to Re"), simple multiply 100 cps by nine, then divide by eight.

$$100 \times 9 = 900 \div 8 = 112.5 \text{ cycles}$$

Finally, it is through the harmonic series that we begin to understand the nature of **Tone Quality** or Timbre (pronounced 'tăm-ber'). Tone Quality depends on the degree of complexity of vibration; that is, the number of harmonics present and their relative intensities to each other. It is tone quality that enables us to distinguish the difference between any instruments that are sounding the same pitch. It is that which gives the clarinet its clarinet-ness the flute its flute-ness or accounts for the distinctiveness of each human voice.

A tone without harmonics sounds cold, lifeless and without character. Pure tones containing no harmonics are rare occurrences in the world of sounds. In the natural world the closest we can come to pure tones are: a flute played softly in its highest register, a child's singing voice in the upper register, and a tuning fork. However, pure tones (Sine tones) can be electronically generated in sound laboratories by acoustical scientists and in electronic music studies by composers. In an experiment conducted some years ago by Bell Laboratories, a tape recording was made of a piano, french horn and violoncello all producing the sound pitch, middle "C". The tape recording was then processed through a sound filter that eliminated all of the harmonics of each instrument. When the process was complete and all that remained was the fundamental pitch with no harmonics, the three instruments were indistinguishable from each other.

The quality or timbre of a tone results from a blend of the complex wave motion of the fundamental frequency plus its harmonics. We are able to discuss differences between musical instruments or between two voices because each instrument and each voice accentuates some harmonics and attenuates others. Additionally, the timbre changes for each instrument or voice as it moves from note to note or from low to middle to high register, or from soft to loud dynamic. We hear these harmonics in the composite effect of the tone, and they are the cause of the infinite number of possible variations in timbre. The greater the number of harmonics present and the stronger they are, the more rich, brilliant, cutting or even strident the tone quality becomes.

The louder the tone, the more complex it becomes; also the lower the tone the more complex—and therefore richer—it becomes. If tones become too complex or too great in irregularity of vibration form, the result is "noise". Sound with no distinguishable fundamental frequency, such as the hiss of a steam pipe, or ocean surf, or the roar of a jet plane, is called "white noise" because it contains all of the frequencies and harmonics of the sound spectrum. It is comparable to white light which contains all colors of the spectrum within it. White noise, then, stands at the opposite extreme of the sine tone; between them lies the incredibly rich and endless palette of our sound world, from the deep tones of the pipe organ to the crystal clear tones of the upper register of the piccolo.

Wave Motion

Sound, unlike light, cannot move through a vacuum; it needs a medium to carry it from its place of origin to our ears. Sound waves also contrast with light waves in two other respects. First, light waves can be directed from their source in a straight line without necessarily illuminating anything behind it — an obvious example being a flashlight — whereas sound moves outward in spherical waves from its source in all directions. Consequently, no matter where we might be in relation to a sound source — behind it, above it, below it, in front of it, or beside it — we hear it.

Second, sound unlike light can move through solid substances such as walls, steel, wood and the human body. Obviously, however, the most common medium for sound is the air around us.

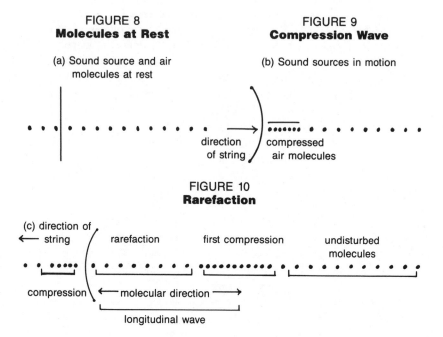

FIGURE 8
Molecules at Rest

(a) Sound source and air
molecules at rest

FIGURE 9
Compression Wave

(b) Sound sources in motion

direction
of string

compressed
air molecules

FIGURE 10
Rarefaction

(c) direction of
← string

rarefaction   first compression   undisturbed
molecules

compression ←— molecular direction —→

longitudinal wave

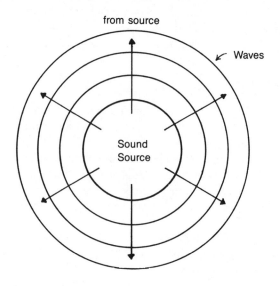

FIGURE 11
Diffusion of Sound Waves

from source

Waves

Sound
Source

Longitudinal Wave Motion

Air consists of molecules (themselves consisting of conglomerates of atoms) that, when at rest might look somewhat like this::::::::. When disturbed by a sound, these molecules respond by moving back and forth, alternately compressing and rarefying the space between them. (fig. 8) Pictured in Figure 8 is the hypothetical condition of both air molecules and the sound source, a string, in a state of complete rest — a condition of no movement. (fig. 9) When the string is set into motion and begins its first cycle the air molecules nearest to the string are compressed. When the string moves to the second phase of its motion these same molecules spread wider apart in what is called rarefaction, but the wave action continues to move outward in a domino-like action which causes the adjacent molecules to become compressed. (fig. 10) The motion of the molecules is confined to a slight back and forth movement at the same rate as the vibrating string; it is the wave motion itself that continues to move outward in a motion that can be compared to the ripples in a pond when a pebble is thrown into it. (fig. 11) Sound waves, therefore, spread outward in every direction and are thwarted in this tendency only when an obstruction is placed before them. This spreading out in spherical waves is called diffraction.

A simple sound wave consists of a pulse of compression and a pulse of rarefaction. The frequency of a sound wave is measured by the number of complete waves to pass a given point in some second. The sound wave's **Period** is the amount of time required for it to pass a given point. If one counts 440 waves in a second, that is its frequency; its period is 1/440 of a second. These sound waves are in fact waves of pressure which can be felt. When these pressure waves reach our ears, our ear drums (called the "tympanic membrane") respond to the pressure by vibrating at the same rate as the sound wave, whose pressure rate was determined by the original sound source.

Speed of Sound

The rate of speed in which sound travels through air is determined by the temperature of the air and is independent of the sound's frequency. Thus the low rumble of thunder and the scream of a factory whistle travel at the same rate. At 32 °F sound travels through air at the rate of 1088 feet per second. The rate increases by 1.1 feet per second per one degree increase in temperature and decreases by 1.1 feet per second per one degree decrease in temperature. At 44 °F the speed of sound increases to 1100 feet per second (750 miles per hour), which is still very slow when compared to the speed of light, 186,000 *miles per second*. It takes only between eight and nine minutes for the light from the sun to reach the earth, yet a sound originating from the sun would not reach us for 591.4 days — and then only if the temperature "out there" were a constant 44 °F which, of course, it isn't!

As a carrier of sound waves air is not nearly as efficient as other materials such as wood, steel, or water. The molecules in these materials are much closer together and have greater elasticity. Sound travels through water approximately five times faster and with greater force than through air. For this reason the sound of a whale at sea can be heard for miles beneath the water and music played through underwater speakers has a stronger force. Remember also that our body chemistry is at least 75% water and that sound may be traveling through us at all times. (One of the areas of study, as yet unexplored, is the possible therapeutic application of underwater sound waves on a human body which is also immersed in water.) Sound travels through wood and steel with even greater speed and is amplified as well. A wristwatch cannot be heard in a room at a distance of twenty feet, but if a wooden rod were placed with one end touching the watch and the other end placed against your ear the sound would be transmitted through the rod and the watch could then be heard quite easily. Wood and metal, of course, are the principal materials from which we make our musical instruments.

Wave Length

Sound waves are not uniform in size but vary according to frequency — the higher the frequency the shorter the wavelengths. The distance from one compression pulse to the adjacent compression pulse is equal to one wavelength. To find the wavelength of any sound we simply divide the speed of sound by the frequency. Below are some representative frequencies and their wavelengths calculated with the speed of sound at 1100 feet per second.

	frequency	wavelength
Lowest audible tone	20 cps	55 feet
Lowest C on piano	32.7 cps	33.6 feet
Middle C	261.6 cps	4.2 feet
Concert "A"	440 cps	2.5 feet
Highest "C" on piano	4,186 cps	2.6 inches
Highest audible tone	20,000 cps	.55 inches

The longer the wave, the farther it can travel because longer waves have both more energy and the ability to bend around obstacles such as walls or trees. Sounds of short wavelengths have less energy to carry them great distances and are easily deflected by obstacles. This explains why we hear only the bass drums and tubas of an outdoor band playing at a great distance away. When the band moves closer to us, or we to it, the trombones, trumpets, clarinets, and finally cymbals, flutes and piccolos can be heard.

Resonance

If you were to place ten tuning forks of the same frequency near each other in a standing position and then strike one of them so that its tone would sound, the remaining nine tuning forks would also sound. However, if you were to add one more with a different frequency and strike it, the original ten tuning forks would remain silent. A singer standing before a wine glass matches her pitch to the exact frequency of the glass and shatters it with her voice. Soldiers marching along a road approach a bridge and are trained to "break step" to avoid any possibility that the frequency of the marching cadence may match the frequency of the bridge and cause it to shatter beneath them as they cross. A violin string held between the hands and plucked does not sound very loud, but when it is placed on the violin it can be heard throughout the concert hall. The sound of the string has been reinforced by the body of the instrument; the sound-post beneath the bridge connects the top and bottom of the body causing the hollow space inside the instrument to vibrate.

All of these examples demonstrate the principle of "resonance" — the ability of a substance such as wood, air, metal, and living flesh to vibrate sympathetically to a frequency imposed from another source. The ability of a substance to resonate sympathetically is the result of its elasticity. Among the most elastic substances are air, water, some woods, the human body and our earth itself. (Other factors, such as shape and molecular structure, contribute to the resonating ability of any material.)

All material substances have natural resonating frequencies. If you tap the edge of a good quality wine glass, the resulting tone is the natural frequency of that glass. Other examples include the wooden "keys" of a marimba as well as all bells and organ pipes. These are rather obvious examples, yet other materials have their own natural frequencies — materials such as table, chairs, buildings, rocks, bridges. The natural frequency of any substance is determined by its weight, mass, shape and molecular construction.

We can divide resonating substances into two types: those that resonate only with their natural frequency, such as tuning forks, and those that have the ability to resonate at a variety of frequencies. The first is "free" resonance and the second is referred to as "forced" because the sounding frequency forces its tone upon the resonating body. Forced resonance is by far the most important of the two for musical purposes. Two of the main components enabling us to hear music, the air that carries the sound impulses and our tympanic membrane (ear drum), both respond to forced resonance. Water also responds to the forced resonance as do all of the materials from which we construct our instruments. But beyond this, the Earth is a resonator as well as the air that surrounds the Earth and the water of our oceans, seas, lakes, rivers and ponds. Therefore, every sound made on the Earth potentially resonates through it and round it — every note of music, every cry of despair or joy, the sound of the new born and dying, the shout of anger and the entonings of love, sounds of war and of celebrations, of earthquakes and of our thoughts malevolent and benevolent. (Of course we don't hear them all with our physical ears, but perhaps on some level we are influenced by them.

The Microcosmic World of the Atom[9]

One of the basic tenets of the early mystic schools, of the principle Eastern religions and of the philosophers and scientists (the two were once synonymous) of ancient Greece was that the universe is an interconnected web of vibrating energy. What appeared to our senses as solid consisted, in fact, of groupings of very small moving particles. To these philosophers all things were in a state of constant motion, constant flux. They believed, therefore, that the "material" world is energy.

It was also believed that all of the energy of the universe was created at the instant of the creation of the universe. Energy, the cause and result of the creation of the universe, was always involved with motion, the total energy involved being always conserved.

Recent advances in the study of physics demonstrates that modern science is finally catching up to those ancient mystics! Quantum theory now states that matter is always in a state of motion. This implies that energy is "locked up" in the "mass" of an object and that mass can, therefore, be transformed into other forms of energy. In other words, "mass" is a form of energy! The smallest components of our material universe, what used to be referred to as the primary building blocks, are atoms. Atoms consist of a nucleus at the center and smaller particles called "electrons" which circle the nucleus at a speed of 600 miles per second. The number of electrons in an atom of an element determines that element's chemical properties. Electrons are retained by the nucleus by electronic forces which pull them inward while centrifugal force, the result of their velocity, enables them to maintain an orbital distance. Atoms were once compared to the solar system — a star at the center with planets moving around it. More recently it has been discovered that the electrons create standing waves around the nucleus. Because of their extremely high velocity the individual electron cannot actually be seen; only the wave created by the electron is observable. In appearance, a closer analogy might be the planet Saturn with its rings, except that "Saturn" would be extremely small and the "rings" would be more like a visual illusion.

The diameter of an atom is one hundred millionth of a centimeter while the nucleus is one hundred thousand times smaller than the whole atom. The nucleus is made up of neutrons and protons packed so densely that they are caused to move at a rate of 40,000 miles per second. The nucleus has been characterized as "tiny drops of an extremely dense liquid which is boiling and bubbling fiercely".[10] Molecules, mentioned earlier, consist of large assembledges of atoms packed tightly together in various densities, which account for the relative "hardness" or "softness" of the "material" world.

Finally, there is no more impressive or dramatic a description of the atom than that provided by Fritjof Capra in his book, *The Tao of Physics*:

"In an orange, blown up to the size of the Earth, the atoms of the orange will be the size of cherries tightly packed into a globe the size of the Earth...Blow up the atom to the size of the largest dome in the world, St. Peter's Cathedral in Rome. In an atom that size the nucleus would be the size of a grain of salt, a grain of salt in the middle of the dome of St. Peter's and specks of dust whirling around it in the vast space of the dome—this is how we can picture the nucleus and electrons of an atom."[11]

FIGURE 1

1. External ear
2. Auditory canal
3. Eardrum
4. Hammer
5. Anvil
6. Stirrup
7. Oval Window
8. Cochlea
9. Acoustic Nerve
10. Round Window
11. Eustacian Tube

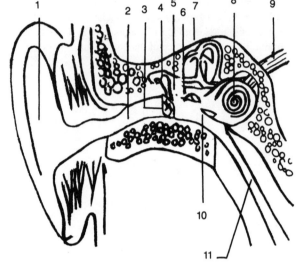

FIGURE 2
Middle Ear

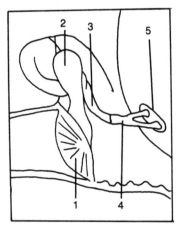

1. Eardrum
2. Hammer
3. Anvil
4. Stirrup
5. Oval Window

FIGURE 3
Inner Ear

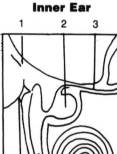

1. Foot plater of stirrup against oval window
2. Saccule
3. Endolymph duct
4. Round Window
5. Cochlear duct
7. Cochlea

CHAPTER TWO

The Process of Physical-Psychological Hearing

We have examined in some detail two of the three components that enable us to experience the environment of sound: the action of the source of sound — vibration, and the process by which sound is moved from its source. It now remains for us to examine the process through which we internalize sound by means of our faculty of hearing. Since hearing is both a physiological and psychological response to the stimulation of pressure waves we shall examine both, beginning with the physical characteristics of the ear.

Our sense organ for hearing has three parts: the **outer ear** consisting of the external parts, the ear canal extending an inch and a quarter into the head, and the eardrum (tympanic membrane) which is about a quarter of an inch in diameter and three-hundredths of an inch thick and located at the end of the ear canal; the **middle ear** consisting of three small bones called "hammer, anvil, and stirrup"; and the **inner ear** containing the "cochlea" which looks like a very small snail shell one-quarter inch in diameter at its open end. (fig. 1)

The purpose of the outer ear, shaped like a spiral, is to "catch" vibrations traveling through the air (or water if one is immersed) and to channel them into the ear canal. Its structure is such that it is most efficient for channeling sound waves in front of us and less so for waves behind us. (Perhaps this is the result of evolution when our survival required a highly developed ability to both see and hear possible danger before us. The fact that there are a few people today who can "wiggle" their ears invites speculation that at one time in our evolutionary development we all might have possessed the ability to move our ears as do many mammals today.)[1] We hear binaurally and the distance between our two ears enables us to locate the direction of a sound's source and to calculate its distance from us. Thus we are able to distinguish foreground sound from background sound and to "pick out" specific sounds from what otherwise might be an undifferentiated flat "wall of sound".[2] The current theory as to why binaural hearing allows

FIGURE 4
Cochlea, cross section

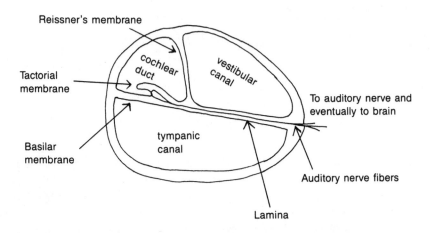

FIGURE 4a
Cochlea, uncoiled and also as if cut through lamina so as to lay it open:

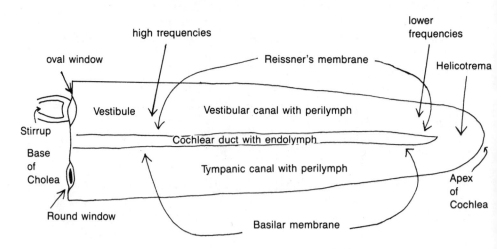

us to locate directions of sound (and it is still unproven), is that sounds originating on one side of us reach the ear on that side a fraction of a second sooner than the other side whereas a sound directly in front reaches both ears at the same instant. Regardless of whether this theory of binaural hearing can be proven, the fact remains that binaural hearing is an important factor in our ability to differentiate the various components that characterize a musical composition — melody from harmony, melody from melody when played at the same time, foreground material from supporting material — and to follow the various rhythmic, harmonic and melodic ideas as they flow from one instrument to another.

The sounds that we hear are directed through the opening of the external ear and into the ear canal, a funnel-like passage that terminates at the eardrum one and a quarter inches inside the head. The ear canal is shaped to concentrate the pressure waves and direct them to the eardrum.

Consider for a moment the marvelous and miraculous ability of the tympanic membrane, a translucent wisp of elastic flesh, one-quarter inch in diameter and three hundredths of an inch thick, which can accurately transmit every vibration of every instrument of a large symphony orchestra (over 105 performers) both individually and as a whole at every fraction of a second — every note of every instrument plus all the harmonics of every note and every sound characteristic of every instrument, and all the new frequencies created by the harmonics of all these instruments as they interact with each other! Now add to this a chorus of 500 voices, a children's choir, eight soloists and an organ, timpani rolls, bass drum and three well placed strokes of a giant orchestral gong. Into this incredible complexity mix the extraneous rustlings, coughings, sneezes of a concert audience and, for fun, a jet plane flying overhead from left rear to right front — all of this complex sound channeled without distortion into a thin channel in our head and into a thin membrane smaller than the head of a thumb tack that responds by vibrating with all those frequencies.

There are many mysteries concerning the functioning of our senses and one of them is how such a small piece of human anatomy can register and transmit all of those sounds without any effort on our part. For us to be able to hear the sounds just described our eardrum must physically vibrate all of the frequencies. It does so because the eardrum, like the violin string, can vibrate as a whole and in all of the segments necessary to accommodate that massive sound. In other words, the complex pressure waves created in the air by this musical performance cause the eardrum to vibrate with the same pressure pattern and actual physical movement or complex of movements made by the sound source. But the mystery doesn't end here. For although we can describe what happens, we cannot comprehend how it happens. We can describe the motion of the eardrum; we cannot comprehend how so tiny a surface can vibrate with such complexity.[3]

Located directly behind the eardrum are the three small bones of the middle ear. Less than half an inch in length, the hammer, anvil and stirrup — so called because of their resemblance to their namesakes — transmit the vibratory actions of the eardrum to the cochlea of the inner ear. One end of the hammer rests against the eardrum while the other end is in contact with the anvil. The anvil touches the end of the stirrup while the other end of the stirrup rests against a small opening to the cochlea called the oval window. The total distance from the eardrum to the oval window is one centimeter. Because we live in an environment of constant sound, both externally and internally, these bones are in constant motion from before birth to death — even when we sleep. The louder the sounds, the greater is the movement of these bones. As we age, the hammer, anvil and stirrup tend to deteriorate somewhat, resulting in some hearing loss of the upper frequencies as the bones become more rigid. The three bones of the middle ear are the only part of the skeletal system that do not grow in size. They are fully mature at birth. (fig. 2)

The footplate of the stirrup rests against the oval window which is the entrance to the inner ear. Just inside the oval window is an irregularly shaped chamber called the vestibule at the end of which is found the cochlea. A very small shell-shaped chamber less than half an inch in diameter at its larger end, and less than one and a quarter inches in length when uncoiled, it is in the cochlea that the physical pressure waves — as vibrations — are transformed into electrical nerve impulses that are carried by the auditory nerve to the brain. (fig. 3) As can be seen in figure 4 and 4A, a cross section of the cochlea reveals a division into three chambers with the cochlea duct and vestibule canal on top divided by a thin membrane and the tympanic canal on the bottom. Each of these chambers is filled with a liquid substance called "perilymph". Separating the upper chambers from the lower chamber — in a sense floating in the perilymph — is another membrane, the basilar membrane. This membrane contains the organs that transmit the vibrations through the oval window causing the perilymph to vibrate. (It should be remembered that vibrations through liquid are much stronger than through air!) Studies indicate that the area near the base of the cochlea is more sensitive to higher frequencies; the area near the apex of the cochlea is more sensitive to the lower frequencies. The "round window" is covered with a thin membrane that vibrates with the movement of the perilymph.

Located on top of the basilar membrane (which consists of 10,500 transverse fibers) are the micro-structures which mark the end of the journey of physical vibration from the sound source — 30,000 deiters cells, each one joined to a hair cell around which are wound several auditory nerve fibers. (fig. 5) Each fiber contacts several neighboring hair cells. Resting on top of each hair cell are between eight and twelve auditory receptor cells (cilia). These are stimulated by vibrations in the endolymph when the hair cell is subjected to a mechanical deformation — due to the up and down displacement of the basilar membrane — as the hair cell reacts to pressure from the tympanic canal's perilymph which generates an electrical charge. This electrical charge stimulates the entwined auditory nerve fibers to fire a pulse to the auditory nerve, which is transmitted to the brain. Exactly how this occurs is not known, although several theories have been deve-

FIGURE 5
Micro-anatomy of the cochlea

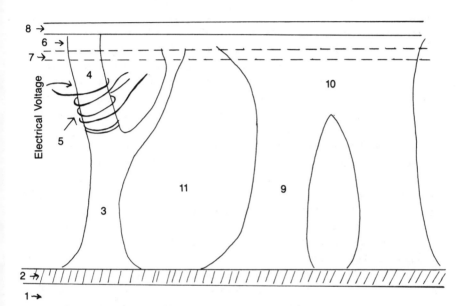

1. Tympanic Canal with perilymph
2. Basilar membrane marked with its transverse fibers (10,500).
3. Deiters cell (one of 30,000).
4. Hair cell (one of 30,000).
5. Auditory nerve fibers (several of 30,000). Several auditory nerve fibers are entwined about the lower end of each hair cell, and each fiber contacts several neighboring hair cells.
6. Cilia (hairs) of hair cell. When hair cell is subjected to a mechanical deformation (due to the up-and-down displacement of the basilar membrane as it reacts to pressure from the tympanic canal's perilymph) it generates an electrical charge which stimulates the entwined auditory nerve fibers.
7. Reticular membrane—dotted lines are meant to suggest that it is merely a mosaic consisting of the headplates which terminate the branches of the Deiters cells, the extensions of arches and the collars through which the cilia of the hair cells protrude.
8. Tectorial membrane—cilia probably maintain contact with Tectorial membrane during excitation of the hair cell.
9. Rods of Corti (two of 4500).
10. Arch of Corti.
11. Entire superstructure above basilar membrane is known as Organ of Corti.

loped over the years. Of these the one which is considered to be the most viable is known as Wever's Volley-Place Theory.

In order to illustrate this complex theory let us make three assumptions for the sake of convenience. First, let us assume that there are six auditory nerve fibers wrapped around a hair cell. Second, let us assume that we are hearing a frequency of 1200 cycles per second at low intensity. The Volley-Place Theory is derived from several observations. First, when a nerve fiber "fires" it needs a small amount of recovery time before it is ready to respond again. Thus there is a maximum limit to the number of times a nerve fiber can "fire" an electrical impulse per second. The limit appears to be a factor of its placement on the basilar membrane and of the intensity of the impulse. At the place of greatest sensitivity along the basilar membrane the maximum firing rate of a nerve fiber is 200 times per second if the intensity is low. However, the same nerve fiber can be forced to fire at a rate of 300 times per second by increasing the intensity of the sound. Yet the nerve fiber can fire at this rate for only a short time before fatigue sets in. Once fatigue sets in, the nerve fiber ceases firing altogether for a period of time during which we experience hearing loss. The greater the intensity and the longer its duration at that intensity, the greater is the necessary amount of recovery time for that nerve fiber. Repeated exposure to sounds of high intensity will result in permanent damage to these fibers.

The second part of the Volley-Place Theory states that because the limit of a nerve fiber is 300 firings per second, frequencies above 300 cycles require that several nerve fibers cooperate in a relay volley system. If this was not the case, so the theory states, we would be unable to hear frequencies above 300 cycles. In fact, high frequencies and high intensities require the participation of many nerve cells and nerve fibers. The higher the frequency and/or the greater the intensity, the more nerve cells are involved.

Twelve cycles of our frequency of 1200 c.p.s., representing a time span of 0.01 second, is shown in figure 6A. At low intensity each nerve fiber rests for five cycles after each "firing". Fiber (a) fires on one, fiber (b) on two, fiber (c) on three, fiber (d) on four, fiber (e) on five, fiber (f) on six at which point fiber (a) fires once more on seven and the process repeats itself, 200 times per second. In figure 6B the greater intensity causes two nerve fibers to fire at the same time, resting the three cycles before firing again. Thus each fiber fires a total of 300 times per second. We can see from this illustration that the perception of relative loudness and softness is determined by the number of nerve fibers and hair cells that are caused to fire. The greater the energy of the sound waves, the more nerve fibers are excited.

The resulting electrical charges are carried along the auditory nerve to the thalamus that rests on top of the brain stem. From the thalamus the nerve impulses are relayed to the cortex where they are registered according to their frequencies. The function of the thalamus is to integrate all incoming sense data, which now are received as electrical impulses, and relay them to appropriate areas of the cortex.

Wrapped around the thalamus is the limbic system. Although not fully understood, it is believed that the limbic system contributes to our emotional response to playing or hearing music. A deeper understanding of the thalamus, limbic system and cortex may reveal the answer to the question of why we respond emotionally to music. The answer may involve an understanding of the inter-relationship of the auditory nerve, thalamus, limbic system, cerebral cortex, and the glandular system.[4]

We have followed the journey of a sound from its source, through air, into the three parts of the ear and into the cerebral cortex of the brain which is its final destination. Having completed the physical journal of sound, we will now examine the psychological phenomenon of hearing. The physiological process we have traced thus far is common to all members of the human species regardless of environment, race, or cultural considerations. All sounds within one's environment follow this path, yet only a portion of these sounds reach the level of our conscious awareness. When these sounds are consciously perceived the physiological process of hearing becomes a psychological process. A sound becomes consciously perceived when it is of sufficient loudness to catch our attention or when our hearing is in a state of heightened awareness.

Acoustical scientists have derived a means of measuring loudness levels that covers the entire range of hearing from zero to 120 decibels. Zero decibels is referred to as the "threshold of hearing" and is the point at which a sound is just barely heard. At 120 decibels we experience what is called the "threshold of pain"; it is the point which sound becomes so loud as to cause physical pain. Prolonged exposure to a sound at 120 decibels may cause permanent damage to the delicate structures of the middle and inner ear. In a quiet room a whisper might measure about twenty decibels; a medium sized room in which three or four people are talking in normal voices might measure between fifty and sixty decibels; the sound of a pencil dropping to the floor would not be heard. It would be, therefore, below the threshold of hearing. However, if the room is empty, the sound of the dropping pencil would be easily heard. Sounds in the range of zero to forty-five decibels require an increasingly heightened aural sensitivity on the part of the listener resulting from physical and mental relaxation, mental alertness and interest, and an emptying of the mind's preoccupation with cognitive thinking. For example, as these words are being written it is nearly one o'clock in the morning. I am sitting near an open window in a house where there is no traffic. There is soft spring rain and my radio is quietly playing a Schubert string quartet. Although my consciousness is aware of both the rain and the music my mind is occupied with the writing of these thoughts so there are long moments when I hear neither the rain nor the music. If I pause from writing and listen to the music, the rain becomes background. However, I do have another choice and that is to relax and open my hearing facility to enable me to hear both the music and the rain as complementary to each other and as equal components of my environment at this time.

Of course, as I begin writing again, both the rain and the music fade into the background and disappear from my conscious awareness. Yet the sounds are still traveling into my ears, along my auditor nerves to my brain at the same loudness level. It is only my perceptual awareness that has changed.

Hearing, then, is as much a matter of the mind as it is a matter of the brain. Once a sound enters our awareness and we choose to give it some attention, a very personalized psychological hearing process begins. Our first step is to subject the sound to a memory check based on our assessment of the sound's characteristics. We determine whether that sound (or music) has been encountered before, if so under what circumstances, and what was the response at that time. Figure 7 illustrates the path of our process of psychological hearing.

Following a memory check the process of evaluation begins as we assess our physical, emotional, cognitive and spiritual reactions. Here a sampling of questions are put forth: What does the sound do to my body, breathing, heart rate, muscles? How does the sound affect me emotionally? Is it interesting to me at the present time? What happens to the sound? Does it satisfy a kind of spiritual need? Does it have any recognizable syntax? For answers to these questions we call upon our cultural conditioning and consult our personal biases as part of the evaluation. On the basis of this internal process we either approve or disapprove of the experience. Finally we give an external response — one in which we either leave the environment of the sounds, ignore the sounds or continue to listen. In either case, the experience is recorded as another piece of information in our memory banks for possible future reference.

Music results from our biological, affective, cognitive and spiritual processes and is an inherently human activity. Likewise, we respond to music on all four levels. Biological response involves body processes such as breathing rate and depth, heart rate and the like. Affective response involves emotion. Cognitive response involves aesthetic satisfaction and stimulation. A spiritual response is tranpersonal in that we experience something transcendental. We feel a wholeness greater than individual awareness and a unity of universal forces and human experience. A complete musical response is one that occurs at all four levels. The degree to which music manifests biological, affective, cognitive and spiritual processes depends on cultural conditioning, social values and personal bias. The ability to respond to music on all four levels is a matter of personal choice.The American composer Harry Partch (d 1974) wrote in 1947:

> Music, 'good' and 'not good', has only two ingredients that might be called God-given: The capacity of a body to vibrate and produce sound and the mechanism of the human ear that registers it. These two ingredients can be studied and analyzed, but they cannot be changed; they are the comparative constants. All else in the art of music, which may also be studied and analyzed, was created by man or is implicit in human acts and is therefore subject to the fiercest scrutiny — and ultimately to approval, indifference or contempt. In other words, all else is subject to change.
>
>   Implicit in the man-made part of the musical art are (1) an attitude toward one's fellow man and all his works; (2) a source scale and (3) a theory for its

FIGURE 6a
Wever's Volley-Place Theory

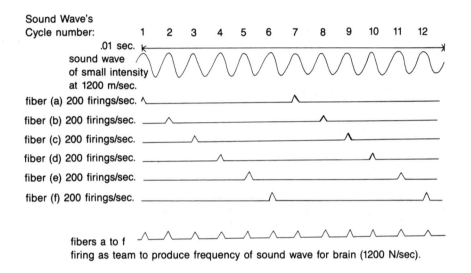

fibers a to f
firing as team to produce frequency of sound wave for brain (1200 N/sec).

FIGURE 6b

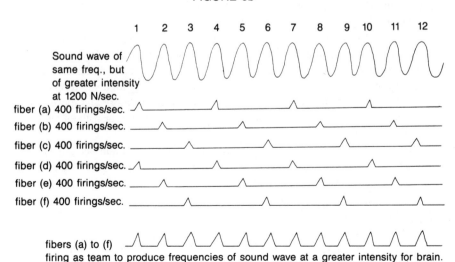

firing as team to produce frequencies of sound wave at a greater intensity for brain.

Use; (4) more than occasionally a vocal design; (5) a complexity of organized tones which we call a composition; (6) a musical instrument or instruments; (7) a powerful emotional reaction to the composition.[5]

The characteristics listed by Partch are subject to infinite variation throughout the musical languages of the world and they account for the incredible richness of musical expression available to us. We are limited only by our willingness and openness to fully experience different musical languages and to be enriched and expanded through that process.

Beneath the complexities of the musical differences which occur on a surface level, the same emotions, concerns and thoughts find expression throughout our world's musics. All we need do is to choose to hear.

Preparation for Hearing

"Hearing means breathing."

—Charlotte Selver—
founder of Sensory Awareness Training

It is important to remember that our senses receive and respond to sensory stimuli. As such, we cannot project them outward. We can, however, restore their efficiency as receivers through an active-passive process of relaxation. When we wish to rest our eyes we massage our facial muscles, we close our eyelids and we diminish visual stimuli by entering a dimly lit room. In other words, we can voluntarily control the amount and variety of what we see.

Such is not the case with hearing. Because there is no direct way to regulate or terminate the amount of incoming sound, we resort to the secondary method of increasing the tension of our jaw, scalp and neck muscles. Most of the time we are not aware of this condition or that our hearing has become restricted. We may not even notice that we seem to require ever increasing loudness levels while the amplitude knob on the home stereo finds itself turned more and more to the right. We sacrifice texture, timbre and pitch subtlety for raw power without realizing that we are doing so.

Our condition, however, is not irreversible. There are a number of steps we can take to restore our hearing to its fullest capacity through a method that I have termed "Sound Awareness Training".

Physical Preparation

The first step in the restoration of hearing involves easing the tension of the eyes and the facial muscles around the eyes. These suggestions are most effective while lying down, so find a comfortable space away from areas where other activities are taking place and away from bright lighting. Close your eyes and as you begin to follow the inhalation and exhalation of air as you breathe, allow your jaw to relax so that your mouth is slightly open. Begin to breathe through both mouth and nose at the same time in slower, deeper and gentler breaths — allowing, but never forcing — and as you do so bring your hands to your eyes, palms down. Gently cover your eyes, allowing your hands to relax and mold themselves to the shape of your face. Continue this process for several minutes, removing and replacing your hands over your eyes. When your eyes feel relaxed, when your face feels more open and the verbal chatter in your mind has ceased, bring your hands to the floor and remain quiet while the sensation of your hands on your face slowly evaporates. Repeat this process but this time place your palms over your ears. As you inhale, visualize that the air is now flooding your ears, the top and back of your head, and that it is traveling down the back of your neck, throat, and into your lungs. Rest again as before.

Next, begin to gently massage the facial muscles around your eyes and then massage your outer ears, remembering to breathe as described earlier. Massage the area in front of your ears, in back of the ears, and the mastoid bone of the skull as well as the bottom of the skull all around the back of the head. From there proceed down the back and sides of the neck where most of the tension accumulates that tends to restrict our hearing. As you do this visualize that your ear canals are expanding so that you can sense two large canals — one from each side of your head — meeting in the center of your head. Then visualize that at this meeting place another sound channel begins to grow downward through your throat, into your torso, dividing at the pelvis and proceeding down your legs to your feet. With every inhalation visualize that this channel expands slowly until it reaches your skin, penetrates your skin and extends beyond your body boundaries. Bring in all sounds around you into this space. Take several minutes to do this. Without judgement examine and enjoy all entering sounds as they flood your entire mind and body and as they merge with your personal environment of internal sounds.

Now extend your ears outward into and beyond the room you are in, through the windows, above the buildings and trees, mountains and clouds, away from the Earth, beyond the moon, the sun, and the solar system. Reach for the stars with your ears!... Now reverse the process, slowly approaching the Earth once more, past the clouds, the wind, over the trees and into the place where you are...past your own breathing and back into your body once more.

Take time to experience this fully. Then if it's convenient, listen to some music, at a low amplitude — something simple, perhaps, that is of moderate tempo. Listen for the silences between the notes, go through the notes until you can experience the music from the other side of the sounds.

Set aside twenty or more minutes a day to repeat this experience and give pause during the day's activities to hear the sounds around you. For example, try to hear the clouds as they move across the sky, or when talking to someone hear the message behind the words. Try to examine each sound rather than to simply identify it. Working with a partner can also be very rewarding. Here the key words are: breath, quietness of mind, awareness, and presence in a non-judgemental experiencing of sound.

A sound, being a manifestation of energy, is a living organism with its own life span. Every sound has its conception (preparation), birth (attack), growth (the time it takes to reach its maximum loudness), old age (decrease of loudness), death (the point at which the sound ceases, and an afterlife (memory of the sound). Yet within the world of sounds relatively few are organized into what we commonly regard as music. When we liberate ourselves from our conditioned perception of what is or is not music we begin to discover a far greater variety of music around us. We possess a marvelous ability to perceive unity in any "random" series of sounds. It is only the limitation of our prejudices that cause us to disregard that unity. Relish the opportunity to hear both very soft and very loud sounds; these invite you to expand your awareness beyond the narrow band of what is generally considered comfortable. Soft sounds require complete attention and openness while loud ones intrude upon our complacent ears and drive out all thoughts. When this occurs we no longer listen to the sounds. Rather, we acquire the sensation of peering out at the world from within the center of the sounds.

Generally we give little attention to soft sounds and try to avoid loud ones. However, it is not the loud sound that causes discomfort. It is our resistance that creates tension and it is the tension that results in discomfort. The way to experience a sound at the threshold of feeling is to physically relax. Tension causes the muscle construction that decreases blood and oxygen supply. Refraining from resistance allows sound to flow freely through us. By surrendering to the sound we let it fill our head and merge with the energy of our bodies.

True hearing is fully receiving without judgement. In relinquishing control, our minds are still — free of expectation, free of verbal monologue, free of fantasies, free of fear. Hearing in the moment, ego is circumvented; future and past give way to continuous successions of present. We are drawn into the center of the sound and to the sound beneath the sound.

FIGURE 7

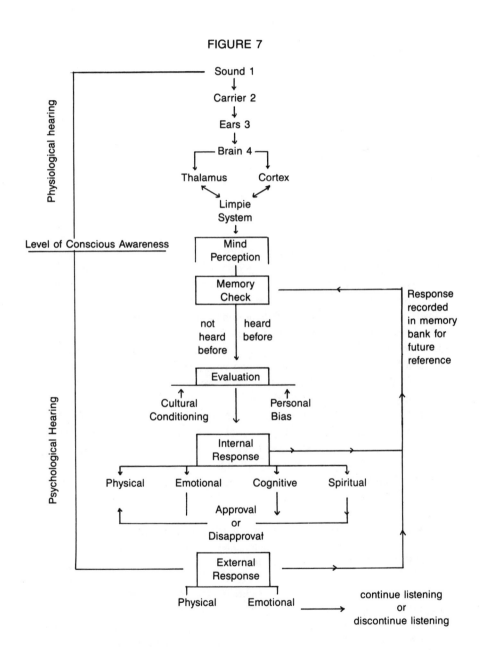

CHAPTER THREE

The Vibratory Nature
of the Human Body

The human body consists of a large number of interlocking and interdependent vibrational systems of various frequencies and densities within an environment of fluids which are encased by a highly elastic perforated outer covering. Known as the **dense physical body**, it is the sum total of all the organisms of which it is made, and a vehicle for spiritual evolution in the physical world. The substance of the body is a virtual symphony of frequencies, sounds, and biological, mental and emotional rhythms in a state of continuous flow which seek to achieve and maintain the state of perfect balance and equilibrium.

Within the dense physical body is the muscular system, the skeletal system, the blood circulation system, respiratory system, digestive system, endocrine system, nervous system, excretory system, reproductive system, and various fluids. All of these structures and fluids consist of atoms. These atoms form molecules which, in turn, form the various cells of the muscles, bones, organs, glands, nerves, blood and other fluids. A highly magnified film of a cell shows a constant movement that folds within itself, though the external shape is maintained. As Dr. Guy Manners describes it:

> Where there is movement, there must be friction and where there is friction, there must be sound. However minute it may be, the sound has got to be there. So therefore you've got the sound in that little cell.[1]

Each cell of the human body, then, produces a frequency or resonating harmonic. These cells combine and eventually form a body structure, such as a liver. As a result of the harmonic of each cell, the body part with which it is associated produces its own harmonic. But here we have a problem, because all cells are basically the same. How do they know to form themselves into a liver and not a lung? Dr. Victor Beasley, a member of a team of research scientists who are investigating the human body as an electro-vibratory phenomenon at the University of the Trees, offers the following explanation:

> All functions of the human body are electro-chemical in their operations. A cell, like all units comprised of physical, atomic substance, has a magnetic moment which, in part, results from the interaction of its electro-chemical constituents. In fact, Dr. Oliver Reiser has speculated that there is a resonance which holds between the DNA in the chromosomes of the cell nucleus and the RNA residing in the cytoplasmic envelope which surrounds the nucleus. . .Consequently, each cell can be viewed as possessing its own immediate magnetic environment, or magnetic field, which combines with the fields of like and adjacent cells, thereby giving rise to the magnetic field of a particular system within the human body.[2]

Expressed more poetically, Dr. Guy Manners, an osteopath, rayologist and cymatic therapist practicing in England, offers this explanation:

> Every cell is like a father and it produces a son. If the father cell is working as a part of the liver he only knows the signal of the liver. He can't do anything else. . .So therefore one cell educates the other to take its place and gradually take over. So, according to the form and the shape of the liver you have a collection of cells that do nothing else but reform themselves as liver cells. Therefore you have a harmonic of the liver. Now the heart is entirely a different shape. The cells are the same but because you have a different shape, you have a different harmonic.[3]

The atoms that form each cell contain electrons that are in constant motion and which therefore radiate electromagnetic waves. These waves are measurable as frequencies, the rate of which vary according to the particular form of matter. It would appear, then, that all matter exhibits its own natural rate of vibration and that the frequency is dependent on the oscillation rates of the electron charges. Atoms possessing the same frequency rate tend to combine and strengthen each other through the principle of resonance.

> If two independent systems, both having the same naturally occurring frequency, are joined together in phase, resonance occurs with the result that their maximum and minimum values are reached simultaneously. Both systems vibrate in unison. Under these conditions, the resultant waveform values, created by the union of the two frequencies, exceed that which either could produce independently.[4]

This phenomenon occurs in all forms of matter, both inert and living cells. Cells whose natural frequency rates are the same combine to form the various structures and systems that are an integral feature of our physical existence. Each structure is a harmonic of the cells through which it is formed and maintained. It may be said, then, that sound creates the structures of our bodies.

Itzhak Bentov[5] states that the atoms of our bodies vibrate at the rate of about 10^{15} c.p.s., that the molecules, formed of atoms, vibrate at the rate of 10^9 c.p.s., and that the frequency response of cells is 10^3 c.p.s., a step down in range of six octaves you arrive at the frequency of 7.8 c.p.s. which some researchers have identified as being the frequency of the human body.[8] If these calculations are correct, they may indicate that as the various systems of our bodies — and all matter as well — becomes more dense, and as they gain more mass, the natural frequency of the structure also decreases. Therefore the frequency of the nervous system may be of a higher rate than that of the organs. The organs, in turn, may be higher than that of the bone structures.

Experiments undertaken at the Cymatics Institute in Switzerland indicate that there is some feasibility to this hypothesis.[6] A single drop of water dropped onto a plate — was subjected to sound of increasing frequency rates and photographs were taken to record any changes occurring in the appearance of the water as a result of the frequency changes. The experiment demonstrated that the shape and form of the water changed radically as the frequency of the sound was changed. As long as the frequency remained constant, the resulting shape of the drop of water was held indefinitely, and the chemical property of the water did not change. As the frequency was increased, a more etherial appearance began to emerge, rendering the drop of water unrecognizable. In the final photograph, it can hardly be seen at all, yet it is still there. At each frequency change the water kept its external form but within the water itself, the molecules continued to move. Further experiments with other liquids displayed exactly the same patterns of change. Dr. Guy Manners, in reflecting on this experiment, posed the following question:

> Is it feasible, then, and is it possible that you and I — all of us in here — living in this dimension and perpetrating this sound which holds you in the shape and the form that you are? It could be. And if the shape and the form, the vibration that is round this planet changes, we could all mutate? We really don't know.[7]

Thus far, the emerging concept of our physical bodies is one wherein each atom emits its own natural frequency rate which, through resonance, combines with similar atoms to form the molecules whose natural frequency is a harmonic of the atoms. Molecules of the same harmonic form the cells of the various structures and fluids, each of which emits its own natural frequency. In every case the external shape of the structure is maintained as long as the frequency for each remains constant, while within the structure there is constant movement. All are maintained through the principle of resonance and the resulting interaction of harmonies. As each structure increases in density and gains more mass, the natural harmonic decreases in frequency rate. Although still highly speculative, and not yet accepted by medical practitioners, early results of experimenters such as Guy Manners, Hans Jenny, Victor Beasley, and Itzak Bentov indicate that there might indeed be some basis of truth to this concept.

Bio-Physical Resonance

Experiments conducted by Itzak Bentov and his associates have identified five resonating systems within the human body:[6]

1. The heart-aorta system produces a standing wave oscillation of seven cycles per second in the skeleton, which is caused by the ejection of blood from the heart into the aorta. This wave causes a minute corresponding movement in the body.

2. Responding to this movement, the skull causes an up and down movement of the brain and produces reverberating acoustical plane waves of 1,000 c.p.s. through the brain.

3. These waves activate standing waves in the third ventrical (12,000 c.p.s.) and the lateral ventrical (4,000 c.p.s.) of the brain.

4. The sensory cortex of the brain is stimulated by standing waves in the cerebral cortex. These frequencies are in the audio range.

5. A pulsating magnetic field is produced in each hemisphere of the brain.

In addition, Bentov characterizes the fundamental frequencies of the brain at 4,000 c.p.s., the circumference of the skull at 2,250 c.p.s., the whole body length at 375 c.p.s., trunk and head at 750 c.p.s., and heart sounds at 2,000 c.p.s.[9]

Other sounds found within the human body result from the actions of the various systems and include:

1. the sound of the circulation of blood through the veins and arteries,

2. the sounds of our nervous system,

3. the sounds of our breathing,

4. the sounds of our digestive system,

5. the sound produced by the action of the heart, and

6. sounds that result from any movement of our bones.

These sounds are in the audible range and can be heard easily by inserting ear-plugs into our ears.

Our brains emit frequencies that respond to our mental and emotional states. Research on these frequencies, or brainwaves, as they are called, began in the 1920's and has recently blossomed into the biofeedback instrument industry. Researchers have recorded brain waves that range from .5 c.p.s. to 22 c.p.s. and have divided this range into four categories based on what appears to be four distinct correspondances between the brain wave rate and the state of conciousness of the individual producing it.[10]

Beta waves range from 13 to 22 c.p.s. and accompany cortical activities of thinking. They are present when one's attention is focused on the external world.

Alpha waves range from 8 to 12 c.p.s. and accompany the state of relaxed wakefulness. Alpha waves become stronger and more regular when the eyes are closed and visual imagery ceases, but they are blocked by sensory stimulation, conceptual thinking, strong emotions or the effort of trying to produce them. Studies have shown that experienced meditators produce alpha waves while meditating.

Theta waves range from 4 to 7 c.p.s. and are produced as one drifts towards sleep or when one enters deep meditation. Hypnogogic imagery is very often present in the transition from lower alpha waves to upper theta waves.

Delta waves range from .5 to 3.5 c.p.s. and are present during sleep. One psychologist claims that by playing relaxing music into which a subaudio frequency of 3.5 c.p.s. has been added below the level of conscious hearing, he is able to guide people into deep relaxation while retaining a state of wakefulness.[11]

One theoretical explanation of the origin of brain waves is that they result from the continuous rhythmic swing of electro-magnetic polarities in the cerebral hemispheres of the brain.[12] Any slight change in body or mind state causes a change in wave rate. What is significant, however, is that through the brain wave rate a feedback loop system appears to take place between the brain, the rest of the physical body, and the mind — an integrated system of body/mind, the one inseparable from the other: when the body relaxes, the brain wave rate lowers; when the brain wave rate lowers, the body relaxes. The process can be initiated in our mind by allowing a change in wave rate or by allowing relaxation of the physical body through breathing techniques. Once the process is initiated, the mind responds and the process continues as the brain wave rate approaches 7 c.p.s. or lower. Bentov states that "in meditation the skeleton and all inner organs will move coherently at about 7 c.p.s."[13] If this is correct, then 7 c.p.s. is the rate of maximum efficiency of brain/body, leaving the mind to attend to other things such as healing or experiencing union through meditation.

FIGURE 1

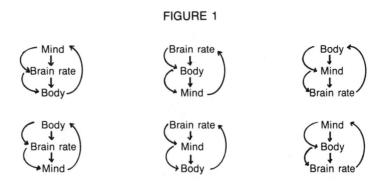

The Etheric Body

Emerging from the dense physical body and extending about three inches beyond is a web of energy that completely surrounds us. It has variously been called the "bio-plasmic field", "electro-magnetic field", "electro-static field", "corona discharge", or just simply "the aura", and for the past three hundred years Western science and medicine have denied its existence. Yet belief in its existence as well as the conviction that one can be taught to see it and gain information from it as an indication of a person's physical, emotional and spiritual health has persisted among many non-Western philosophies, wholistic healers and Western occultists.

> When we look at a human being we see a head, a torso, neck, two arms and two legs. But do we see that person? We only see what our eyes (and beliefs) allows us to see. We don't see the aura or the electronic field around that body, the bio-plasmic field or electro-magnetic body. But no matter what you call it, it is there and until comparatively recently we didn't even believe it was there. Well, now we know it's there but we can't see it because our eyes have not been trained to be sensitive to the vibrations set up within that field.[14]

Occultists such as C. W. Lendbetter[15] and Alice Bailey,[16] and non-Western spiritual leaders such as Paramahansa Yogananda[17] have written extensively about the etheric field during the first part of this century, but it was the work of Professor Harold Saxon Burr, a neuro-anatomist and for 43 years a faculty member of the Yale University School of Medicine, that gave scientific validity to what had previously been refuted by medical practitioners. Burr devoted forty years to the investigation of the etheric field in a wide variety of life forms. As a result of his investigations, Burr concluded that the body's etheric field "serves as a matrix or mould which preserves the 'shape' or arrangement of any material poured into it, however often the material may be changed."[18] He also demonstrated that abnormal fluctuations in the voltages of the field can give advance warning of disease before it manifests in the physical body. The etheric field is an electro-magnetic vibrational field that shields and energizes the dense physical body and integrates it with the Earth's energy fields. It fluctuates continually in response to vibrational waves with which it comes into contact. The etheric field is found around all living organisms, of both the plant and animal worlds, and gradually fades upon the death of that organism. The etheric field can be easily perceived as a whitish hue if you gaze at or around a person.[19]

Although not yet verified through scientific investigation, two additional auric bodies extending beyond the etheric body have been identified by the vast majority of occultists writers and psychic healers. They are identified as:

The Emotional Body (Psychological Aura)
Also known as the astral body or the desire body, the emotional body is said to extend 2 to 4 feet beyond the etheric body and contains three sub-divisions

within it. Characterized as being less dense than the etheric body, the designated function of the emotional body is communication. It is said to change color in response to our emotional state. Because the emotional body responds to and accumulates the energies of our emotions, physical disease can be detected in the emotional body before it manifests in the physical body. When emotions are not expressed and dispersed, accumulations of great energy force are retained in the emotional body and are reflected to the physical body through the etheric field. Occultists writer Alice Bailey has stated that about 90 percent of disease is emotional in origin.[20]

The Mental Body

The mental body extends from the emotional body to distances of eight feet. It is lighter in color and less dense than either the etheric body or the emotional body. It responds to our mental activity and is believed to absorb electro-magnetic frequencies present in the Earth's atmosphere.

The purpose of this short exposition of our human environment has been to demonstrate that we consist of frequencies and rhythms of various densities and time rates, a web of pulsating vibrational energies that give shape and energy to our bodies, thoughts and emotions. We are a resonating system in process rather than a stable solid mass.

Insofar as all order, whether in matter or thought, evolves from chaos through rhythms themselves can be seen to reverberate through different dimensions of manifestations. We can look at what we take to be ourselves in a more expansive light. Today's physics teaches us that human flesh is not solid, but a lattice of force-fields which is not dissimilar to the lattice of thoughts and feelings which move through our minds. . .Our bodies now emerge as diaphanous webs of pulsating form, in constant flux, which change and fall apart as soon as their underlying energies are distorted or withdrawn.[21]

PART TWO

*The Application of Tones
for Therapeutic Purposes*

"Between five and five-thirty (p.m.), we were still talking when the swami suddenly said, 'Now sit in meditation. In five minutes I will leave my body. Its time is over. This instrument which is called body is not capable of giving more than I have already attained, so I will leave it behind.' Five minutes later, he sang out "Aumm..." and then there was silence."

Swami Rami; Living with the Himalayan Masters, p. 441.

"At the exact moment of death, if a person's own note is sounded, it will co-ordinate the two streams of energy and eventually rupture the life thread, but the knowledge of this is too dangerous to transmit yet and can only later be given."

A. A. Bailey; Treatise on White Magic, p. 506.

"A French engineer, Professor Gavraud, became fascinated by sound and, intrigued by the whole range of low frequencies produced by the French police whistle with a pea in it, he built a giant six foot version of it powered by compressed air. The unfortunate technician who first tested this whistle died instantly, a post mortem revealing that his internal organs had been thoroughly scrambled by the sound."

Lawrence Blair; Rhythms of Vision, p. 117.

"...each time a new soul descends into the ocean of the manifested realm, it generates a vibration which is communicated to the entire cosmic ocean which means all created realms, entirely and heavenly, physical and super-physical. As each of these vibrations bring into resonance a host of consonent tones throughout the universal, their unimaginable interferences produce globally the symphony of the spheres referred to by Pythagoras. Each creature...is a crystillization of a part of this symphony of vibrations. Thus we are like a sound petrified in solid matter and which continues indefinitely to resound in this matter."

Pir Vilayat Khan quoting from the Hekaloth, a Hebrew esoteric book on the Heavenly Spheres; Toward the Qne, p. 229.

"Music is considered a vital source of spiritual transformation, and vibrations are recognized as cosmic manifestations of a spiritual principle. The Lamas (of Tibet) have developed a science as well as an art of sound. They carefully cultivate sensitivity to musical pitch and tone and to the moods thereby created which they believe have the power to heal or, if misused, cause illness, according to the vibrations involved."

Dom Cyril von K. Krasinski; Die Geistage Erde; quoted by Elsie Mitchell in Sun Buddhas, Moon Buddhas (Salem, MA, John Weatherhill, Inc., 1980), p. 21.

CHAPTER FOUR

The Principles of Healing Through Sound

It is written in the *Hekaloth*, a Hebrew esoteric book on the Heavenly Spheres, that when a new soul incarnates it sends forth a vibration that resounds throughout the entire cosmos — the earth and heavens — which continues to sound throughout the incarnated life of that soul.[1] In his book, *Living with the Himalayan Masters*, Swami Rama cites two occurrences in which he personally witnessed in which Hindu swamis discarded their bodies by chanting "Aum" while in meditation. Checking the bodies for signs of breathing or a pulse immediately after, he found the bodies to be completely lifeless.[2] In *A Treatise on White Magic* (1934), author Alice Baily, in describing the process of death, suggests that the chanting of specific tones is a part of the "ritual of transition" of the dying person.[3] Sant Kirpol Singh, a Hindu mystic, has stated that "in his nameless state he is in neither light nor darkness, neither sound nor silence, but when he assumes shape and form, light and sound emerge as his primary attributes."[4]

These are important clues to help us understand the use of tones in the healing process. First, these thoughts offer insight into esoteric concepts of sound. Second, they suggest that humans, indeed all manifested beings, come into the world with the aid of an actual frequency, maintain a frequency throughout life, and exit from this life by means of a frequency. Third, they hint that the frequency of each human is different. Fourth, they also hint that the whole of the cosmos and each being within the cosmos is maintained through the principle of resonance.

By way of speculation, let us consider that in realms beyond our known physical reality, there exists one principal frequency, an energy source that cannot be perceived by our senses because either its frequency is too high or its essence is beyond the gross physical realm. Let us then consider that before birth each of us is enfolded in this frequency. As we approach manifestation as separate beings, our vibration rate decreases and is resonated by the principal frequency. We maintain a separate identity through the lower vibration rate during the course of our earthly life, yet we always resonate in sympathy with the principal frequency. We leave this life through harmonic resonance with that frequency until, beyond the realm of the limitations of physical reality, we are merged once more into the unity of the primal vibration.

Now consider the possibility that there is a distinct band of frequencies which is the realm of the spirit, a slightly lower band of frequencies for the soul level, another frequency rate which accommodates and transmits thoughts (a possible correlation with Carl Jung's "unconscious collective: and with Alexander Elliot's concept of a global "mythosphere"), another for the realm of emotions. Imagine further that in addition to permeating the Earth, these frequency bands surround each of us, nourishing, sustaining, resonating and intermingling with our etheric body and with the various frequencies and rhythms of our physical bodies. Perhaps, then, we may conceive of a system of complex interconnected vibrational structures forming and reforming themselves as they are resonated by one primordial frequency according to capacities as determined by the densities of their molecules. The greater the density, the lower is the corresponding frequency and the more susceptible it is to vibrational influences imposed by other structures. Thus, the frequency of spirit is less susceptible to variation than that of mind; the mind less so than the emotional plane. The slower vibrational rates of the physical body are the most susceptible to frequency variation.

A Therapeutic Application of Frequencies

There appear to be several advantages to the process of healing by use of specific frequencies. First, sound acts directly on the physical body and frequencies may be directed to specific parts of the body in need of attention. Second, the application of specific frequencies, whether they are produced by the voice, a musical instrument, an electric tone generator, or even by a pitch pipe, does not meet resistance in the person being treated as the result of cultural or personal biases; therefore, the question of aesthetics does not impede the healing process. Third, when administered under laboratory conditions, treatment can be carefully monitored and data can be accurately gathered and evaluated. Fourth, treatment is entirely painless and there appear to be no negative side effects.

The therapeutic application of frequencies is based on two principles: that sound is a vibratory energy that interacts with the vibratory energy of body structures through resonance, which is defined as the interaction of two bodies vibrating at about the same frequency; and that each structure of the body has its own natural resonating frequency. Illness results when this natural frequency is altered by frequencies that are foreign to it. A change of frequency results in a change of energy; a change of energy results in a change of frequency, for they are related to each other.[5] After determining the natural frequency of the structure in question, that frequency can be introduced to the body structure and, through resonance, cause it to return to its natural frequency. Thus the body structure is restored to healthfulness and harmony. In cases where the injury is severe, cells can be regenerated.[6]

The process of healing with specific frequencies utilizes two approaches. One employs frequencies imposed from a source outside of the person being treated by either a musical instrument, the voice, or electronic instruments that have been designed for the purpose, and is generally administered by a specialist. The second employs self-treatment for the prevention of disease or to correct a condition that has already manifested itself. In this method the person's own voice is used as the sound source. Both appear to have long traditions and have been found in most cultures. In the case of Western culture this form of treatment appears to have been employed in the healing centers of Egypt and Greece.[7] With the advent of the Christian era, these centers died out and all activities ceased or degenerated into superstition, pseudo-alchemy or folklore. Not until the beginning of the twentieth century has interest and scientific inquiry been directed toward a serious examination of the therapeutic use of vibration. Several approaches and methodologies have been developed since the 1920's, all of which are still in the process of testing and refinement. Those presented in this chapter have two traits in common: all of them utilize frequencies that are imposed on the body from an outside source and the frequencies are generated by specially designed electronic instruments.

Radionics[8]

Radionics was developed in America in the early twentieth century by Dr. Albert Abrams, M.D. (1862-1924) and refined by Dr. Wallace MacNaughton of Schenectady, New York. The practice of Radionics has met with substantial resistance by the Food and Drug Administration and is not accepted by the American medical profession. It has, however, been firmly established in England where the Radionics Association of England was founded in 1960. Radionics is based on the principle of oscillatory frequencies and employs a simple machine, called a Pathoclost, to detect, diagnose and modulate the fundamental energy patterns of the human body. The basic premise of radionics is that each individual organism radiates and absorbs energy through an extended electro-magnetic force field that surrounds it. In humans this field is very complex and is associated with the various organs and systems of the body. Any change in the condition of the body is reflected in a change in the force field. Radionics specialists claim to be able to determine the origin of the change in force-field by diagnostic methods. Once the ailing body part is discovered, the frequency rate being emitted by the body part is determined. The frequency rate is then duplicated by the Pathoclost and beamed back to the body part. It is a basic premise of radionic therapy that if the vibratory frequency radiated by two substances is identical, the frequencies will neutralize each other. Duplicating the radiations of the diseased tissue neutralizes and dissipates the vibrations of the disorder and weakens the molecular bonds of the diseased cells to literally "break up" the disease. In this treatment method the frequencies are above the level of human hearing. Therefore, no sound is heard. Radionics is related to Radiesthesia, e.g., divining and dowsing, and utilizes some of the principles of Color Therapy. The work of Abrams and Mac-Naughton is being further developed by Mark Gallert, N.D., and Dr. Robert Massy.[9]

Sound Creates Structure (The Science of Cymatics)

In the eighteenth century a German physicist, Ernst Chladni, mounted a thin metal plate on a violin, placed a small amount of very fine sand on the plate, and drew his bow across the strings. When he sustained one tone for a long period of time he discovered that the sand moved into geometric patterns of interlocking and concentric circles. Changing the pitch resulted in the movement of the sand particles into other organic shapes — spirals, radiating wheel spokes, and hexagonal grids. In so doing, Professor Chladni accomplished two important tasks. He demonstrated that sound does indeed affect physical matter, and he established the basis for the new science of **Cymatics** — the study of the effects of sound waves on physical matter.

Ernst Chladni's experiments remained an interesting curiosity until a twentieth-century Swiss scientist, Hans Jenny, began the series of experiments which were to occupy him for the rest of his life. Using electronic sound oscillators, metal plates, microphones and sophisticated photographic equipment, Jenny experimented with pure sine tones (tones that do not contain harmonics) of various frequencies, with recordings of European classical music, and with vocal sound — both singing and speaking — and photographed the patterns as they emerged from such materials as sand, iron filings, water, mercury, and other liquids. He discovered that the evolving forms repeated themselves in predictable ways and resembled the growth patterns of organic living organisms: chromosomes, cells, molecules, bone tissue, growth rings in trees as well as crystals. He demonstrated that music produces a visible texture that resembles the weavings of cloth. He discovered that when the syllable "O" was spoken into the microphone, the sand on the metal plate took the shape of "O". When the syllables of the ancient languages of Sanskrit and Hebrew were pronounced, the sand took the form of the written symbols for those sounds, whereas our modern languages did not produce the same effect.

Hans Jenny remained the pure abstract scientist throughout his work. It was only toward the end of his career that he commented on the biological aspects of sound. Near the close of his two-volume work on Cymatics he concludes:

> Throughout the animal and vegetable kingdoms, Nature creates in rhythms, periods, cycles, frequencies, reduplications, serial phenomen, sequence, etc. This is the style in which natural structures are built and it is ubiquitous...The very origin of the word *tissue* (Latin, texere = to weave) is a significant comment

on the conditions obtaining: cells are arrayed in rows, one pattern following another wherever we look. The intercellular structures take the form of frameworks, networks, grids, families of elements continually repeated and following each other in regular sequence, forming a woof and weft, whether looked at with the naked eye, through the light microscope, or through the electron miscroscope.[10]

In summarizing his own work, Jenny states that:

We have the certain experience that harmonic systems such as we have visualized on our experiments arise from oscillations in the form of intervals and harmonic frequencies. . .we are familiar with the style of nature which is characterized by rhythmicities and periodicities, so that we can speak of biological periodicity, and even biological oscillation in the strict sense. . .We have knowledge of the interplay of factors in the organic world. . .If biological rhythms operate as generative factors at the interval-like frequencies appropriate to them, then harmonic patterns must be necessarily forthcoming. . .if harmonic configurations appear in organic nature then what we see before us is the result of rhythms, intervals and frequencies of the generative factors. . .How Nature proceeds in these matters, that is the question.[11]

It was Jenny's conviction that biological growth was the result of vibration and that the nature of the vibration determined the resulting structures. He speculated that each cell, as a result of vibration, generated its own frequency while several cells of the same frequency would combine to generate a new frequency that would be harmonic to the first. Likewise, the organ that was made up of these cells would produce its own frequency, and the body, as a composite of all of its structures, would also resonate its own frequency. The resulting frequencies would be the result of harmonics, perhaps as found in the natural harmonic series, so that all parts of the whole be assured of compatibility with each other. Jenny concludes:

. . .if one holds that harmony is at work even in embryology in the generative phase, the actual processes must nevertheless be seen in their frequencies and intervals. So many questions concerning the effects produced by these rhythmicities and periodicities remain unanswered. . .How do the generative factors act to determine the embryogenesis of organisms which present harmonic forms throughout? Since the formative style of nature in all its aspects is rhythmic, periodic and cyclic, how do living intervals, sounds and frequency spectra act in embryology? Time and effort should be devoted to experiments to enable these generative realities to be seen and recognized.[12]

In other words, according to Jenny the key to healing the body with specific tones lies in our understanding of how frequency acts upon genes, cells and other structures of the body. Only then will we know how to determine the exact frequencies for each individual human being. When we can do this with accuracy we may begin to impose healing frequencies from outside sources with reasonable assurance of favorable results and with no risk to a patient.

Dr. Jenny suggests two methods of developing the science of Cymatics. He first suggests that we engage in the study of biochemistry, bioelectronics, biodynamics, and biostructure as a way to understand the relationship of body and frequency, a method that suggests highly sophisticated experimental laboratories with complex and sensitive equipment. The second method, which he proposes on the final page, is to look more deeply into the human larynx and ear to discover the primal cause of vibration.

> We will look into the larynx, which potentially contains the whole range of cymatics in its capacity and is therefore truly and really the Primordial Word. What is this primordial Word? That is what we bring our minds to bear on as if a mystery, what we seek to approach methodically in cymatics, what we will dedicate ourselves to, using all our powers of sight and hearing and with modern science as our basis. One thing is clear: we are not in pursuit of a phantom but are directing our perceptual powers on the organ of speech and also on the organ of hearing which is closely bound up with it, both of which are invested with an almost all-pervasive enigmatic quality. In our research we move towards a creative world, towards a world-creating power. . . in admiring and respecting those visions of a world of harmonics (we feel) that a responsive chord has been struck, for he carries in his heart the new cosmos as the mystery of the primordial word seeking revelation.[13]

And so Dr. Hans Jenny, like so many before him, having begun his work as an empirical scientist seeking to understand the essence of life itself through scientifically controlled observation, became a true mystic near the end of his life.

The Therapeutic Application of Cymatics

From the experimental laboratory of Hans Jenny, the therapeutic application of Cymatics is being expanded, developed and refined in England. It is not possible to know how many are involved in the development of Cymatics Therapy, but one of its most important pioneers and spokesmen is Dr. Peter Guy Manners, osteopath and rayologist of Evesham, Worcestershire.

As in Radionics, the basic principle in Cymatic Therapy is that all material units — atoms, molecules, cells, organs — are in a state of continuous vibration. The wave forms resulting from vibration are neither random nor chaotic but produce patterns of complex unity. Manners states that:

> Careful observation of structures excited by vibration and sound shows that, when they move, they invariably move as a whole. They do not disintegrate or fragment, but move collectively. It is therefore legitimate to speak of a total or wholistic process. Again, we see unity in the way structural patterns and dynamic processes appear in one and the same configuration. All are sustained by the underlying vibratory process.[14]

Each unit has its own frequency of vibration and produces its own characteristic wave pattern as the result of its frequency. The frequencies of larger units are the algebraic sum of their smaller components. According to Cymatic therapy, disease is the result of a change in the fundamental frequency of vibration. This change can occur in any part of the body but will affect the whole. Cymatic Therapy treatment involves the restoration of the entire unit to its natural vibratory rate by duplicating the frequency with electronic oscillators and applying this frequency to the unit. In his own words Dr. Manners states that:

If we take readings of the muscle structure we can get a signal, a harmonic, a sound will come on. We know that any deviation from the correct signal in the muscle structure or bone formation is an indication of disease, a malformation, a change. So therefore how do we remedy the situation? By administering pills, tablets, medicine? That's yesterday's medicine. We can find new ways. If you just think for a moment, the whole of the medical profession has built its theories on the basis of a theory of Louis Pasteur. I'm not decrying him, he was a great and important man. He was one of the cranks of his time. But I am quite sure that if he were here with us today, he would agree that we shouldn't have stood still in the theory he had postulated a hundred years ago. We should advance to new thoughts. He showed us how to protect ourselves against the invasion of virus and bacteria and from that we evaluated something which he at no time said — that disease is caused by that virus, that bacteria. Oh, if we take someone who has died of smallpox or something and we examine the body, we will find those viruses or those bacteria in that system. But we are of the opinion now that it is not a cause of that disease, but the result of that disease. The cause is an imbalance, the harmonics of the body have been disturbed... There is a harmonic of the heart, the liver, the bones, the muscles and so long as they're all playing in that harmony, we are in harmonic pulse. We are healthy. But if any part looses its tune or goes out of phase then we are in trouble. Until we could reproduce these harmonic signals — even though we believed it — we could do nothing about it and we had to rely solely on medicine.[15]

For Cymatic Therapy treatment an instrument called an "applicator" was built that could be brought into direct contact with the surface of the skin. The frequencies for the body structure that is to be treated are computed according to a code by a small computer installed in the instrument. The instrument then computes these frequencies into a harmonic of five frequencies. The harmonic is exactly identical to that which exists in the human body. Dr. Manners states that the reason for five frequencies is that single frequencies are dangerous because a single frequency can nullify the action of the peripheral nerve.

The applicator uses a frequency range of 60-70 c.p.s. to 30,000 c.p.s., most frequencies for muscle structures, for example, being in the 247-619 c.p.s. range. The resulting harmonic is generated by oscillators and recorded on a cassette tape as treatment is being administered.

The effect on the patient is characterized as being quite pleasant as it penetrates, the sensation being similar to that produced by an electric massager except that the sounds produced are the natural frequencies of the body. The average treatment length is ten to fifteen minutes, but if longer there are no adverse effects because the frequency corresponds to the natural frequency of the area.

Dr. Manners has utilized Cymatic Therapy for rheumatic conditions, arthritis, fractures and rebuilding bone sockets, muscle strain, whiplash, slipped discs, fibrositis, and paralysis, but treatment is by no means restricted to these conditions. Cymatic Therapy is a new healing method, barely twenty years old, and is therefore still in the experimental stage. Dr. Manners is willing to share the results of his work with medical practitioners and responds to all serious inquiries.

If sound creates structure as Hans Jenny and Peter Guy Manners assert, then one might assume that it is possible to create a replica of a body structure by imposing the natural frequency of that structure into some form of inert matter such as water or liquid plastic. Dr. Manners recently commented on this question in the following way:

> We are able to create replicas of the organs of the body. It's not fantastic, it can be done. We were giving a lecture not so long ago and there were physicists and scientists in the audience. And they said,
>
> "Do you, are you saying that the sound that we can hear on your instruments, that is the sound that is created by a cell that is in the body multiplied many thousands of times so it becomes audible?"
>
> "Yes, it is."
>
> "Well then if this is so, can you create a cell?"
>
> "If you mean by that, can we create a living cell, no. But can we create a replica of exactly what it looks like doing exactly what it does? Yes, very easily. We'll show you on these photographic slides a cell magnified many thousands of times under the microscope and then we'll show you almost identical the same thing made by man."[16]

I have personally seen these slides and they are indeed very convincing.

The instruments used in radionic and cymatic treatment still rely heavily on pre-transister and pre-computer technology. Their prototypes, designed and assembled in the 1950's and 60's, were primitive, cumbersome and often unreliable. Further development depends greatly on the ability of radionics and cymatics researchers to incorporate state-of-the-art technology in redesigning the machines for greater sensitivity, mobility and ease of use. The development of more sophisticated instruments will result in greater refinement of both theory and application. Only then can it be clear whether radionics and cymatics will become a major therapy or remain as yet another interesting footnote in the development of sonic healing.

Ultra-Sonics

Whereas radionics and cymatics lie at the outer fringes of therapeutic sound technology, the more recent field of ultra-sonics has been fully embraced by the medical profession. This fast-developing medical procedure has already found applications in physical therapy, diagnosis, surgery, dentistry and its use in birth control has reached the experimental stage.[18] Because the frequencies used in ultra-sonics exceed the upper limit of human hearing, a full discussion of this medical practice lies beyond the parameters of the present book. But ultra-sonics shares with radionics and cymatics a reliance on electronic technology and a procedure of introducing frequencies into the body with instruments designed specifically for that purpose. All three require a trained specialist to diagnose and administer the therapy and, most significantly, all three treat the physical manifestation of the condition rather than a cause that might be located elsewhere in the anatomy or psyche. However, ultra-sonics differs from radionics and cymatics in that the higher frequencies of ultra-sonics are used to generate heat which can penetrate to the deep tissues of the body.

Diagnostic Uses of Ultra-Sonics

The diagnostic application of ultrasound has already begun to replace x-ray photography that can destroy cells through radiation.[19] The diagnostic use of ultrasound includes the assessment of the stages of pregnancy,[20] investigation of diseases of the bladder, kidneys, liver, ovaries, pancreas and brain tumors. In ultrasonography the deep structures of the body are "represented by measuring and recording the reflection of pulsed or continuous high-frequency sound waves."[21] Ultra-sonography is a method of scanning the internal organs of the body, a process that is similar in principle to sonar scanning of the ocean floor. More recent developments in ultra-sonography include:

Echocardiography — for studying the structure and motion of the heart. Ultra-sonic waves are directed through the heart and are echoed when they pass from one type of tissue to another. This procedure is used to detect atrial tumors and pericardial effusion, measure the ventricular septa and the ventricular chambers, and to determine mitral valve motion abnormalities and congenital lesions.[22]

Echoencephalography — to study the intra-cranial structures of the brain. This process shows ventricular dilation and any major shift of midline structures resulting from expanding lesions.[23]

Echodiography — replaces X-rays for the visualization of the internal structure of the body.[24]

Treatment of Diseases and Surgical Applications

The use of ultra-sonics in surgery and for the treatment of disease appears to be in its beginning stages and research is underway throughout the United States, England, Italy and Australia. Among the diseases that have been successfully treated are Meniere's disease,[25] Parkenson's disease,[26] Hypodermitis Scherodermiformis,[27] and Herpes Zoster Pain.[28] Ultrasound has also been used for bruises, strains,[29] simple low back pain,[30] and back pain resulting from a prolapsed intervertebral disc.[31] The list of surgical applications is already impressively diverse, as can be seen from the following list:

> Removal of Tumors[32]
> Removal of Renal Stones[33]
> Removal of Kidney Stones[34]
> Hyperthermia Therapy for Cancer[35]
> Mastitis[36]
> Ophthalmic Surgery[37]
> Partial Slenectomy[38]
> Healing of Surgical Wounds[39]
> Brain Surgery for Removal of Tumors[40]

Postscript — The Need for Caution

As a child, I saw a film which documented the destruction of a newly-built suspension bridge during a violent rainstorm. As I watched, the road across the bridge began to move in a longitudinal wavelike fashion, similar to what occurs when a rope, fastened on one end, is shaken at the other end, causing a wave to travel its length. In the film, the wave motion of the road gradually increased in size until, at the height of the storm, the road broke apart and fell, in sections, into the water below. Many years later I saw the film again and was provided with the explanation that the strength of the wind made the wire cables of the bridge vibrate like a giant harp and that the resulting frequency caused the road to vibrate in sympathy through the principle of forced resonance.[41]

When I was a graduate student, one of my professors read a newspaper article to our class that described the activities of a group of French scientists who were attempting to perfect what was referred to as "the ultimate doomsday machine." Based on the principle of resonance, the device was designed to produce a frequency at a loudness level sufficient to rupture our internal organs. The article concluded by stating that the project was abandoned because the device would also kill its operators due to the fact that sound waves move outward in all directions from their source — a motion which is similar to what occurs when a pebble is tossed into a pond.[42]

In *Rhythms of Vision*, author Lawrence Blair reported the experience of Professor Gavraud, a French engineer, who became interested in the effect of subaudio frequencies on the human body. Having discovered that the whistle with a pea in it — used by French police — produced sub-audio frequencies, he built a six-foot long version of it powered by compressed air. According to Blair, the technician who first tested it was killed instantly, his internal organs having been ruptured by the sound.[43] In the book *Supernature*, biologist-author Lyall Watson confirmed the accuracy of this incident and cites other examples of the destructive potential of vibration.[44]

More recently, at a public lecture Dr. Guy Manners, who knew Gavraud, supplied further details of Gavraud's work: "Everything he developed proved in testing to be destructive." According to Manners, many of his assistants died when "a short blast of sound ruptured the liver." Among the experimental instruments he built was one that could split concrete ten feet thick by creating the frequency of its molecular structure. When Gavraud died of natural causes, all blueprints for the instruments were banned, his laboratory was disbanded, and all photographs were confiscated by the French government. Dr. Manners exhibited one of the few remaining photographs of Gavraud's machines.[45]

When Manners sought approval from British authorities to use his cymatics applicator for therapeutic purposes, he was asked if it had any destructive potential. His response took the form of a question: "Has there ever been a device invented by man that could not be turned to destructive purposes?"

The point which I wish to emphasize here is that scientific investigation of the effect of frequency on the human body and psyche is relatively new. Although our motivation has been to search for beneficial applications of frequency, such investigations always carry the potential for destruction with them, either through ignorance or by design. Our understanding of frequency waves and the role they play in our physical universe is as yet unsophisticated. In view of Professor Gavraud's disastrous experiments, Dr. Manners' simple question serves as a poignant warning to us all.

CHAPTER FIVE

The Power Within
Maintaining Health
Through The Voice

The most ancient means of music healing is that which occurs through our own voice, for in singing there exists an immediate communion with the subliminal recesses of our minds, when we are reminded of our common origins, experiences, needs and aspirations. Our response to a natural singing voice is a total response — biological, emotional, mental and spiritual — because of its ability to unite body, mind and spirit by its resonance. Legends pertaining to the role of the voice in both healing and in the creation of the world abound in the world's mythologies and attest to the esteem with which the voice is universally regarded.

Musicologist Alfred Sendry cites one such legend in his discussion of Egyptian music:

> In Egyptian mythology, the earth was created by the gesture of a god whose name is not revealed. This gesture, reproduced in a hieroglyphic sign, is identifical with that by which the god Hesu created music. The name "Hesu," translated literally, means "Singer."[1]

In the creation myth of the Hopi people, a song creates life on earth:

> Spider Woman took some earth, mixed with it some tuchvala (liquid from mouth: saliva), and molded it into two beings. Then she covered them with a cape made of white substance which was the creative wisdom itself, and sang the Creation Song over them. When she uncovered them the two beings, twins, sat up and asked, "Who are we? Why are we here?"[2]

The earliest therapeutic use of the voice was, no doubt, for the singing of songs and chants — the rhythmic and melodic effect being primarily a sensory and emotional one — and it is still practiced by the shamans of the world in much the same way as it has been for thousands of years. The power to cure everything from emotional-mental disorders and wounds, to the ravages of plague has been attributed to the use of songs.

When people think of the therapeutic value of music, the vast majority think of songs that express feelings of transpersonal love or unity with a benevolent universe. Consequently, we are left to speculate on whether it is the music that is doing the actual healing or the thoughts expressed in the words. Is the effect of a healing song dependent on whether we sing it to ourselves or whether it is sung to us? Does a healing song work as effectively when it is removed from any ritual that might surround it, or does the song require a ritualistic context in which it forms a part of a greater whole? Does a healing song have any power for healing when it is removed from its cultural context? Finally, when we speak of a healing song we realize that we refer to a series of pitches organized into rhythmic phrases which become the vehicle for words that convey ideas. And at least in Western European cultures, all three elements are supported by a changing harmonic structure. The question remains as to which of these elements is the most potent. Is it the individual tones, the meter, the words, the harmony, or is it a combination of all of these plus a new element that is greater than the separate parts?

If the singing of healing songs is the more obvious use of the healing power of the voice, I am convinced that it is by no means the only one. There is much to suggest a second approach that emphasizes the sustained vocalization of individual pitches for the purpose of resonating specific body areas to which the voice is directed. The advantages of this method are obvious: for one who is vocalizing in this way, sensory feedback is immediate and can be effectively monitored; it focuses awareness inward and increases concentration; it slows and deepens the breath. It vibrates and stimulates the entire physical system as it regulates blood flow and increases oxygenation, tones the nervous system and affects gland secretion. Our verbal thoughts fade, our emotions become quiet, and our voice is always available. The method requires total involvement and concentration with the process, a commitment of will, conscious awareness of the breath, a heightened awareness of hearing, and a highly sensitized internal feedback system.

The employment of the voice for personal health has developed into two specific and ancient techniques. There are two additional procedures that are of more recent origin. They are: healing techniques of mantra Yoga; Tantric Yoga with its utilization of the seven energy centers of the body (Chakras); a method of vibrating the internal organs and gland system through the use of pitch, resonance and vowels; and the application of the voice for the healing of others.

Mantras

On a superficial level, any short verbal phrase that is constantly repeated becomes a *mantra*, the repetition of which sinks into our unconscious minds and influences our thoughts, perceptions, and actions. *Mantras* are planted, like seeds, in our conscious mind, and through repetition and acceptance they send their roots into our unconscious minds. Once implanted, they can exercise power over us until they are replaced by a new mantra. Once a *mantra* is firmly planted in the unconscious it can influence us even when we are unaware of its presence. a *mantra* is usually planted by another person or, in the broadest sense, it may form as a result of encounters with the people and events in our environment. Speaking also in the broadest sense, a *mantra* can be either negative or positive in its effect on us. The earliest bestowers of *mantras* are usually our parents, and the earlier a *mantra* is planted in us the more power it has over us.

The origin of *mantras* is to be found in conceptions set forth in the Hindu *Rig Vedas* and the *Upanishads*. Reputed to be thousands of years old, the *Vedas* and *Upanishads* constitute the two fundamental spiritual writings that form the philisophical basis of Hindu and Buddhist thought.

Mantras are formed on the concept of *Nada* — intelligible sound — also referred to as *Shabd* in Tantra Yoga writings. *Nada* is the primordial or inner sound, the essence and origin of all manifested and unmanifested creation. There are two forms of *Nada*: *Ahata* or "struck sound", that which can be heard and which "gives pleasure", and *Anahata* or "unstruck sound", that which can only be heard by Yogis whose senses are withdrawn from the external world. *Anahata* leads to liberation. *Ahata*, "struck sound", is born of the union of breath and fire and is the mirror of *Anahata*.

Out of *Nada* is formed the system of fifty distinct "mother" vibrations (*Matrika*) that form a language of "manifest *Matrika*" known as *Sanskrit*. *Sanskrit* has an alphabet of fifty letters called *Varnas*, a world which means "colors". Each of the *Varnas* has a definite color affinity and is the foundation of ever changing reality which is consciousness. Thus consciousness, unmanifested sound, manifested sound, form, color and the elements of fire, water, earth, air and ether are all interconnected. Each one of the fifty *Matrika* manifests an energy (*Shakti*) that can be released through vibrational activity of which there are three types:

> Pranayama — breath control
> Mantra — sound
> Alchemy — the five elements

Mantras, traditionally in the Sanskrit language, are formed from these fifty *Matrika*, also called *Bija-Matrika* — seed-mother — and are combined according to their natural relationship. The *mantra* thus formed are mental sounds created or received for special purposes. Repetition of *mantra* is called *Japa* of which there are three types: repetitions spoken aloud, repetitions in low tones, and silent repetition. The third is considered to be the most effective. When a *mantra* is combined with a specific breathing discipline, the vibrational activity of the two unify and gradually bring about a transformation of consciousness. *Mantras*, then, are sound formulas that are formed by carefully combining *Bija-Matrika*.

Govinda states that

...all *mantras* are held to be modifications of an original underlying vibration which sustains the whole energy pattern of the world and which is another form in which the principle can be recognized...*the energies concentrated by mantras can be directed to specific magical purposes, including healing.*[3]

According to Pandit Usharbudh Arya, a teacher of mantra and meditation, the early developers of *mantras*, "tried out all the various sound patterns and carefully recorded the impact that the practice of such meditative thought left on the very subtle recesses of their mental personalities."[4] The chanting of *mantras* is said to have two desirable effects on the mind:

1. clearing away the undesirable tendencies of the mind, and
2. cultivating the desirable tendencies of the mind.[5]

There appear to be two types of *mantras*: single syllable seed *mantras* that work on the subtle levels of vibration and carry no discussive meaning, and multi-syllable discussive mantras of evocative power. The latter form of *mantras* are often associated with deities and are prayers for aid. The power of these *mantras* most often depends on the culture or religious background of the individual, whereas seed-syllable *mantras* create vibrational sound patterns in space that sets in motion "the respective psychic forces or *chakras* and frees (the individual) from the restrictive entanglements by loosening the knots into which (he) has bound (himself)."[6] The chanting of seed-syllable *mantras*, then, is the "repetition of sounds which have power due to the vibration of the sound itself."[7]

The chanting of *mantras* is said to release a liquid essence — a "nectar" — in the pineal gland (located in the center of the brain and called "the seat of the soul") that results in an alteration of consciousness. According to Yogi Bhajan, a teacher of Kundalina Yoga, the components of the *mantra* are organized so that the tongue hits the roof of the mouth in a definite rhythm that releases the nectar.[8] Therefore the recitation of the *mantra* in its proper rhythm is of utmost importance. It appears that the cumulative effect of *mantras* is in their psychological influence on the mind, both conscious and unconscious, that results in healing and transformations.

The chanting of *mantras* is generally monotonal and syllabic. The rhythm is generally dictated by the rhythm of the word sounds. There is very little melodic elaboration, for the *mantra* works from continuous repetition, the object in some traditions being to repeat the *mantra* as many times as possible within a short time. Generally no more than three tones are used: the principle chanting tone, the tone immediately beneath it and the tone immediately above it. These auxiliary tones are used for inflection and phrasing. Chanting is not intended to appeal to the emotions or to the aesthetic sense. Its purpose is not to produce a melody in the usual sense of the term. In other words, *mantras* are not to be considered musical expressions but are kept melodically simple. With these considerations in mind, here is a list of a few traditional healing *mantras*, their translation, and their specific purposes.

Hindu Mantras of Evocative Power

1. **Removal of Fear**

   Aetathe Vadanam Saumyan Lochanatraya Bhushitam Patu Nah Sarva-Bhootebhyaha Katyayini Namostute.

   Protect us from all fear, of three-eyed Goddess of bright face. Katyayini, salutations to you.

2. **Removal of Worries and Pain**

   Savva Badha Prashamanam Trailokyasya Akhilaeshvari Akhilaeshvaril Acvameva Tvaya Karyam Asmadvairi Vinaashanam.

   O Divine mother, ruler of three worlds, let all my grief and misery come to an end.

3. **For cure of illness, take a little water in a cup, chant this mantra, and then drink**

   Aushadham Jahnavee Toyam Vaidyo Narayano Harihi.

   The holy water touched by God is the best medicine. Lord Narayana is the best physician.

4. **For cure of seemingly incurable diseases; to avoid all accidents by air, fire, vehicles, snake bite.**

   Om Tryambakam Yajamahae Sugandhim Pushti Vardhanam Urvaarukamiva Bandhanaan Mrityormuksheeya Maamritaat.

   Bless me with health and immortality and sever me from the clutches of death even as a cucumber is severed from its creeper.

5. **For Divine Wisdom and Power**

   Om Eim Hrim Klim Chamundayai Vichhe Namaha.

   Salutations to Shakti, who showers blessings of wisdom and power.

6. **For Blessings of Faith, Intelligence, Fame, Wisdom, Longevity, Health and Radiance**

   Shraddham Medham Yashaha Prajnam Vidyam Budhim Sriyam Balam Ayushyam Tejami Arogyam Pehimae Havyavahana.

   Bless me O cosmic Fire with faith, intelligence, fame, wisdom, education, understanding, wealth, strength, longevity, radiance, health. Salutations.

7. Happiness of all People in the World and for Universal Peace.

Sarvesham. Svastirbhavatu Sarvisham Shantirbhavatu Sravesham. Purnambhavata Sarvesham Mangalambhavatu Om Sarve Bhavanta Sukhinaha Sarve Santu Niramayaha Sarve Bhadrani Pashyantu Maa Kaschid Dukhabhag Bhavet.

May all be happy. May all be peaceful. May all attain perfection. May all be blessed. I pray for happiness for all. Let all be free from misery. Let me see all beings living joyfully. Let no one be suffering in this world.

8. The Gayatri Mantra

OM OM OM (3 breaths)
Bhuh Bhuvah Svah (breath)
Tat Savituh Varenyam (breath)
Bhargah Devasya Dhimahi (breath)
Dhiyah Yah Nah Drachodayat (breath)

Meaning:

Om
Supreme Divine, Thou art the
Creator of this universe,
Of earth, space, and heaven.
We adore *Savitah**
That radiant splendor
Thy pure form — the source of all creation.
We meditate upon Thy Divine radiance.
Thee we behold.
Inspire all our thoughts,
Guide our soul, Open our inner eye —
The eye of Wisdom.

Savitah — that which gives birth. *Savitah* is the creater of the five elements: Earth, Water, Fire, Air, Ether.

Short *Mantras*

1. "RA"

Raises energy, brings strength and energy in a hurry.

Procedure: Take deep breath, hold for a few seconds. Exhaling, chant out loud ERRRRRAAAA. Exhale any air that remains in the lungs. Repeat two more times. Chant loudly and forcefully.

Result: Expands aura, increases flow of circulation, brings vitality.

2. ANI-HU

Brings in the quality of empathy with others. Good for group chant.

3. HOO (who)

Increases focus and concentration. Is placed in center of the head. Balances scattered energies of body.

4. HU (hue)

Invokes purity; builds energy.

Procedure: a. deep breathing 5 times.
            b. Exhale HU 5 times (5 breaths)
            c. Repeat up to 15 times.

5. SO-HAWNG

Balances mental and emotional energies. Unifies mental and emotional vibratory rate. A silent mantra.

Procedure: a. Say first part while breathing in. A wind sound, does not use vocal chords.
            b. Say second part while breathing out. Does not use vocal chords.
            c. Repeat 5 to 10 minutes.

Comment: May experience unusual physical feelings as emotions are skaken loose.

6. THO

Alters energy patterns around body and brings healing.

Procedure: a. Breath in deeply and hold breath. Exhale fully.
            b. Repeat.
            c. Third time breathe in deeply, then exhale forcefully saying aloud "Thoooo". Emphasis is on the "TH" with "OOO" trailing to whisper.
            d. Exhale all remaining air.
            e. Breath normally for a minute or two.
            f. Repeat a-e up to 4 times at any one time.

Comments: Can be done silently after having done at least once aloud. Breath in through nose, out through mouth. Direct concentration to areas in need of balance.

Thus far our discussion of *mantra* has concentrated on traditions foreign to our own; hence their effectiveness on us may be greatly diminished because we don't share the cultural or emotional context within which they were created. This is especially true in the longer *mantras* that enlist the aid of deities about whom we may know nothing. There is little use of *mantra* chanting within Western religious traditions and certainly no clearly defined theory such as is found in Vedic and Tantric chant, for example. However, for therapeutic purposes short *mantric* phrases can be devised in one's vernacular language that may produce positive results by altering one's consciousness or by changing one's relationship to a particular situation. The negative *mantras* of our childhood, which may still influence our adult actions, can be replaced by a positive *mantra* that is more beneficial to our health and psychological well-being. We probably all have at least one *mantra* that has limited us in some way. Search your memory and find it, then examine how you have been affected by it. Formulate a new *mantra* that transforms the message of the old one and repeat this new mantra at specific times during the day. Observe the results after seven days.

If we are willing to accept the Tantric philosophical principle that sound creates form, a concept that Hans Jenny's experiments appear to validate, then we might also be able to conclude that the power of *mantra* lies in its ability to create new vibrational patterns that, through resonance, can stabilize our mental attitudes and physical energies.

> All the objects that we see and feel in this universe, from thought or idea to matter, are sounds of a particular concentration. Every object consists of a certain density of sound more or less compelx and varying from case to case...Sound is the reflex of form; and form is the product of Sound.
>
> by repetition of *mantras* (thought-forms) and their *japa* (rhythmic concentration on them), one can remodel one's entire physical, mental, and psychic nature.
>
> The power of *mantra* consists in the effect of its pattern of sound-waves. Under vibration small particles of matter, as one can prove by experiment, group themselves into definite geometrical patterns and figures, corresponding exactly to the quality, strength, and rhythm of the sound. The physical sound patterns produced by *mantras* are capable of coming into sympathetic vibrations with sound patterns which constitute physical phenomena.[9]

These Tantric concepts have not yet been fully investigated by Western scientific method, although current research in physics may be leading in that direction. My personal experience in daily practice of North Indian vocal music and chanting over a period of several years, and my observation of others who have been similarly engaged compels me to conclude, albeit subjectively, that there is considerable transformational power in the vibrational forms created through the practice of *mantra*.

Tantra Yogic Concepts of Human Subtle Anatomy, The System of Chakras and Vibration[10]

According to the teachings of Tantra Yoga, the human subtle anatomy is composed of a system of *Nadis*, *Pranas* and *Chakras* which sustain and control the vitality of our physical and spiritual life. The *Nadis* are a system of subtle channels that underlie our nervous system. They originate at the crown of the head and spread, like veins, throughout the body and terminate at special places in the sense organs, including the hands and genital organs. There are three principle *Nadi*: a left channel — *Pingala Nadi*; a right channel — *Ida Nadi*; and a central channel — *Sushumna Nadi*, also called Mount Meru and "the central pathway". The central pathway follows a path of the spinal column and has three layers:

> The *Vajra Nadi* runs from the navel to the top of the head and is responsible for the regulation of the flow of electrical energy within the body.
>
> The *Chitrina Nadi* is found within the *Vajra Nadi* and runs from the base of the spine to the top of the head. It carries the cosmic energy force through the central axis of the body.
>
> The *Brahma Nadi*, considered the most subtle of all the *Nadi*, is encased within the *Chitrina Nadi*. It is the pathway of the unstruck *Anahata — dhvani* "sound" of inner being awareness.

The three principle *Nadi* are associated with color and with matrix sounds called *Ali* or vowel vibrations, as well as other qualities as shown:

Pingala Nadi	Sushumna Nadi	Ida Nadi
Tha-breath	*Hatha-Pranayama*	Ha-breath
Moon	Fire	Sun
Female	Together	Male
Magnetic	Timeless	Electrical
Ali-16 vowels	*Bindu*-central point	*Kali*-34 consonants
Semen	Thought of Enlightenment	Blood
White	Blue-Black	Red
Yin	Balance	Yang

Pranas are the vitality essences or currents of vital energy that run through the *Nadis*. Four specialized branches of yoga have developed from Tantra Yoga that concern themselves with the control and release of *prana* through the *Nadis*: Kundalini Yoga, Laya Yoga, Kriya Yoga, and Nada Yoga. All of them are concerned with breath and sound.

Chakras (from Sanskrit language meaning "wheels") are a series of mandala-like discs or energy vortexes that are strung along the central pathway (*Sushumna*). *Chakras* serve as the focal points for receiving and distributing the subtle energies of the body as well as the incoming energies of the environment as they are filtered through the etheric body. There are seven major *chakras* and 21 minor *chakras*. The major *chakras* are said to govern the endocrine gland system, one of the four principle agents of distribution in the physical body,[11] and are found in the same general area as the glands.

No.	*Chakra*	Location	Gland	Relationships
7	Crown	Top of Head	Pineal	
6	Ajna	Forehead	Pituitary	
5	Throat	Throat	Thyroid	
4	Heart	Heart	**Thymus**	**Center**
3	Solar Plexus	Navel	Pancreas	
2	Sacral Center	Genitals	Gonads	
1	Base of Spine	—	Adrenals[12]	

In addition to the relationship of the *chakras* to the seven major glands of the body, esoteric teachings reveal that each *chakra* is associated with a meaning, a quality, a color, an element, a sense organ, and a *mantra* sound that when sung, can balance and energize the *chakra*. There have been many writings about *chakras* from the many traditions that utilize them. Different sources agree with each other on some points and differ on others. Likewise, not all traditions acknowledge all seven *chakras*. Tantra, for example, traditionally acknowledged four with the remaining three added after the tenth century A.D.

Muladhara is located at the base of the spine and is associated with the adrenal glands. It is the root support for the body, its quality being solidity, physical survival, and security. Its element is earth; it is associated with smell. Of the writers consulted, the majority gave its color as yellow and its *mantra* sound as "Lam". Other colors cited were: crimson, dark purple, and red with white. Other mantra sounds were given as "Bhuh" and "Shivum Shanti" (meaning "Peace and Benediction").

Swadhisthana (Hindu) and *Apana* (Tantric) *chakra* is located in the lower pelvis near the sexual organs and is associated with the gonad glands. Its quality is creativity and sexuality. Its element is water; its sense association is taste. Traditional Hindi teachings assign to it the color vermilion, but other colors associated with it are silver and violet. *Mantras* for this second chakra are: "Vam" (Hindu), "Bhuvah", Bam, "Um" and "Mano ramon".

Manipura chakra ("Samana", Tantric) is located at the navel and is associated with the pancreas. Its quality is expansiveness, will and power; its element is fire and it is associated with the sense of sight. The majority of sources give its color as red, but others give it the colors of red/yellow, blue and purple/red. All sources give its *mantra* as "Ram".

Anahata ("Prana", Tantric) is located at the heart and is associated with the thymus gland. The heart *chakra* is located at the center of the body and is the mid-*chakra* with three *chakras* below it and three above. It is therefore considered the chakra of fusion, the place where the energies of the lower centers begin their transformation from concern for personal needs to a more expansive and encompassing concern for the larger humanity. It is, then, the center of spiritual love, compassion and light. Its element is air; its sense association is touch. Its color is variously given as sky blue, green, "color of smoke", pink, peach, and enerald-blue. Its mantra is given as "Yam" (Hindu), "Maha" (also "Hindu", "Om" and "Soham".

Vishuddha Chakra ("Udana", Tantric) is the fifth center. It is located in the throat and is associated with the thyroid gland. Its qualities are abundance, purity, knowledge, and power of speech. It is also associated with special wisdom. Hindu tradition gives its element as space, whereas Tantra gives its element as air. Its sense association is hearing (Hindu) or touch (Tantra), and its color is given as mauve, purple, blue, green, and reddish violet. Most sources give its *mantra* as "Ham" or "Aim".

Ajna Chakra (not utilized in Tantra) is found in the center of forehead at the level of the eyebrows and is associated with the pituitary gland. Commonly referred to as "the third eye," its qualities are clarity, inner command, and spiritual insight. Two of the seven sources consulted associated this chakra with mind and thought. In traditional Tantra Yoga, this center was not added until much later — after the 10th century A.D. No sense organ is assigned to it, and its color is given as white, orange or green. Its *mantra* is given as "Ham" (Hindu), OM (two sources), and "Pragna" which means "Wisdom with Compassion".

Sahasrara Chakra ("Vyana", Tantric) is found at the top of the head and is commonly referred to as the "crown *chakra*". It is associated with the pineal gland, its quality is higher consciousness, and its element is ether. In Tantra Yoga it is associated with hearing. Its color association is given as white, blue, golden yellow, and blue white. Its *mantra* is variously given as "Om", "Am", "Satya", and "Om arkum namah" ("I bow to the worthiest energy which I am").

As one moves upward from the lowest *chakra* to the highest, the vibrational energy quality of each chakra becomes progessively more subtle. Chanting the associated *mantra* from lowest to highest aids in maintenance of the *pranic* energy flow by freeing any accumulated energy blocks, stimulates the associated gland and raises the Kundalini force which is said to lie dormant in the first *chakra*. There is a definite physiological and vibrational relationship between the second (lower pelvic) *chakra*, and fifth (throat) *chakra* and the sixth (third eye) *chakra*, as well as a balancing relationship between the first (base of spine) *chakra*, and the seventh (crown) *chakra*. Likewise, there is a physiological relationship between the gonad and thyroid glands and between the thyroid and pituitary glands.

Association of Chakras and Pitches (Tones)

No traditional source gives any hint of actual chanting tones to be used with each *chakra* nor any clue as to intervalic relationships between the seven *chakras*. Until recently it has been fashionable to claim that one simply moves up the major scale in ascending order for each *mantra* beginning on the pitch "C" as the tonic note. Thus:

Chakra 1	C	Mantra 1
Chakra 2	D	Mantra 2
Chakra 3	E	Mantra 3
Chakra 4	F	Mantra 4
Chakra 5	G	Mantra 5
Chakra 6	A	Mantra 6
Chakra 7	B	Mantra 7

I find this to be an unsatisfactory solution to the problem of finding the proper tones of each *chakra* for the following reasons:

1. The proposition that we all resonate to the same pitches is unlikely. It is more likely that each individual will have a different resonating pitch that may not even be one of the designated pitches of our tuning system.

2. The idea that seven *chakras* correspond to the seven tones of our major scale is entirely too simplistic, too convenient, and I think, a bit capricious because;

3. Chanting mantras to tones was done long before the invention of our equal tempered scale, indeed before the concept of a scale was developed and

4. Our major scale is primarily of European origin, whereas the concept of *chakras* comes from Hindu and Buddhist teachings. Many different types of seven tone scales have been developed over a thousand year period. Eastern scales employ tuning systems that are very different from our own.

5. Our Western major scale dates from the middle of the sixteenth century and the equal tempered system of tuning emerged at the beginning of the eighteenth century and has been standardized only with the last 50 years.

6. The frst scales to be developed were probably four and five tone scales, and they were based in the relationships of the natural harmonic series.

7. Early forms of chant, both Eastern and Western (predating the Gregorian chant of Christianity), utilized only three notes. Vedic chanting (India), the oldest continuous tradition of sacred chant, still uses only three tones.

8. The fourth and seventh scale degress of our major scale cannot be derived from the harmonic series.

More will be said on pitch relationships as they relate to the seven *chakras* when we consider the glands more specifically in the next chapter.

By means of breath-control (*Pranayama*) and vibrational activity (*Mantra-yana*), it is possible to influence the subtle and physical body.[13] This is considered the essence of Tantra Yoga; the two primary methods of achieving this and are through Sexual Tantra and by chanting the mantras for the chakra centers. The purpose in influencing the vibration rates of the subtle and physical body is to maintain the health of the body and for the transformation of body energies into the higher spiritual realm.

We have two basic systematic methods for mantra chanting of the seven centers.

In both cases the procedure is to chant each *mantra* in ascending order, beginning with the base of the spine from two to fifteen minutes for each center, using a kind of rolling rhythm. The proper pitch is located according to that which produces the greatest resonance in the heart and throat area, and is maintained as the principle tone throughout. From my own experience I have found that the pitch slightly higher than "C#" to works very nicely and that chanting a fourth or fifth above it for the fourth *chakra* adds vitality at the halfway point. Experimentation, however, is very important both with regard to pitch selection and to rhythm; we must be guided by our intuitive sense, for we really know more about this than we may realize if we simply trust ourselves instead of looking to "outside authorities" for guidance.

The following are two principal *chakra mantra* systems in ascending order with suggested rhythms for each which I have found to be particularly attractive. While chanting, attention is concentrated on each corresponding *chakra* and the breathing is deepened into the pelvic area.

Suggested Tempo: 136 m.m.

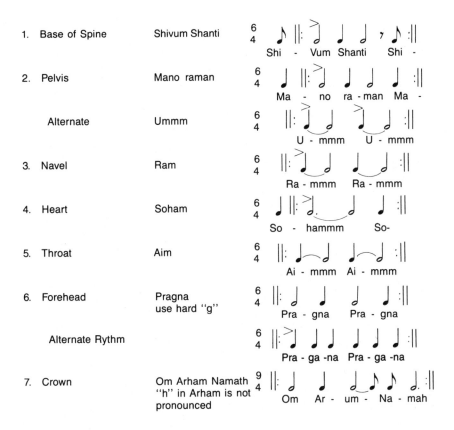

1.	Base of Spine	Shivum Shanti
2.	Pelvis	Mano raman
	Alternate	Ummm
3.	Navel	Ram
4.	Heart	Soham
5.	Throat	Aim
6.	Forehead	Pragna use hard "g"
	Alternate Rythm	
7.	Crown	Om Arham Namath "h" in Arham is not pronounced

Suggested Tempo: 132 m.m.

CHAPTER SIX

Toning Organs and Glands With the Voice

Singing regulates, sustains and deepens the breath, increases the sensitivity of the auditory system and refines the internal sensing process. Singing can resonate the entire physical body and electro-magnetic field, fully engage the mind, and give the emotions a vehicle for expression and produce an overall sense of well-being. When we combine the singing of sustained pitches with specific vowels and directed concentration we can, in addition, revitalize our internal organs, tone our endocrine gland system and calm our nervous system. In short, the quality of our voice can be a reflection of our emotional, physical, and spiritual condition — our healthfulness.

Over the centuries many methods for training the voice have been devised to meet the rigors of public performance for the various styles that are part of our musical culture today. All of these styles present the student with an idealized model of good vocal sound to which the student aspires. Some of these styles utilize techniques and mannerisms that are more healthful and more natural than others. But the training and packaging of the voice for public performance is very different in method and purpose from those considerations that presently draw our attention.

The truly natural healthful voice that we seek does not employ a training method *per se*, but results from a highly individual process of continuous discovery, for the restoration and maintenance of healthfulness is a part of the process itself. One's natural voice gradually emerges as restricting tensions are released, as the internal structures of the body become more involved in support, as breathing becomes fuller and deeper, and as more of the resonating potential of the body is filled with sound. The natural voice has none of the cultural mannerisms that have become associated with "good" singing; there is no imposed vibrato, there are no extraneous tensionful jaw movements, no stretching of the neck muscles, no look of anguish in the face, no restriction of the throat, no rigidity in the shoulders, no compacted barrel chests resulting from improper use of the thoracic diaphragm. One's energy is concentrated in the lower torso and not in the chest, which must be free of tension so that the lungs may expand fully and effortlessly. The fullness, flexibility and resonance of the voice results as a matter of course when we allow these tensions to evaporate, and the emerging sound will be expressive, full and vibrant.

Here, then is a catalogue of the tensions and self-imposed constructions that impede the emergence of an individualized natural voice. In essence, these constructions are blockages in energy flow that respond very well to breath and voice.

HEAD

Tightness of scalp
Sense of compactness of brain
Rigidity of facial muscles
Tension around eyes and ears
Squinting
Tightness of lips
Insensitivity of mouth
Inflexibility of tongue
Tightness of jaw — both sides and underneath
Compacting of skull on the top of the spine

NECK AND THROAT

Rigidity and loss of sensation of glottis
Restriction of back of throat
Chronic tension of neck muscles (impairs hearing)
Inflexibility of vocal diaphragm
Tension in area around thyroid gland
Rigidity of area around parathyroid glands and base of throat

SHOULDERS

Rigidity of shoulders

CHEST

Rigidity of upper chest — lack of expansion
Constriction in thymus and heart area
Restriction of movement of lower ribs
Bank of tension surrounding entire rib cage
Rigidity, constriction of thoracic diaphragm

ABDOMEN

Rightness of abdominal muscles from sternum to pubic bone
Chronic tightness of stomach
Chronic tension of genitals, sphincter muscle and intestinal tract
Tightness of hip sockets
Constriction of pelvic floor

Lest this list lead us to despair, we must remember that these constrictions are learned responses which we have created and nurtured. We can, if we wish, relinquish them by re-educating ourselves through directed relaxation, breathing, sensory awareness and singing with the utmost gentleness and compassion.

Breath and Voice[1]

The key to reclaiming a natural voice lies with a full use of the entire breathing process. Anatomically, the breathing apparatus is a totally contained volume of muscular power which involves the trachea, lungs, thoracic diaphragm, ribs, abdominal muscles, back muscles, pelvic diaphragm (more commonly referred to as the pelvic floor), sphincter muscle and the organs contained between the thoracic and pelvic diaphragms.[2] When the breathing apparatus functions without restriction a subtle expansion and contraction can be felt in the buttocks, throat, neck and scalp as well. When you inhale, the lower abdominal muscles and the pelvic diaphragm are drawn outward and downward to increase the abdominal/pelvic cavity while the back, lower ribs and thoracic diaphragm expand to create a vacuum in the thoracic cavity. The lungs respond by expanding, which allows the air to fill the vacuum when the throat is open. "When you inhale, you increase the vacuum and therefore the lungs expand to allow the air to fill the vacuum. When exhaling, you reverse the vacuum and the air is drawn from the lungs; it's a matter of air pressure caused by a reduction of the thoracic cavity."[3] In exhalation the thoracic diaphragm is released, the abdominal muscles and lower ribs contract (apply pressure to the internal organs) and the pelvic diaphragm is drawn upward. The thoracic diaphragm responds with a lengthening (eccentric) contraction which decreases the thoracic cavity thereby causing air to be released from the lungs. In the process of breathing, the lungs function like an active sponge that actually sucks the air in and then lets it out. "The lungs have an active role in breathing. They are not some passive tissue, they can double the amount of air by the lungs taking an active role. A useful and accurate image of the entire breathing process is to envision an expanding balloon in the belly."[4]

    If you place your fingers under you rib cage near the sternum and then cough, your fingers will be pushed out by the action of your thoracic diaphragm. This action can be felt all around the rib cage. Now stop the cough halfway; do not release the diaphragm but feel where it is. Next, consciously initiate the action of the thoracic diaphragm separate from the breath, hold it briefly, then inhale, expand the diaphragm further and exhale. Repeat, but this time as you inhale, allow the full length of the abdominal muscles to expand before the exhalation. In this last experiment perhaps you noticed a downward movement at the bottom of the pelvic cavity as you expand your abdominal muscles; this is the downward expansion of the pelvic diaphragm and this action is essential in full, effortless breathing.

We have not yet completed our series of breathing experiments, however. This time repeat the previous experiment, but before expanding your abdominal muscles contract your sphincter muscle until after your exhalation. Did you notice how this inhibits the outward expansion of the lower abdominal muscles and the downward expansion of the pelvic diaphragm? Now repeat the experiment, but this time consciously release the sphincter muscle and allow it to expand as well. Was there a noticeable difference in the capacity of the lower abdomen and pelvic cavity for expansion?

The purpose of this series of experiments is to bring to conscious awareness a breathing process that functions effortlessly if we have not hindered it in some way. The initiator of the breathing cycle is the thoracic diaphragm which must be activated before breathing or there will be a tendency to pull in the diaphragm — a tendency which soon becomes habitual. As long as the thoracic diaphragm is pulled in for breathing there will be a restriction in the process.[5] Another important, but often overlooked observation with regard to the breathing cycle is that it is a three-part cycle, not a two-part cycle as many have been led to believe. Rather than being a simple inhale-exhale rhythm, breathing is actually an inhale-exhale-rest rhythm. The rest phase of the cycle serves as a recovery period for the muscles used in breathing and is also the period in which the mind is more quiet. Simple observation will verify this.[6]

The vocal diaphragm (or vocal fold),[7] located in the trachea near the base of the pharynx directly behind the thyroid cartilage, consists of two bands of yellow elastic tissue (inferior thyro-arytenoid ligaments), each of which is covered by a thin layer of mucous membrane. (Fig. 1) Each band is attached in front of the thryroid cartilage and in the back to the artenoid. When the vocal diaphragm is not engaged, it remains open and relaxed, allowing air to pass freely through the trachea and into the pharynx. When we speak or sing, the two bands of the vocal diaphragm are stretched across the trachea, thereby closing the aperture. The exhaling air, now obstructed in its passage to the pharynx, creates pressure against the vocal diaphragm and forces the edge of each band to release in minute, rapid puffs. The more the air is held under pressure by the breathing apparatus, the more powerful is the sound emitted and the longer it will last. The air that escapes between the two bands is the exhaust from the pressure against the vocal diaphragm; to the degree with which this air is released, in terms of both volume and rapidity, no sound will be produced.

Variation in tension of the vocal diaphragm occurs from the pivot motion of the **crico-thyroid** and **thyro-arytenoid** cartilages which cause the pitch change

FIGURE 1
Looking down the Larnyx from above

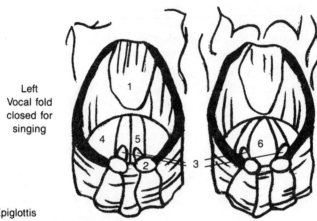

Left
Vocal fold
closed for
singing

Right
Vocal fold
relaxed for
breathing

1. Epiglottis
2. Cornicutate Cartiledge
3. Arytenoid Cartiledge
4. Vestibular Fold
5. Vocal Fold (diaphram)
6. Glottis

FIGURE 2
Tension of Vocal Fold

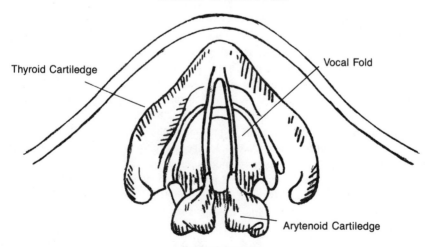

Thyroid Cartiledge

Vocal Fold

Arytenoid Cartiledge

Back of throat

in speaking and singing.[8] (Fig. 2) The vowels used in singing are formed primarily by the shaping of the pharnyx, and secondarily by the shaping of the tongue. Full resonance is achieved when the total pharnyx is used; secondary resonance occurs in the mouth and sinus cavities.

The ability to sense and to use fully all of these separate but interconnected parts of the vocal process is what gives the voice its strength, its richness and its flexibility. (Fig. 3) To describe all of the aspects of the process of vocalization and breathing in greater detail would increase the size of this book unnecessarily. Much of this work requires verbal explanation accompanied by actual demonstration and guided exploration within a class setting. Others who have made the study of voice and breath a lifetime occupation have produced books which contain suggestions for further explorations.[9]

Interrelationship of Voice and Internal Organs

Our internal organs support the sound of our voice and simultaneously receive the benefits of a vibratory massage. (Fig. 4) The organs involved are: lungs, heart, liver, spleen, pancreas, intestines, kidneys, bladder, rectum, and internal sexual organs. Through a process of vocalization the vitality of each organ can be maintained while all of the organs become more smoothly and freely integrated with each other. According to Bonnie Bainbridge Cohen

> All three aspects of voice production — pitch, vowel and intensity — are supported by the organs and breath. Their color or quality of expression is dependent upon which organs are involved in the support of the breath, and the manner and degree of which they are involved. The central organs support the fighting efforts of strength, directness and quickness and the peripheral organs express the indulging sustainment.[10]

In voice classes taught at the School for Body-Mind Centering (1978-81), it was discovered that the vocal quality changes when different organs are called upon for support. It is feasible, therefore, that one could diagnose a voice to identify which organs are supporting it and which are not. It is also possible to develop the skill of using the voice to actively tone a specific organ or group of organs at will.[11]

Inayat Khan, a highly respected musician and Sufi leader of India during the first part of this century, may have been alluding to the influence of the organs and endocrine glands on voice quality when he identified the three principal voice types as the:

> *Jelal* voice, indicating power;
>
> *Jemal* voice, indicating beauty;
>
> *Kemal* voice, indicating wisdom.[12]

FIGURE 3
Nasal, throat and mouth cavities utilized in Vocal Production

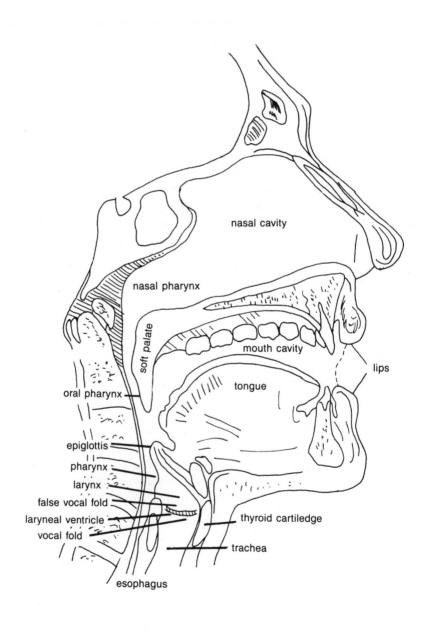

In addition, he described five qualities of the voice that are associated with the particular character of a person:

Earth quality, "hope-giving, encouraging, tempting;"

Water quality, "intoxicating, soothing, healing, uplifting;"

Fire quality, "impressive, arousing, exciting, awakening, horrifying;"

Air quality, "taking one far away from the plane of earth;"

Ether quality, "inspiring, healing, peace-giving, harmonizing, convincing, appealing, intoxicating,"[13]

Accordingly, one could possess a *Kemal* voice with a fire quality, a *Jelal* with an earth quality, or any other combination of qualities. However, Khan neglects to mention that a person's voice might, at various times, display characteristics that indicate gland and organ support as a reflection of one's emotional, physical and mental condition, or that a sensitive singer could greatly increase the range of expression with the effective support of the glands and organs.[14]

The process of learning to tone the internal organs requires a concentrated use of the voice combined with an ability to direct one's concentration to them. It is necessary, therefore, to have a visual image of each organ and its exact location in the body. To begin, breathe in through the nose with your throat fully open, employing the inhalation process described earlier in this chapter. The result will be an "hhh" sounding whisper. As you exhale through your mouth, gently vibrate the area of the body directly over the organ with your fingertips and, with an actively open throat, begin to make a an "hhh" — stop — "aah" sound, at first in a whisper, as you begin to explore the point at which your breath engages the vocal diaphragm. Then, with each breath, allow the vocal sound to become more full and the break between "hhh" and "aah" to be less pronounced until you achieve a smooth transition from "hhh" directly into "aah." Allow your fingers to rest as you focus your attention on areas where vibrations seem to be resonating such as head, throat, upper or lower chest, or abdomen. Be guided by the process and respond through your sensory feedback system. The sounds that emerge may not necessarily be "musical" ones; you may experience moments of discomfort from time to time resulting in coughing, sneezing, or itching spells. Trust your intuition to indicate whether to continue or to rest. Experiment with different pitches and vowels as you search for combinations that produce fuller resonance. Alternate between tones that sustain for the entire exhalation, and tones of short duration — several in one breath — because each initiation of the tone is very important.

Vocalizing requires an enormous amount of focus, attention and effort. Yet, if you are focused directly and your breath-voice process is operating efficiently, the result will be a sense of effortlessness and a fuller, richer sound.

FIGURE 4
Placement of internal organs that are effected in singing

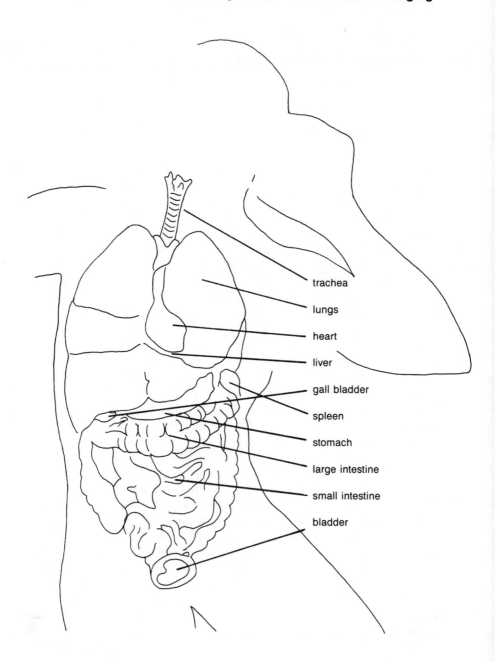

As you explore, pay attention to any special resonating pitches produced by your voice. These will be recognized by their greater strength and richness, possible indications of natural resonating frequencies with therapeutic potential. It is helpful to have someone work with you who can support your vocalizing by matching your pitches and calling your attention to significant changes in vocal quality. Alternate between singing with your eyes open and closed in order to balance awareness of both your internal and external environment. For some it will be more comfortable to begin with eyes closed and finish with eyes open; for others the reverse will be true. It is a matter of choice and, perhaps, personality. Use different positions for singing also: lying down, or moving your arms, or walking, standing or in various yoga positions.

Try to devote half an hour or more per day to this process, concentrating first on general areas of the body and eventually on specific organs as your sensitivity becomes more refined. The sequence of the organs will vary from individual to individual depending on your own nature. Likewise, the sequence will vary from day to day depending on your mood and physical condition. After working with a specific organ or sequence of organs, always complete your session by returning to general areas again.

Some Thoughts on Vocal Range

The fully flexible voice is capable of an effective range of three octaves. Our traditional range classifications, Bass, Baritone, Tenor, Countertenor, Alto, Soprano, and all the various sub-categories (mezzo, lyric, and so forth) are restricting categories. We need not be limited by them. *Every* voice has a pelvic quality, deep chest quality, upper chest quality, throat quality, head quality and "fal-setto" quality. It is possible to move effortlessly from one to the other. The extreme limits of one's vocal range will have a softer quality to them that, with practice and effective use of the support mechanisms, can be strengthened. The "falsetto" voice is not normally intended to be a loud voice. However, with proper control of resonance — achieved in the mouth, nose and sinus cavities — this voice quality can be used expressively without undue stress to the vocal diaphragm itself.

Suggestions For Extending Your Vocal Range

First, find the pitch that is the interval of a fifth or sixth higher than the lowest pitch that you can sing. Consider this pitch as your tonic note. Using either the Western "do, re, mi's" or the Indian equivalent "Sa re ga" sing the descending from of the major scale to the lowest note you can sing and then sing the scale up to the tonic once again. The following example will clarify the procedures:

Step I

Scale Degree:	8	7	6	7	8'*	8	7	6	5	6	7	8'
Western Syllable:	do	ti	la	ti	do	do	ti	la	sol	la	ti	do
Indian Syllable:	sa	Ni	DhaNi		Sa	Sa	Ni	DhaPa		DhaNi		Sa

8	7	6	5	4	5	6	7	8	8	7	6	5	4	(3)	4
do	ti	a	sol	fa	sol	la	ti	do	do	ti	la	sol	fa	mi	fa
Sa	Ni	DhaPa		Ma	Pa	DhaNi		Sa	Sa	Ni	DhaPa		Ma	Ga	Ma

5	6	7	8'	8	7	6	5	4	(3)	(2)	(3)	4	5	6	7
sol	la	ti	do	do	ti	la	sol	fa	mi	re	mi	fa	sol	la	ti
Pa	DhaNi		Sa	Sa	Ni	DhaPa		ma	ga	re	ga	me	Pa	DhaNi	

8'	8	7	6	5	4	(3)	(2)	(1)'	(2)	(3)	4	5	6	7	8
do	do	ti	la	sol	fa	mi	re	do	re	mi	fa	sol	la	ti	do
Sa	Sa	Ni	DhaPa		ma	ga	re	sa	re	ga	ma	pa	DhaNi		Sa

* ' = breath mark

As you arrive at the pitches that are below your pitch range, relax your vocal diaphragm as much as you can, continue to exhale air, form the syllable with your mouth and lips and *think* the pitch that you are not able to sing. Do not stop until you have sung the entire sequence; sing without force, lightly, at a moderate tempo — perhaps one syllable per second. Pronounce each syllable clearly, sounding each consonant distinctly. Allow your voice to resonate into the lower chest and the pelvis. Repeat the sequence several times and invent some patterns of your own. Be consistent about doing this every day for at least thirty minutes; the best time of day to do this exercise is early in the morning after having something warm to drink but before eating breakfast. In about a week you will discover a noticeable change in your lower register. Your voice will acquire more resonance and more depth in both singing and speaking. You will also find that your original lowest pitch has more sound to it and eventually your range will be extended to the tonic note ("do" or "Sa") an octave below your original tonic note.

Step II

The range from your original tonic to the tonic an octave above is probably your strongest range, so proceed to the upper tonic as follows:

1	2	3	2	1'	1	2	3	4	3	2	1	1	2	3
do	re	mi	re	do	do	re	mi	fa	mi	re	do	do	re	mi
sa	re	ga	re	sa	sa	re	ga	ma	ga	re	sa	sa	re	ga

4	5	4	3	2	1'	1	2	3	4	5	6	5	4	3
fa	sol	fa	mi	re	do	do	re	mi	fa	sol	la	sol	fa	mi
ma	pa	ma	ga	re	sa	sa	re	ga	ma	pa	dha	pa	ma	ga

2	1'	1	2	3	4	5	6	7	6	5	4	3	2	1'
re	do	do	re	mi	fa	sol	la	ti	la	sol	fa	mi	re	do
re	sa	sa	re	ga	ma	pa	dha	ni	dha	pa	ma	ga	re	sa

1	2	3	4	5	6	7	8	7	6	5	4	3	2	1
do	re	mi	fa	sol	la	ti	do	ti	la	sol	fa	mi	re	do
sa	re	ga	ma	pa	dha	ni	sa	ni	dha	pa	ma	ga	re	sa

As before, when you reach your highest pitch, continue to exhale, form the syllable with your mouth and tongue, let your voice drop off and *think* the pitches you cannot sing. Do not stop until the entire sequence is completed. As you approach your highest pitches it will be natural for you to change from a chest voice to a "falsetto" voice and your voice may become quieter as you do so. Pay special attention to the break between the two and practice making a smooth transition, keeping a uniform quality to your voice.

Step III

Complete your practice with the following exercise beginning on your original tonic. Again, *think* the pitches you cannot yet sing.

original tonic —

Lowest Octave

1	7	6	5	4	3	2	1	2	3	4	5	6	7
do	ti	la	sol	fa	mi	re	do	re	me	fa	sol	la	ti
sa	ni	dha	pa	ma	ga	re	da	re	ga	ma	pa	dha	ni

Middle Octave / **Upper Octave**

(1)	2	3	4	5	6	7	1	2	3	4	5	6	7
do	re	mi	fa	sol	la	ti	do	re	mi	fa	sol	la	ti
sa	re	ga	ma	pa	dha	ni	sa	re	ga	ma	pa	dha	ni

original tonic

Upper Octave / **Middle Octave**

1	7	6	5	4	3	2	1	7	6	5	4	3	2	(1)
do	ti	la	sol	fa	mi	re	do	ti	la	sol	fa	mi	re	do
sa	ni	dha	pa	ma	ga	re	sa	ni	dha	pa	ma	ga	re	sa

If you do this every day, within a month to six weeks you will have a three octave range, plus a fully flexible voice, excellent breath control and a full command of pelvic resonance, chest resonance, throat resonance, head resonance and restoration of your "fal-setto" voice.

Vowels and Vocal Resonance

Whereas variation in the tension of the vocal diaphragm controls pitch and the pressure of the breath against the vocal diaphragm regulates the intensity of the sound produced, it is the resonating capacity of the pharyngeal cavities (nasal,

FIGURE 5
Three-dimensional Cross

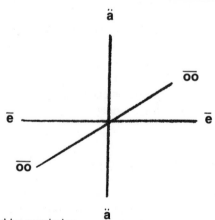

Examples of common vowels through the shaping of the pharyngeal cavity in dimensions and planes.

Dimensions

Dimensions	Vowels	Key Words
vertical	a	father, car
sagittal	oo	tool, hoop
horizontal	e	even, meet

oral and laryngeal) that account for the tone quality of the voice. Each of the interconnected cavities can be shaped to produce the different overtones which, in turn, create all the vowels of human speech and song. According to Cohen:

> These three connecting cavities can be shaped into an infinite variety of spatial forms, each registering different overtones. Those overtones which are produced by the shaping of the total pharyngeal cavity, we call vowels. Therefore, vowels are (the result of) the overtones of any pitch picked up by a specific shaping of the resonating chamber.[15]

It is the subtle manipulation of the tongue that shapes the pharyngeal cavity to produce the variety of vowel sounds used in our many human languages. Of these, three have been identified as the key vowels: *AH, EE* and *OO*. Philip Lieberman of Brown University, who has made an extensive study of the anatomy of human speech, notes that at least one of these vowels is found in every language while most contain all three. The reason, he believes, is that AH, EE and OO are the most stable and easily identifiable of the vowels, remaining intelligible despite individual variation in enunciation.[16] If we examine the anatomy of the vocal tract, we can see why this is so. The larynx is located deep within the throat which "makes the pharynx almost as long as the oral cavity, with which it forms a right angle."[17] Therefore in producing the vowel *AH*, the tongue is drawn backward to narrow the pharynx while the oral cavity remains open; to form the vowel *EE*, the pharynx is left open while the oral cavity is narrowed by raising the back of the tongue. In forming the vowel *OO*, the oral cavity and the pharynx remain open but are separated from each other by a constriction between the raised back of the tongue and the back of the palate. All other vowels emerge from subtle variations of these three extreme tongue positions.

As a result of related but quite independent experimentation, Bonnie Cohen has placed these primary vowels on a three dimensional cross based on the shaping of the vowel in the pharyngeal cavity. (Fig. 5)

Based on the premise that there is an ideal place in the pharynx corresponding to the pitch produced by the vocal diaphragm, her experiments consisted of moving the pharynx in various ways to observe what vowels emerged from the process. With this approach she discovered that a vertical stretch of the pharynx produced *AH*, a horizontal stretch produced *EE*, and a sagital stretch produced *OO*. By differentiating the pharyngeal cavity into three resonating areas (nasal, oral and larngeal) she further observed that the proper placement of the vowel varies according to the pitch and the intensity with which it is sung — proper placement meaning the area of fullest resonance for a specific vowel sung at a specific pitch. For example, in falsetto register vowels sung at high pitch and low intensity will receive their primary resonance in the nasal pharynx. However, when intensity is increased, the primary resonance will shift to the oral pharynx. This is not to negate the role of the tongue and the mouth in the formation and resonance of vowels, but they are considered to be secondary resonating areas.

From these experiments Ms. Cohen has formulated the hypothosis that "the fullest resonance of the vowels occurs when pharynx, which is the major adjusting resonating chamber, is fully aligned with the pitch being produced. Therefore, flatness of vocal quality is really a suppression, or covering, of the resonant capacity of a vowel and results from a mismatch of the pharynx with the pitch."[18]

DIAGRAM X

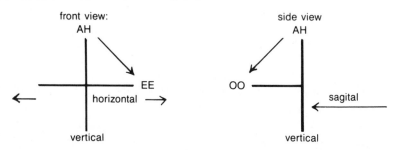

Thus far, our discussion has been restricted to a consideration of vowels on a one dimensional plane: vertical *AH*, sagital *OO* and horizontal *EE*. But when we move from vertical to horizontal, as from *AH* to *EE*, or from vertical to sagital, as in AH to OO, we form a two dimensional plane. As we make the change from *AH* to *EE* in one continuous breath by widening the pharynx at the level of the oral cavity, we pass through a number of vowel sounds — at the midpoint of which the vowel *I* (as in kite) will emerge. However, if we change to *EE* from *AH* by narrowing the pharynx at the level of the oral cavity, a different set of vowels will emerge. In both cases we have moved from the vertical to the horizontal plane. but in the former we have moved through what Bonnie Cohen refers to as the outer curve. In the latter, we have moved through the inner curve.

DIAGRAM Y
Vertical Plane

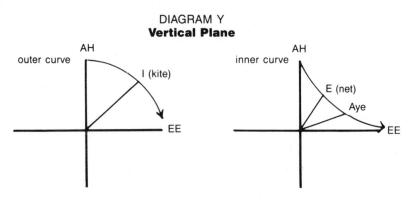

As demonstrated in the illustration that follows, there are six possible combinations, each with an inner curve and an outer curve variation. From these all of our vowels are derived. (Fig. 6)

FIGURE 6
Planes (combination of two dimensions)

Planes	Two Dimensions Primary—Secondary	Vowels*	Key Words
vertical (fig. 3)	vertical to horizontal	overcurve: $\bar{\imath}$ ä ⟶ ē undercurve: ē ā ä --→ e	(ä) father, car (ī) kite, mile (ē) even, meet (ĕ) net (ā) ape, date
sagittal (fig. 4)	sagittal to vertical	outward curve: ōô o̅o̅ ⟶ ä inward curve: u o̅o̅ ⟶ ä	(o̅o̅) tool, hoop (ō) over, tone (ô) horn, fork (ä) father, car (u) up, cut
horizontal (fig. 5)	horizontal to sagittal	outward curve: ū ē ⟶ o̅o̅ inward curve e ē ⟶ o̅o̅	(ē) even, meet (ū) use, cute (o̅o̅) tool, hoop (e) French o̅o̅

Application of the Vowels in Two Dimensions

When vowels are combined in two dimensions with arm and hand movements that externalize the change from the first plane to the second, our understanding of the resonating effect of the vowels increases dramatically. This process can have a very positive effect on our posture, vitality, physical and mental presence and energy balance as well. For *AH*, when sung properly has a lengthening effect on the body; *EE* has a broadening effect and *OO* produces the effect of depth. These effects can extend beyond the limits of the physical body to the electro — magnetic field that surrounds it. Two illustrations can serve as a model of the process. (Fig. 7 and 8 here) To move from the vertical *AH* to the horizontal EE following the outer curve, begin with your arms, fingers and thumbs extended fully above your head — the upper arms should be parallel to your ears — with your palms facing inward toward each other. Slowly move your fully extended arms downward in an arc, gradually rotating them until the palms of both hands face frontward, and your arms are fully extended outward from your sides, parallel with the shoulders. At the same time, move continuously from a pure *AH* at the beginning of the sequence to a pure *EE* at its completion, moving through the long *I* vowel at the midpoint. The entire sequence should be completed in one exhala-

FIGURE 7
Vertical to Horizontal: Outer Curve

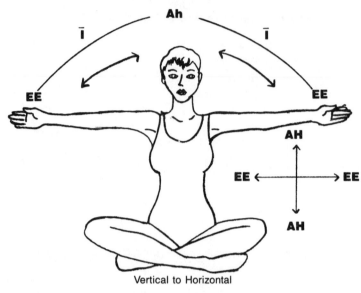

Vertical to Horizontal

FIGURE 8
**Sagital to Vertical
Outer Curve**

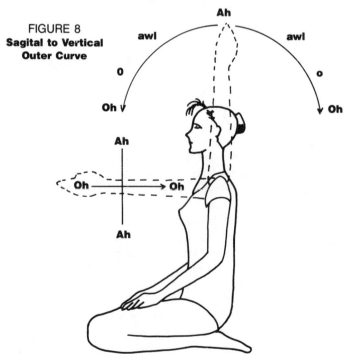

tion. Pause in this position to inhale, then sing *EE* to *OO* as you bring your extended arms forward toward each other in an arc until they are extended in front of you, arms parallel with palms facing. To complete the sequence, pause for an inhalation, then raise your extended arms upward in an arc, parallel with each other and palms facing until they are again extended over your head and you are singing *AH* once more. Although you may experiment with different pitches for each sequence, sing only one pitch for each complete sequence. Daily repetition of these sequences will produce a lasting effect, though it must be kept in mind that the effective potential of any therapeutic application of vowels depends on their proper placement. The slightest deviation from the intended vowel will render its application less predictable and therefore less effective.

The employment of vowels as an aspect of the healing process is hardly a new idea; indeed, one of the earliest references comes from Chinese healing practices. Traditionally, the vowels are arranged according to their relation to the principles of Yin and Yang. The vowel "A" (as in father) is considered to be most Yin; "E" (pronounced "Aye") is next most Yin; "I" (pronounced as in "tree") is more Yang; and "O" (as in "bowl") is more Yang. "U" (as in true) is considered to be the most balanced, containing equal amounts of Yin/Yang energy. By singing these vowels in the proper sequence the healing energy is accelerated for administering to oneself or to another who is ill. One's health, therefore, is enhanced through a balance of Yin/Yang energy by singing the sequence of vowels regularly, beginning with the most Yin and concluding with the balancing vowel.

The following instructions are given for the singing of the vowels:[19]

1. Sit in meditation posture.

2. Bring palms of hands together in "prayer" position. Thumbs touch each other but are separate from hands.

3. Lightly touch the throat (beneath the thryroid gland) with the tips of the thumbs.

4. With eyes closed, breath in and out slowly several times.

5. Begin to sound A E I O U (Ah-Aye-Ee-Oh-U) as you exhale.

6. Repeat several times as you begin to feel a change on Ki energy between both hands.

The syllable "Su" may also be used to activate healing energy. The procedure repeats numbers 1, 2, 3, 4, and 6, or you may raise both arms at the elbows with the palms facing inward as shown in the illustration. (Fig. 9)

FIGURE 9
**Chinese Meditation Posture for Singing of
Vowels for Yin/Yang Balance**

The Effects of Vowels on the Body

Many attempts have been made to relate the vowels to specific body areas. Although there seems to be some measure of uniformity among the various systems that have emerged, differences of perception do exist. These differences may be due to the fact that the resonating qualities of vowels are dependent on the individual, due in turn to such variables as the size and shape of the resonating cavities, breath support, intensity, pitch and one's ability to shape the pharynx. One of the more plausible of the many possibilities is given below and is intended more as a starting place for individual explorations.

MM — resonates the crown and back of head when sung in upper register or in falsetto.

EE — resonates the frontal area of the skull and the nasal cavities

AYE — resonates the throat and seems to stimulate the thyroid gland

AH — resonates the upper chest, heart and thymus area.

OH — resonates the upper abdominal area. A medium to low pitch seems to be most effective.

OO — resonates the lower abdominal area surrounding the naval and into the upper pelvic region.

UH — resonates base of spine and pelvic floor.

In personal exploration, I have found that the initiation of the vowel is very important. I suggest, therefore, that before singing vowels on a sustained pitch, one should first experiment by sounding each vowel several times, alternating between a breathy whisper and a normal speaking voice. The pressure of the breath against the vocal diaphragm followed by its sudden release helps to focus attention and direct the energy.

The Relationship of Pitch, Vowel and Endocrine Gland System

Related to the resonating effects of vowels, one may also explore possible correlations with the endocrine gland system. The endocrine system includes seven major glands that secrete many hormones used to regulate specific bodily functions.

> Pineal — a small structure located near the center of the brain. Referred to as the "seat of the rational soul" by Descartes, the pineal gland regulates the hormonal changes that usher in adolescence.[20]

> Pituitary — located in the front of the brain above the roof of the mouth. It regulates the secretions of the adrenals, gonads, pancreas and thryroid.

> Thyroid — located in the throat. It regulates the rate of metabolism, growth and mental development.

> Thymus — located in the chest above the heart. Its function is related to the immune system.

> Pancreas — located in center of body above the naval. It regulates blood sugar and functions in the digestion of food.

> Gonads — in women located halfway between the navel and pubic bone, and in men located outside the body in the testes. They regulate reproduction and sex characteristics.

> Adrenals — located on top of each kidney. They prepare the organs for fight by increasing heart and breathing rate.

In exploring possible correlations between the endocrine glands, pitch and vowels, a suggested procedure is to place a hand over the area of the gland — to help focus your concentration — initiate the sound, then remove your hand, initiate the sound again and observe the difference. An alternative to this procedure is to lightly vibrate the area over the gland with your hand as you sing.[21] There are a number of systems of correlation between glands, pitch and vowels, none of which have, as yet, been validated. The system presented here is an example of but one among several others. Again, focused experimentation will determine which of them is the most valid for you.

By combining the glands, the vowels and the pitch relationships of the harmonic series, we have a complete system for health maintenance.[22] Drawing the pitch relationships from the harmonic series, specifically the 2nd, 3rd, 4th, 5th, 6th, 7th, and 8th harmonic, we find that the natural relationship of the base of the spine, and the solar plexus and of the crown is reflected in the corresponding octave relationships of the 2nd, 4th, and 9th overtones of the harmonic series that are assigned to them. The thymus receives the fifth harmonic and stabilizing effect of the major triad while the pituitary receives the 7th harmonic.

The harmonic series is suggested because it is derived by nature. We do not, therefore, become involved with the shortcomings of artificially created scales. The use of the harmonic series does require at least a two-octave vocal range, however, which one should try to acquire. The fundamental pitch (or first harmonic of the series) lying a full octave below our 2nd harmonic, is below our vocal range. We might consider this to be our own fundamental as well. According to the law of the harmonic series, if the upper overtones are sounded, the fundamental note is also present. For our purposes, even though we may not actually hear the fundamental, its presence can be felt as the stabilizing force. It remains only to determine your individual resonating pitch. At present there is no accurate way to do this; all that can be suggested is a process of trial and error — in other words, experimentation. For the purpose of demonstration, the fundamental tone "A" has been selected as a place to begin. Here, then, is the full system presented:

Gland	Body Area	Harmonic	Interval	Vowel	Suggested Pitch	
Pineal	Crown (7)	8th	octave	"MM"	A	
Pituitary	Brow (6)	7th	minor 7th	"EE"	G	Upper Octave
Thyroid	Throat (5)	6th	P. 5th	"Aye"	E	
Thymus	Heart (4)	5th	Major 3rd	"AH"	C#	
Adrenals	Back	4th	octave	"OH"	A	
Pancreas	Abdomen	3rd	P. 5th	"OO"	E	Lower
Gonads	Pelvis	2nd	octave	"UH"	A	Octave

Anchor — Below vocal range — Fundamental —   A

Working with Partners and Groups

All of the vocal explanations and procedures of this chapter lend themselves to work with partners in groups of two or three people. These include breathing work, exploration of vowels, and toning of glands and organs. In working with partners one becomes the initiator and the others are the helpers. The support of partners helps to overcome timidity toward one's own voice — the result of negative conditioning. The helpers support by vocalizing in unison, matching pitch and vowels and breathing in the same rhythm as the initiator. In learning to vibrate glands and organs, helpers can lend physical contact with their fingers or hands directly over the area being vibrated and either lightly touch or massage-vibrate the area. Through observation, helpers can observe areas of restricted breathing, help to release the restriction and observe changes in vocal sound as specific areas begin to resonate. What is sought is a gradual emergence of a natural voice with the full support and active participation of the pelvic and thoracic diaphragms and of all the organs and glands, plus the ability to tone each organ and gland at will. This is a key to consistent health; for when it is accomplished, there is a free flow of bodily energy, stagnation — a cause of illness — is less likely to occur and the resulting vitality promotes a sense of emotion, mental and spiritual well-being.

The following order is recommended.

1. Freeing of breath restrictions and full utilization of the diaphragms.

2. Vowel work, beginning with head sound "ee" to throat "Aye," chest "ah," solar plexus "oh" to lower abdominal "oo." Activization of directional planes — vertical, horizontal and sagittal.

3. Vibration of organs beginning with heart and proceeding to lungs, liver, spleen, stomach and intestines.

4. Vibration of glands and gradual vitalization of glands to support resonance of voice beginning with thyroid, thymus, gonads, pancreas, adrenal, pituitary and pineal.

5. Combining voice, organs, glands, vowels and harmonic series as suggested.

Droning

Droning is a procedure that allows one person to improvise using an agreed upon scale while another sustains a vocal drone on the tonic pitch. The two (or three) participants should sit facing each other as close to each other as possible. When the person improvising comes to a resting place he/she intones the drone pitch and the partner begins an improvisation. The process continues as "droner" and "improviser" alternate until the droner joins the improviser in spontaneous unison improvisation.

In bringing this chapter and this part of our investigation to a close, it is helpful to draw a few of the main principles into focus once more. According to traditional Indian medicine, the three animating principles of the body are: the fire energy that gives warmth through the expanding principle of motion in all living things; the hidden energy of the air that is the sustaining energy and activator of the fire energy; the blood stream that maintains the chemistry of life and conveys the vital energies throughout the body. Restriction or inhibition of the free flow of one of these creates an imbalance that affects the other two.

There are three additional agents of energy distribution: the electro — mag—

FIGURE 10

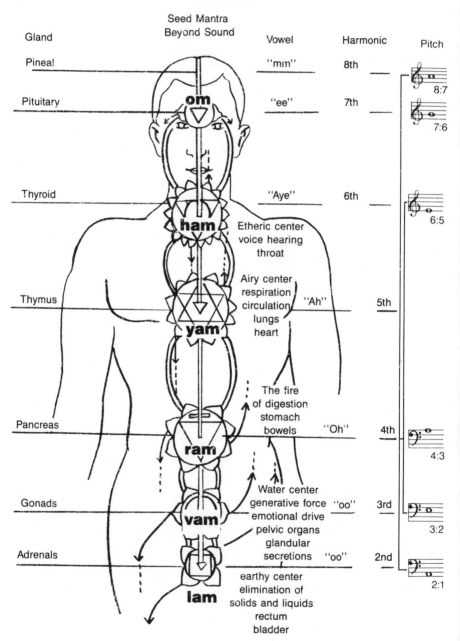

netic energy field with its seven energy centers that serve as points of reception and distribution throughout the physical body; the vast network of the nervous system; the endocrine gland system with its seven major glands. These systems are interdependent and respond to our emotional and metal states. The agents of energy distribution are connected to the three animating principles through the blood stream which, in addition to maintaining the chemistry of life, is also responsible for the circulation of oxygen and food throughout the body. Disease is considered a disharmony or lack of alignment in one or both of these systems. The introduction of specific tones to areas where blockages occur can release the cause of the blockages, restore the body to a balanced flow of energy and restore wholeness and unity.

CHAPTER SEVEN

Methods and Procedures in Sound Healing

The first requirement in learning the process of healing with tones is to experience the effects of various pitches on one's own body directly, and many of the suggestions of the previous two chapters are designed to do just that. It is an arduous labor but a most necessary one for those who aspire to work with sound in a healing capacity. Singers of India devoted at least one hour each day to the singing of a single pitch as a regular part of their vocal practice in order to study the effect of each pitch on their physical bodies. Numerous stories tell of legendary singers who accomplished miraculous cures and could change weather conditions with certain *ragas* came about as a result of this practice. There is, for example, a "rain" *raga* — so called because the first time it was sung it caused a violent rain storm in the midst of the drought season. It is said that it rained directly on the singer and his audience who were inside a palace at the time.

The practice of singing a single pitch for such a length of time, and singing the same pitch day after day until its full effect is experienced, is particularly difficult for Westerners because we do not place as much importance on a single tone. We approach this exploration with some curiosity but soon begin to lose interest. Yet with a little self-discipline, our boredom evaporates as the tone begins to take on a life of its own. As the tone reveals its own inner richness in progressively finer detail, we begin to discover a great deal. Eventually a whole new world opens to us, far richer than anything we could have imagined. The longer we remain with that pitch the more specific is our knowledge of its effect upon our physical body and our mind. In this regard there is a marvelous story, reported to have originated with the Armenians, of one old gentleman who loved to play his cello. Day after day, however, he continuously played but one note for hours at a time. This drove the other members of his household to distraction. Finally one of them admonished him, saying that all his friends played many different pitches on their instruments and created beautiful melodies. The gentleman gazed at his admonisher with compassion and replied that all his friends played so many notes because they were still searching for the "right" one whereas he had already found "the note".

By experiencing the full influence of a specific pitch upon our physical body we begin to refine the specific location of the pitch in terms of where it resonates within us. In so doing we may begin to predict with increased accuracy how we may resonate specific organs and glands in others. In addition, we increase our abilities of internal scanning, concentration and channeling, and strengthen our intuitive skills. The remainder of this chapter is devoted to presenting additional procedures that accomplish these goals. It is divided into three sections: procedures that may be practiced individually, procedures intended for increasing group channeling, and procedures that may be applied to another individual for healing purposes.

If you have experimented with some of the practices that were suggested in the two previous chapters you have probably already discovered that certain pitches resonate with greater richness than others, that the different vowels affect different parts of the body, and that the consonants are initiated by differing body efforts. The first purpose of these explorations was to arrive at a personal system for health maintenance to be utilized on a daily basis. The second purpose was to increase sensitivity to the effect of resonance on the physical body so that one may effectively assist another in a healing situation through the process of "channeling". Simply defined, "channeling" is a method of energy transference that by passes the personalities and egos of both the "healer" and the one being healed. The purpose of channeling is, therefore, to remove the restrictions that impede the free flow of energy which is the clearing agent that initiates and sustains the healing process. Susceptibility to illness results when one's natural vibrational energy flow becomes obstructed, the result of which is an accumulation of stagnant energy at one point, and a depletion of energy at the point immediately after it. This produces a condition of imbalance; the longer the condition lasts, the greater is the degree of imbalance and the greater is the threat to one's health.[1] The most commonly acknowledged cause of such obstruction to the body's energy flow is an emotional one, and the first place that the obstruction occurs is in the electromagnetic field that surrounds our physical bodies. If untreated, this eventually manifests in our organs or glands. Once this occurs, our emotional and mental energies are adversely affected and the cycle, being complete, feeds on itself, increasing our discomfort. Channeling has the effect of breaking the cycle by eliminating the effect of the first cause which is rooted in the personality and ego. Channeling also eliminates issues of ego and personality in the "healer" such as the desire to perform well and the resulting fear of failure that might impede the process. Because the process of channeling utilizes the intuitive thought process, its effectiveness depends on the ability of the channeler to eliminate the cognitive thought process with its characteristic running verbal monologue. This is accomplished through the utilization of meditative breathing techniques before and during the process of channeling. Slow and deep breathing is intended to quiet the mind rather than to flood it, as rapid breathing tends to do. Some form of slow and deep breathing is, therefore, a necessary first step to the series of experiments that follow. In these experiments the voice is the primary sound vehicle because it is the most effective sound agent for healing. The only additional equipment suggested is a pitchpipe to check pitches and possibly a pad and pencil to record results and insights.

Increasing Sensitivity to Internal Sound Resonance and the Electro-Magnetic Field

Part I

After approximately five to ten minutes of slow, deep breathing with your eyes closed, begin to initiate a soft sigh with closed lips.[2] The pitch is in the low-medium register — a comfortable range that is near your normal speaking voice. Do not choose a pitch. Rather, let the sound result easily as a natural part of each exhale. From the starting "pitch" level, allow your voice to slowly descend to its lowest possible note and then a little beyond, to relax your throat and increase the flexibility of your vocal diaphragm, timing the length of each vocal "sigh" to match the length of each exhalation. Do not attempt to hold your lowest pitch. Repeat this several times and then switch from a closed lip sound to an open "ah" sound. Repeat this several times and with a pitchpipe, locating the pitch names of any especially resonant frequencies that might emerge.[3]

Returning to the closed lip sound, repeat the same process in the upper — middle register, middle-high register, and the upper-high register. Returning once more to the closed lip "mmm" sound, begin with the highest pitch you can reach without straining and make a slow descending slide into your lowest register, inhaling when necessary. At each new exhalation begin with a pitch just slightly above the one with which you ended the previous exhalation so that your entire vocal range is engaged. Repeat several times and keep a record of any especially resonant frequencies that may emerge. Then, with the open "ah" sound, repeat this sequence also.

Now, with your pitchpipe as a reference, re-explore those pitches that were especially rich in harmonic resonancy using the vocal sequence of "ah — aye — ee — oh — oo — mm" and notice any changes in the location of the resonating areas that may occur. Keep a record of the results of this exploration for future reference.

Part II

Returning to your breathing practice, close your eyes and, hold your open hands in front of you with the palms facing each other about four inches apart. Let your hands remain in this position as you direct your concentration to the space between your hands until you begin to feel an increase of energy between them. As you continue deep concentrated breathing, begin to slowly move your hands about an inch apart on the inhalation and toward each other on the exhalation. Continue this process until your hands are about six inches apart. When you feel a resistant force between your hands, begin to hum a tone with each exhalation and feel how this increases the strength of the force. Select some of the tones and vowels which you discovered in Part I to have had a particularly resonant effect, and explore whether these tones significantly increase the strength of the electro-magnetic field that you have created.

Part III

As you continue your deep breathing and your concentration, rest your left hand on your lap and bring your right hand with open palm facing you to about four inches from your skin over the heart area, solar plexus area or beneath the navel. As you inhale move your hand slightly toward your skin and as you exhale move your hand back. Continue this procedure until you begin to feel a strong force between your hand and your skin. When the resistance force has become stronger, slowly sweep your hand up and down your torso, beginning with the genital area and ending with the crown of the head. As you do this, take notice of where the resistance is stronger and where it is weaker. Repeat both of these experiments and explore the influence of voice tones upon the magnetic force. Make a note of any pitches that significantly strengthen the force or weaken it. Eventually, you will have an intuitive sense of which pitches match the different energy vortexes. After a while, you might explore the use of both hands. For example, with your right hand just below your navel, place your left hand over your throat, retaining a distance of three or four inches between your hands and skin. Add tones to this also.

These explorations are designed to increase sensitivity to pitch, vowels and resonance as they effect the physical body and to create greater confidence in your intuitive processes, greater faith in your ability to channel, and to discover points of reference that can be of value in the process of aiding others. They are, however, merely procedural openings to a process of even deeper understanding of healing through sound. As such, their real value is that beginning with these you may add your own explorations and in sharing your personal discoveries, add significantly to its effectiveness and understanding.

Methods for Assisting Others through Sound

After you have been engaged in self-exploration with sound for a period of time, it is relatively simple to work with another person in a similar way. All of the procedures described thus far can be applied to a partnership situation of two or three people. One's partners can assist by listening for resonating pitches, by adding vocal support to your explorations, and by singing your resonating pitches back to you while you listen. The explorations in this section are designed specifically for work with a partner and, in addition, they are suggestions for applicable procedures in actual therapeutic situations.

Your first task is to get both you and your partner to relax and to clear away emotional and mental activity. Meditational breathing, as previously described, accomplishes both at the same time. Following a short period of quiet non-activity, sit face to face before your partner and while you both have your eyes closed, (closing of eyes encourages the production of alpha brain waves), engage in slower and deeper meditational breathing. During this "clearing" process each of you withdraw into your own internal centers, locating a point of stillness and balance. When you have reached this point within yourself, begin to visualize that with each exhalation your electro-magnetic field expands until it encompasses your partner. When you have connected with your partner in this way, rest a moment and fully experience this connection.

Now, with each inhalation, allow your eyes to open and visually scan your partner; beginning at the top of the head move downward with each inhalation. On the exhalation, close your eyes again and allow this information to be drawn into your intuitive process. Make no judgements and engage in no verbal analytical process. When this phase has been completed, come back to your own center and, quietly breathing, re-enter your own point of stillness. The impressions you have received are now being processed on a non-verbal level.

Ask your partner to lie down on his/her back and then station yourself in a comfortable sitting position at your partner's head. Lightly place your two hands on the crown of his/her head and again with eyes closed, aurally scan your partner's body and electro-magnetic field, listening for sound impressions that might be present. Observe particularly any impressions of frequencies and possible associations with specific areas of the body. Do not be discouraged if you do not actually hear sounds. Rather, you are receiving intuitive impressions by using a portion of your mind that, at least in our culture, we have not developed in any systematic way. Eventually, after perhaps years of experience, you may actually "hear" real sounds. When you can sense intuitively that this phase has been completed, bring your hands away from your partner's head and return to your center of stillness once again.

Now move to the right side of your partner and sit in a cross-legged position facing him/her approximately across from the solar plexus area. With your left hand you should be able to scan your partner from his/her crown to the heart area, and with your right hand from the throat to the area above the pubic bone area at a height of between two and three inches from the skin. Remain in this position until you begin to sense your partner's energy field and then at a leisurely pace move your hand up the torso directly over the chakra centers. When your hand reaches the upper chest area, move your hand back down the torso to the pubic bone area and beyond it another two or three inches, then reverse your direction again. This time bring your left hand to about three inches over your partner's forehead and let it remain there as you continue to sweep your partner's torso with your right hand. Your purpose here is to sense the relative strengths and weaknesses of the various energy centers. Alternate the process by bringing your right hand back to rest over the pubic bone area and with your left hand sweep downward to the heart area and then upward to the crown.

Some areas will have a stronger energy, some will have less. Place one hand over the strong energy centers, the other hand over the weaker centers to transfer energy from strong to weak centers for the purpose of balancing. Singing or humming a pitch will increase the effectiveness of this process. From this point on you must rely on your intuitive sense with regard to procedures in the channeling process. There is no systematic method with regard to placement of hands or selection of pitches. The important factor here is your ability to remove your own personality and ego and respond to the energy with your hands and with whatever tones might be appropriate at any given moment.

The more experience you have, the more trust you will have in your ability to allow yourself to respond to the energy. After a while your hands will move automatically without conscious direction from you and the tones that issue from your throat will not have been consciously selected. Further, with regard to the tones, you are encouraged to sound the first pitches that come to you in the midst of the process, rather than to agonize over whether you have found the correct one. If the pitch you produce is the wrong one, both you and your partner will know it immediately. You can always adjust to a new pitch or remain silent until you sense another. Once the tone feels right your partner can aid in the process by sounding the tone with you. when this phase has been completed, bring your right hand to a point about two inches beyond the pubic bone area and your left hand to about two inches beyond the top of your partner's head and remain in this position for a few minutes as you feel an energy flow from your right hand to your left hand. Remove your hands and quietly rest. Share with your partner any images or impressions you may have received.

In the process just described you have used your partner's energy field and your own. As such, your hands do not have contact with your partner's physical body. However, in situations involving an injury or when your partner is suffering from physical discomfort in a localized area of the body, there is an additional sound healing procedure that may bring relief. It consists of placing your lips directly on your partner's skin over the place of discomfort and humming directly into the area. In the beginning of the process it is recommended that you hum softly as you locate the most effective pitch. Once the pitch is found, and your partner can help you to verify the pitch, you may then gradually increase the energy level of the sound. Your partner can further increase the effectiveness of this procedure by humming the same pitch with you or he/she can remain silent — whichever feels appropriate at the time. This procedure has the effect of redistributing compacted energy, moving it out of the area to restore a more harmonious flow. At least five minutes of continuous humming — or "Om-ing" — is required. This process can be repeated regularly until discomfort is alleviated and should be followed by a brief channeling of the electro-magnetic field.

One additional practice technique that you can experiment with for the purpose of increasing your sensitivity in sound scanning is to have your partner think a pitch without actually singing. When you feel that you can "hear" the pitch, sing it to your partner for verification.

Additional Techniques Involving Partners

The Following technique appears to be of Chinese origin because of its emphasis on balancing of Yin/Yang energy and its use of "Chi" energy.[4]

1. Sitting facing south with your spine straight, raise your arms slowly over your head and look upward as you inhale. Repeat several times. This activates "Chi" energy.

2. Sit in the "seiza" meditation position and bring your hands together in the "prayer" position with your thumbs extended towards you. Bring your hands close to your throat and place your thumbs lightly on your throat below the thyroid gland. While remaining in this position add the sound "Su". Repeat the sound about ten times. There should be an emphasis on the "Ssss" sound and your throat should press outward as you say it.

3. Next, breathe in and out several times with your eyes closed, and then begin to sound "Ah — Aye — Ee — Oh — Oo" on each exhalation. Repeat several times. This has the effect of balancing your energy since you move from the most Yin vowel, "Ah", to the most Yang, "Oh" and end with the most balanced, "Oo". It also increases energy in your hands.

4. Sit in the seiza position behind your partner, both facing south.[5] Both of you begin with your hands in the prayer position. While your partner remains in this position, extend your arms slowly forward until they are fully extended behind your partner's back. Clap twice to clear away any stagnant energy that may have accumulated in your partner's energy field. Then, with your arms fully extended and the palms of your hands facing your partner, move them slowly up his/her spine and down the periphery of his/her back without touching. Repeat this motion five to ten times.

5. Hold your hands over the lung region and quietly sound "Su" seven to ten times. Your partner may sound the "Su" with you,

6. Clap your hands twice and then return them to the prayer position again.

The following examination and basic treatment method can also be effective:

1. Place the palm of one hand on the person you're examining, either at the feet or head. Tap the back of your hand with the other hand's index and mid-

dle fingers. Travel slowly over the entire body, tapping continuously at an even rate. Tap more gently over sensitive areas such as eyes, ears, genitals, or any injuries, adjusting the strength of your tapping to the strength of the area. Was the tapping high or low in pitch? If the area is mostly muscle, ask the person to tense (then tap) and relax (tap again). Did the pitch change?

2. With tuning forks, harmonica or your voice, play a single pitch on or near the area needing attention. If there is no specific region experiment, using your intuition, as to where to apply vibration. Start with a high pitch, then descend a half-step at a time until the person notices an effect. Ask if this effect feels healing; if it does, continue the pitch for several seconds. If it is not described as healing energy, continue searching. Healing energy may be described as warm, cool, relaxing, energizing. Some people will say they feel something when you first begin vibration, yet often this is merely a response to any vibration near the affected area and not to specific healing pitches. Repeat as necessary to other parts of the body. Record the date, time of day, the pitch used, and where applied.

3. The first tapping procedure has opened rhythmic sensitivity of the treated person as well as of your own hands. Begin tapping, following the steps as before. This time, however, alter the speed of tapping. For each area begin with quick tapping and gradually slow down until the healing rhythm for that area is determined.

Experiments in Group Channeling for Healing Purposes

All of the experiments and healing processes described in Sections I and II of this chapter are easily adaptable to group work involving from three to ten or more people; you are invited to devise your own variations of them. For example, in the method of balancing another person's electro-magnetic field that was described in Section II, three or four channelers can participate in the process. When there are four channelers, the person being aided lies on his/her back and the four helpers station themselves at the head, feet and two sides.

The person seated on the right side is the "active" channeler who passes his/her hands over the body of the person being aided and leads the sounding of tones.[6] The channeler seated at the head places his/her hands on the head of the person who is lying down while the person seated at the feet places the palms of his/her hands about two or three inches from the soles of the person's feet. The channeler on the left side is seated opposite the channeler on the right and places both hands,

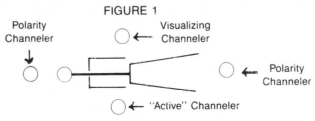

FIGURE 1

Polarity Channeler   Visualizing Channeler

Polarity Channeler

"Active" Channeler

palms up, on his or her own knees. When the "active" channeler sounds the tones, they also sound the same tones; otherwise their task is to quietly channel the energy and support the entire process.

Exercises to Strengthen Sensitivity for Group Channeling

The following two experiments are effective methods of increasing aural sensitivity to the inner sound for group channeling purposes. They can also be used as a preliminary warm-up, a prelude to an actual sound healing session.

Part I

First form two circles of equal numbers of people — an inner circle and an outer circle. Those in the inner circle sit facing outwards with their backs to the center; those forming the outer circle sit facing the center and across from a member of the inner circle. The members of each pair should be close enough to each other so that they can comfortably clasp each other's hands.

FIGURE 2

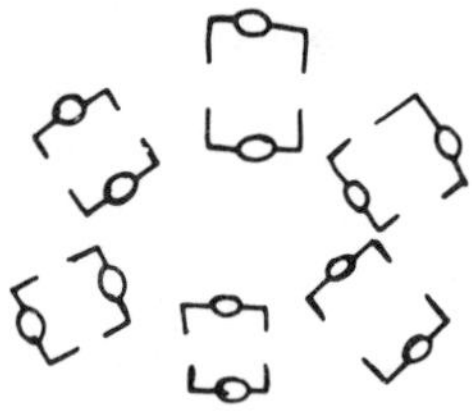

After being comfortably seated, come to inner quietness by breathing deeply into the top and back of your head with your jaw relaxed and your mouth slightly open. Your eyes should be closed and relaxed throughout. As you breathe follow the path of the air as, with each inhalation, the air creates a deeper pathway. Explore the inner spaces created by this pathway — nostrils, head, throat, upper torso, lower torso — and observe what happens in each space until you come to rest at the lowest place in your body that is comfortable. Watch what happens at this place as you relax and breathe. Something moves into your center as you inhale and disperses to all parts of your body as you exhale.

When a larger number of channelers is involved, they form a circle around the person being aided and the "active" channeler in one of two ways as illustrated. When the "active" channeler sounds the tones, all other channelers sound the tones also.

Another very common and powerful group healing procedure is the "Om"

FIGURE 3

OR

circle. When the person for whose benefit an Om circle is formed is present, he/she lies in the center while the singers chant a continuous "Om". The singers chant with their arms extended or slightly bent in front of them with the palms of their hands facing the person in the center. When the person is not present, visualization is utilized. The effectiveness of "Om" circles has been reaffirmed many, many times as a powerful aid to the healing process. Traditionally, all singers chant on the same pitch. However, an interesting variation is to sing the three tones of the major triad either continuously or alternating with unison chanting. The exact length of time for each should be agreed upon prior to commencement of chanting. Since the purpose of group "Om" chanting is to flood the electro-magnetic field of the person in the middle of the circle, the chant should be kept simple, without complex melodic and rhythmic soloistic passages that are calculated by cognitive inventiveness or limited by one's musical habits. The power of these chants does not lie with those sounds produced by human throats but rather by the inner sound that lies beneath the tones being sung. Here we are not creating music; we are creating the resonance for the inner sound, for this is the sound that harmonizes and heals.

Next, bring your hands up in front of you with your palms facing each other at a distance of about two inches. Continue to breathe deeply from your center as you begin to feel the energy force between your hands. After a few minutes return your hands to a position of rest and, facing your partner, breathe in and out from your center a few times.

Raise your arms with your palms facing the palms of your partner at about two inches from your partner's palms and continue breathing until you begin to feel a force field between you. After this force field has gained strength, the partner in the outside circle sounds a tone while both experience the change of energy between the hands that results. Then the partner on the outside remains silent while the partner from the inner circle repeats the tone. Finally, both sound the tone together. This phase completed, clasp your partner's hands and remain in silence for a few minutes, then remove your hands, rest and allow any impressions received to register as a result of sensing each other's presence.

All the people of the inner circle then move to the next adjacent person of the outer circle. Repeat the experiment and sense any similarities and differences that might occur.

Part II

In Part II the two circles are retained. However, the people of both circles do not directly face each other. Rather, a chain-like structure is formed between the two circles so that the right hand of each member of the inner circle meets the right hand of the person to his/her right in the outer circle, and the left hand of each person in the inner circle meets the left hand of the person to his/her left in the outer circle.

In this experiment the energy is passed from right to left hand, alternating from outer to inner circle until the first person is reached again. As before, arms are extended so that the palms of the hands are held about two inches from each other. When everyone in both circles experiences the transference of energy, one person sings a tone that is passed around the circle in sequence until the tone returns to the first person. Next, everyone in the outer circle sings the tone at once as the people of the inner circle receive it, then return the sound as the people of the outer circle receive.

FIGURE 4

There are, of course, many possible variations in all of these experiments using different pitches, different vowels and combinations of vowels both within the circles and in combinations of three, four, or five people. All of them are intended to increase the effectiveness of group channeling for the purpose of healing by utilization of sound and to facilitate the flow of electro-magnetic energy. As such these suggestions are merely starting places for explorations from which one's own individual style will develop.

All methods of healing have established a clearly defined system of general procedures. Healing with the use of sound is no exception. In developing a personal methodology you will want to consider one's relationship to the following phases of sound healing:

> Relaxation
> Clearing
> Tuning-In
> Scanning
> Channeling
> Sounding
> Visualization
> Affirmation
> Closing
> Dis-engagement
> Self-Reflection
> Record Keeping

How you utilize these procedural steps and in what order they occur determines each individual's approach to an effective healing process as a reflection of his or her own inner being.

PART THREE

The Application of Music for Therapeutic Purposes

CHAPTER EIGHT

Historical Perspective

When we introduce a series of varying pitches within a rhythmic framework we create the aesthetic experience of music. A fully dynamic and encompassing art, music creates its own reality of time-space through the flow of kinetic energy which it generates. Music, then, is kinetic energy made audible that effects changes in perception through its influence on human consciousness of creator and listener alike and therefore attracts and engages both the mind and the emotions. As in the therapeutic application of individual tones, music effects our physical bodies through the principle of resonance, but music's primary advantage is that it works with the personal (emotional) level as well as the transpersonal (spiritual) level. The basic premise upon which healing through music operates is that a primary cause of disease is emotional stress and negative mental attitudes that create energy imbalances and blockages. Once manifested, the disease is first treated as a symptom and the cause is sought in the emotional, mental and spiritual life of the afflicted individual. Ultimately, emotional stress may result from our environment or life situation. Health is restored when we are able to give full expression to our natural aspiration for spiritual growth and when there is a balanced and uninhibited flow of energy through all the systems of the body and psyche. Music can facilitate the expression of these emotions and enable us to reaffirm our original healthfulness.

According to Sufi, Inayat Khan, "The existence of illness in the body may be called a shadow of the true illness which is held by man in his mind. By the power of music the mind may become exalted so that it rises above the thought of illness; then the illness is forgotten,"[1]

The use of music for healing may have originated more than thirty thousand years ago. At that time illness was a great mystery, thought to be caused by an evil spirit which had to be expelled from the body and mind of the afflicted. A member of a group or family who was unable to perform tasks within the group because of illness created severe hardship for the other members — perhaps even to the point of jeopardizing the survival of the group itself. Therefore it was imperative that the individual be returned to health as quickly as possible. The return of the afflicted person to health was the concern of every member of the family and each participated in attempting to either frighten or entice the spirit to leave. The earliest form of music healing was probably a wordless wailing vocal chant that was monotonal and rhythmic — the rhythm being based on breath length and heart pulse. The administering group gathered around the patient and chanted for hours at a time. Eventually gourd rattles and drums were added for their value in keeping the healers going and for the special spiritual powers attributed to them.

The process must have been successful for eventually healing specialists began to emerge and became highly valued for their knowledge and skill. These individuals were called upon to lead the healings as well as other rituals. Before long all important occurrences in tribal life were solemnized with sacred rites in which music and dancing played a central role under the direction of the specialist. With this development the long tradition of shamanism evolved. Today, the healing ritual is essentially uniform throughout those parts of the world where shamanism is still practiced.

When treating a patient, the shaman first recites his manner of training by both his spirit teachers and his human teachers. Second, he acquires the necessary assurance that the patient has complete trust in the shaman. Third, the shaman appeals to the patient to concentrate all of his/her energies upon recovery. And fourth, the shaman administers healing herbs to the patient to the accompaniment of special songs to assure the patient that he/she will be restored to health. The shaman uses music to assist the patient in obtaining a maximum concentration of mind and body and to intensify his will to recover and attain physical well being. The patient plays an active role in the healing process. The ritual is aesthetically and psychologically integrated for this purpose. In shamanistic healing rituals there are always at least three participants: the shaman, the patient, and the spirit with whom the shaman communes. Usually there are additional participants: the shaman's assistants, who are always his apprentices, and members of the patient's immediate family, friends and other members of the community. The ritual may last from several hours to nine or more days and concludes with an affirmation song of which the following from the Chippewa Midewiwin is typical:

"You will recover, you will walk again.
"It is I who say it. My power is great.
Through our white shell (emblem of the Midewiwin)
I will enable you to walk again."[2]

The prevailing musical characteristics of shamanistic healing songs are irregularity of accent and unexpected interruptions of a steady rhythm. The singing is mostly monotonal and sung without personal emotion. The rhythm attracts the attention of the patient and may be hypnotic in effect, for one of the purposes of the healing song is to quiet the patient — emotionally, mentally, and physically. The songs are sung slowly — about forty to sixty beats per minute whereas songs of other categories may range from seventy-six to one hundred and four beats per minute. Voice and accompaniment usually coincide rhythmically.[3]

The shamanistic healing traditions survive today among the Indian nations of North and South America, the Arctic regions, Greenland, Siberia, Northern Scandinavia, Africa, Australia, and the South Pacific Islands. The rituals include the administration of herb remedies and healing songs and chants. The purpose filled by music is primarily a psychological one of affirmation and of quieting the mind by altering the state of consciousness of practitioner and patient alike.

The ancient world properly begins with the establishment of the first permanent Sumerian cities around 8000 B.C. and ends with the demise of the Roman state during the fifth century A.D. Within that vast period we find the rise of the great civilizations of Babylonia, Sumeria, Persia, India, China, Egypt, the tribes of Israel, Greece, and the origins of the Christian world.

Of the music of the ancient world we know very little. Although descriptions of musical practice dating to as far back as the Sumerians are available to us, no decipherable music notation exists there prior to 100 B.C. in Greece, and 500 B.C. in China.[4] Whereas the music of India is said to be three thousand years old, a notational system for music did not evolve until much later. The role of music within the religious rituals of ancient Sumeria is described in writings that date from the third millenium B.C. and the earliest example of musical notation dates from this time. In spite of repeated efforts and much speculation it remains undecipherable. Like the shamanistic world before them, most of these civilizations incorporated many gods and goddesses into their religious practice, each deity fulfilling a different purpose. Every nation had several deities for healing and at least one for music. In some cases the deity of healing or medicine and the deity of music were the same. Many temples for worship and healing were built within which the priests resided. The diseased would flock to these temples to implore the gods to restore their health. The music played in the religious and healing ceremonies in these temples was of the most sublime nature, often performed by one singer, a flute and harp or lyre. This ensemble has been found throughout the civilizations of the ancient world where it was regarded as the most appropriate ensemble for the entertainment of royalty, for religious rituals and healing ceremonies. By 3000 B.C. the religious practice of music within the Sumerian temples was fully described in all detail.[5] Here the priests spoke their oracles to the accompaniment of the lyre. Incantations, chanted by the priest, accompanied the administration of curing medicines within these temples.

> All rituals and ceremonies were essentially two-fold; (1) appeals to the deities for assistance. . .; and (2) divination to learn the disposition and the will of the gods. Entreaties to the divinities took the shape of hymns of praise and of prayers that were introductory to incantations, all of which partook of the nature of a curative remedy for present misfortunes, sickness and suffering. The forms of these hymns, prayers, and incantations were built up by the priests from age to age until they became rigid traditional formulas of approved ritual invocation, arranged for all occasions and to be followed without variation.[6]

With the Egyptians we begin to see indications of the esoteric concepts beneath the material accomplishments and public religious rituals.[7] The pyramids, temples, sacred emblems, ceremonies, paintings, sculptures and perhaps also music "often conceal ideas once reserved for a small number of initiates: and the secret of these ideas. . . can be rediscovered by those who study in depth all the types of teachings remaining of the ancient beliefs and the ceremonies they prescribed."[8] For the priests "speaking was a process of generating sonar fields establishing an immediate vibratory identity with the essential principle that underlies any object or form."[9] Gaspar Maspero wrote that therefore within the religious rites of the temple,

> It is the voice which seeks afar the Invisibles summoned and makes the necessary objects into reality. . . But as every one (of the tones) has its particular force, great care must be taken not to change their order or to substitute one for the other.[10]

The music of ancient Egypt is still a mystery. Descriptions of its characteristics, functions and meanings are few and because Egyptian musicians possessed no written notation, we must rely on a handful of surviving instruments and illustrations of musical activities on tomb and temple walls to surmise how the music may have sounded. The principal instrument in religious and court life appears to have been the harp; the musical ensemble most commonly depicted consists of at least one singer — who is the leader — and harps, lutes, long flutes, and double oboes. A trio consisting of a harpist, a flutist and a singer appears frequently in these depictions and must have been the Egyptian version of chamber music. Based on the frequency with which these ensembles appear, musicologist Alfred Sendry suggests that the music was "soft, solemn and sedate, conforming to the *clair-obscure* of the temples, being used as a tonal background for the mystic ceremonies."[11] According to Plato, the Egyptians attributed the origin of their melodies to the goddess **Isis**, and the purpose of these melodies was to govern human emotions and to purify the souls of the people.[12] The extent to which esoteric concepts may have governed music is unknown, and the question of how music might have been used directly for healing purposes cannot be answered since, in both cases, no evidence survives.

Among the ancient Hebrews, music was both a stimulant and a sedative capable of intensifying negative emotions, bringing them to a climax and discharging them from the mind.[13] The writings of the Hebrews are rich in references to music as a healing agent. Through them we detect a shift in attitude concerning the power of music over disease.

For the first time in the Western world, music was used as a form of therapy rather than as a vehicle for various incantations to specific healing deities. Thus it was David's harp alone that brought King Saul out of his depression. In the **Talmud** we find mention of an appliance that caused drops of water to drip continuously on a vessel of metal thereby creating a monotonous buzzing sound that enabled a sick person to sleep and recover.[14] Also mentioned is a song, *shir peg' ayim*, that was capable of serving as protection in times of epidemic.[15] A musician belonging to the Leviteal fraternity was called a "prophet" and a "seer" and the Biblical term "Nabi" (prophet) referred to one who was an interpreter of God's thoughts, a seer who predicted and revealed the hidden events of the future, and a singer and instrumentalist.[16]

From Homer to Pythagoras and his followers, Greek legends pertaining to the healing power of music are abundant and specific. It is reported that Terpandros and Arion, Greek musicians, healed the Ionians and Lesbians by their singing. Hisomenios relieved the Boeatians of their gout by his singing while Empedocles succeeded in calming the rage of one of his guests by the power of his singing.[17] Clement of Alexandria, a well-known Greek scholar (d.c216 A.D.), reports that two minstrels, Hemphian of Thebes and Arion of **Lesbos** were able through their musical skill to lure a fish onto land and also to build the walls of Thebes.[18]

One of the most prominent of the Greek deities was Apollo, God of the Sun, of Medicine and of Music. Apollo was regarded as the founder of medicine, the representative of pure intellect, the god of mental and moral purity and the essence of the Greek idea that the purpose of life is to achieve the purest harmony of soul and body. In him music and medicine were combined as an integrated unity ". . . his rhythmic movement through the heavens produces harmony in the universe, imparts measure and beauty of form; he is the god of poetry, music and dance. . . the dispenser of life and its blessings. . . he purges the soul of its guilt, cleanses the body of ills. . . preserves the harmony of life by dispelling evil."[19] Apollo preserved the harmony of life by divination, music and medicine. Temples dedicated to his son, Aeseulapius, were healing centers where the arts were accorded a large share in the therapeutic technique of temple rites. Music was used to "induce in the patient an ecstatic experience in order to awaken the curative power of the soul and thereby restore the harmonious relation between it and the body."[20] If Apollo was respected, worshipped and called upon in times of need, it was his legendary servant Orpheus who held the affection of the Greek people.

It was he who was able to stop the heavens from moving, cause the animals of the forests to weep and even journey to the Underworld to soften the heart of Pluto by the power of his lyre and voice. A medium for poetry, music and medicine, he is believed to have discovered mysteries, achieved purification from transgressions, and to have discovered cures for diseases and the means of averting divine anger. Standing midway between the Gods and the common people and possessing many of the human frailties, Orpheus was often called upon to intercede in the requests of humans to the more remote Gods.

Legends, mythologies and stories of cures are valued indicators of the esteem with which the Greek people regarded music, but it is the writings of respected philosophers and musicians that give weight to claims of music's healing power. It was through the influence of Homer, Plato, Plutarch, Aristotle, Pythagoras and their disciples that music became a psycho-iatric agent. Homer recommended music "to avoid negative passions such as anger, sorrow, worry, fear, fatigue, and to promote healthful recreation for elevating soul and body."[21] For Plato, the careful regulation of music was of utmost importance for the welfare of the state and the health of the people. He believed "that by changing a musical mode the very foundations of the state might be undermined,"[22] and that when "the soul lost its harmony, melody and rhythm assist in restoring it to order and concord."[23] In Aristotle's view, two of the functions of music were to serve as a catharsis for the emotions and for the building of a strong ethical character.[24]

The central figure in the development of the therapeutic uses of music, whose reputation spanned the Western world for a thousand years, was Pythagoras of Samos. Of his personal life we know little, and since he expounded his teachings orally, we have had to rely on reports by later writers to summarize his concepts. He lived during the sixth century B.C. and apparently travelled extensively with his band of disciples. Both Greek and Persian writers claim that he was born in Syria either in the town of Tyre or Sidon. According to Henry George Farmer, first "by Sidonian and Phoenician hierophants, he [Pythagoras] was initiated into the mysteries of Tyre and Byblos. Later he passed into Egypt where he remained twenty-one years."[25] He was taken captive by King Cambyses and transported to Babylon where he was instructed by the priests. Completing twelve years there, he finally settled in Samos.[26] Pythagoras was a scientist, a metaphysical philosopher, mathematician and musician, he calculated the ratios of the musical intervals and systematized the mathematical basis of the musical scale that formed the groundwork of Western musical theory. Today he is considered to be the founder of musical theory and the science of acoustics, but in his own time and for centuries after he was known as the founder of a philosophy that encompassed music healing, science, mathematics, medicine, nutrition and philosophy. In his teachings he emphasized the ideal life as one of balance, moderation and adherence to certain spiritual values. He believed in a natural vital energy within the human body that the physician assists to restore balance to the body. He believed in a universal law of harmony based on numerical relations that controlled the movements of the heavenly bodies, the laws of music and the inner world — both physical and mental — of human beings. Because the principles of harmony that operated in the heavenly bodies also operated within music and the human species, health involved the proper attunement of body and soul to the universe by means of diet, music and living according to divine law. In Pythagorean philosophy, the laws of music act on the inner world of man through harmony. Harmony of the universe is equal to the harmony of the soul or inner universe of mankind. Therefore melody and rhythm can assist in restoring the soul to order and concord. When the soul is restored to order the body will return to health. By arranging the musical intervals in proper order to reflect the natural order of the heavens, the soul becomes purified and unites with the order of the heavens, nature and the divine. Through the singing of melodies, the emotions and the mind are calmed; when this is accomplished, the inner vitality of the body is restored and healing commences. For Pythagoras, and for the ancient world as well, the human individual is curable as a whole, unified organism. Treatment of only one part of that whole is not only not healing but can actually delay healing. Pythagoras' philosophy was to dominate the field for the next eight hundred years. Whether later writers, physicians and philosophers agreed or disagreed with his concepts, they were required to address and make their peace with them.

When the Romans dominated the areas of Europe and Western Asia they incorporated both the music and the healing practices of the Greeks into their own culture. The religion of the Romans consisted of sacrifice, divination by birds and prediction by oracles. When a Roman became ill, soothsayers and diviners were consulted, for in their view disease was caused by offended Gods or evil spirits. The Greek god Apollo was adopted as a healing deity particularly for his power to avert disease. In addition to divination and dream-oracles held at temples, magic cures were used: words of power, incantations, songs, chants, talismans and amulets.

The extent to which music was a part of these ceremonies is not entirely clear but because mention of music within the various healing practices of the time is sporadic and non-specific, we can assume that music was not a central part of the healing process. As the Greeks before them, the Romans believed in the essential unity of the body and soul. Within this context music was a form of psychotherapy, its function being both curative and preventative. For this reason the playing of music often followed the evening meal; the primary instrument used for this purpose was the harp or lyre, either as a solo instrument or as accompaniment for the voice.

Although music was used by the Greeks and Romans primarily for its psychotherapeutic value, some references regarding the effect and use of music on the physical body can be found. Aulus Gellius, a Roman, mentions that pains in the hips caused by gout can be relieved by listening to music played on the flute in the phrygian mode. Theophrastus believed that epilepsy might be relieved by the sound of the flute. For treatment of insanity, the physician Celsus recommended music — cymbals and other sounds — and Herophilus, a physician of Alexandria, was "able to regulate the arterial pulsation according to the musical scale corresponding with the age of the patient."[27] Unfortunately, we are unable to learn specifically how this is accomplished.

With the collapse of the Roman Empire came the end of the ancient world. New philosophies emerged as science and religion began a process of separation and growing mutual distrust. With the development of alleopathic medicine, based on the study of human anatomy and administration of drugs, the human soul was neglected in the diagnostic process. Music too underwent a drastic change, not only in style, but in conception and use as well. It separated from science and philosophy first and from spiritual connections second. Music was incorporated into and governed by the church as a secular art that must be controlled, tamed and purified. In addition to church music there was, of course, a social music created by individuals for the entertainment and pleasure of the common people, as well as a separate music for the aristocracy. During the Renaissance, music became a craft on equal footing with other crafts such as silversmithing and the like, and only during the Romantic era was it treated as an art. The remains of the ancient esoteric practices of music gradually sank into folklore and superstition, remaining alive only in areas of China, India and Tibet where they continued to be the foundations upon which the exoteric musical traditions of those countries developed. Many Western physicians continued to cultivate an active interest and love of music, many becoming excellent amateur musicians. But for them music was an "after hours" activity from which the practice of medicine remained separate.

The one notable exception to this trend occurred in the eighteenth century in the person of Louis Roger, a physician and amateur musician of Montpellier, France. In 1748 he published a work in two parts, *A Treatise on the Effects of Music on the Human Body* (originally in Latin but translated into French in 1803 and published under the title, *Traite des effects de la musique sur le corps humain*). In Part One he discusses the nature of sounding bodies, sound waves transmitted through air, and the human ear as the organ of sound perception. In the second part, consisting of three chapters, he considers two questions: first, whether music is capable of affecting humans and second, how it does so.

Under the first question Roger writes three chapters, discussing the influence of music on the mind, on the body, and on the union of both, which is the animated body. He proceeds systematically and rationally. The first chapter, based on the principle that the mind has a natural predilection for order and that music consists of ordered intervals of sound and time, enters into a clear analysis of the psychology of musical enjoyment. He discusses the mind's attraction to consonant intervals and chords based on the natural harmonic laws, sense of tonality, the force of the tonic, overtones, and like. Further, he considers the pleasure that the mind derives from rhythmic measure, especially the binary and tertiary, and points out that various rhythms have various emotional qualities and correspondingly various effects on the passions.[28]

In the second chapter of Part Two, Roger sets out to "explain the effect of music on matter, but on matter that constitutes the human body. Here we come upon the psychology of the time and see also how with such a view of physiology the whole question of music's effect on the body is quite plausible and, in fact, inevitable."[29]

"The human body in his view is composed of solids and liquids. The solids are the bones and the softer parts, nerves, muscles, tendons, cartilages. The liquids are the nervous fluid which is actually of aerial nature, the air introduced in the body, and the blood, lymph and other humors produced by secretions. In the first part of the book Roger had discussed the phenomenon of sound vibrations in the air and set forth how they vibrated other bodies. Now he has to show how sound vibrates matter in the human body and with what effects. Naturally the lighter and more elastic the substance, the greater its susceptibility to sound vibrations. Since the air contained in our humors has the same properties as the air outside, it undergoes similar changes by sound vibrations. And since the nervous fluid presumably is aerial, it too is affected by sound just as is air.

. . .The blood and other fluids in the body are also affected, just as the surface of a body of water is rippled by sound. Moreover, since the fluids of the body contain air, they are susceptible to sound on this sense. Roger also considers the effect of sound on the solids of the human body and discusses sympathetic vibration in unison with the original sound.

The vibration of the nerves, of which those of hearing and touch are especially susceptible to music, produces effects in the body itself and transmits sensations to the mind. . . The effect of music on the nervous fluid connects the mind and body, since it is actually the mind that directs the flow of the fluid.

. . .Roger finishes his last chapter with further discussion of music and the mind: how music affects and effects states of mind, and how these, since the mind is master of the body, influence the latter. . . He discusses the aesthetics of composition and the role of ideas in composing music. He cites many cases, recent as well as classical, of music's effects and suggests that if in his day all the known effects are not always found, it is due to the intention of the music composer. With the old composers music served as a double end. It was to please the ear and to affect habits. With Roger's contemporaries music is composed only with a view to please the ear by surprising it with agreeable harmonies. . . But with this one-sided purpose the composers have enervated music and weakened its force by the abundance of ornaments.

Roger further points out that actually that music is most pleasing which stirs passions in us, meaning by this not superficial embellishment but depth of feeling in what satisfies in music."[30]

It is , of course, interesting to note that approximately at the same time as Rogers was presenting his remarkable theories, the physicist Ernst Chladni was involved in his experiments with sand particles, metal discs and violins, as mentioned previously. It is probable that they never met and that they were unaware of each other's work. What is remarkable is that Roger's treatise seemed to have had so little influence on either the musicians or the physicians of his own time, for relatively little of value on the subject of the effect of music on the body and mind was written until well into the twentieth century — basically until the experimental work of Hans Jenny and Dr. Ira Altschuler.

The pace of activity in the field of therapeutic music and music healing is rapidly increasing, giving validation to the prediction made in 1926 by Alice Bailey in the book, *Esoteric Healing*, that music will be one of the principle means of healing by the close of the twenty-first century. It was in 1919 that Columbia University first offered a course on "Musicotherapy" and in 1944 Michigan State College (now a university) designed the first four year course for specialists in the field. Shortly thereafter, the National Association for Music Therapy was founded, followed by the American Association of Music Therapists and, in the 1970's, the American Association of Artist-Therapists. Both the National and American Associations are greatly influenced by the approaches used in Behavioristic Psychology whereas the Association of Artist-Therapists embrace the philosophies of Humanistic Psychology. At the present time only those music therapists certified by the NAMT or the AAMT are approved by the American Medical Association for assignment to hospitals and clinics.

If these three organizations represent the more orthodox approaches to music as a therapeutic force, then there is a growing movement of individuals and small groups who are investigating the more esoteric holistic approaches of music healing. Taking Pythagorean and pre-Pythagorean concepts as a basis, they are studying ancient Western cultures, shamanistic cultures and Eastern cultures that enjoy a long tradition of combining music with healing. Too numerous to mention all of them here, their numbers have increased significantly within the past ten years and their activities and philosophies have begun to infiltrate orthodox medicine and mainstream culture.

Of these, one of the earliest — founded in the 1940's — is the Rudolf Steiner Foundation. Among the many activities undertaken by Steiner, none were more important to him than the development of schools for the education of young children. Central to his concepts of education was the importance of music in the development of the child's spiritual and ethical values. For this he drew from the concepts of the Greek philosopher, Plato. The present day system of Waldorf Schools is based on the concepts established by Steiner.

Simultaneous with Steiner's work was the publication in 1948 of the first important book on the history of music and medicine since Roger's book of 1803. *Music and Medicine* is a classic in the literature and is the source of much of the material of this book.

Activity increased dramatically in the 1970s with the establishment of three institutions: Christopher Hill's University of the Trees for the study of radionics; Stephen Halprin's Sonic Research Institute for the development of stress-reducing music; Dhyani Ywahoo's Sunray Meditation Society that, among many other activities, combines Native American healing tradition, Tibetan philosophy, esoteric concepts of music and the vibrational qualities of quartz crystals.[31] It is also in the 1970's that the term "New Age Music" originated.

It was in the mid 1970s that one of the first college level courses on music and healing was taught (by this author) at Hampshire College in Massachusetts. Enrollments in the course were consistently high. Several alternative college level educational institutions have since incorporated courses in music healing into their curricula. Among them, Lesley College (Boston), Naropa Institute (Boulder) and the New Mexico Academy of Massage and Advanced Healing Arts (Santa Fe) deserve mention. Not to be overlooked is the founding in 1975 of the Institute for Consciousness and Music (Baltimore) and the development of Guided Affective Imagery with Music, discussed in a later chapter, by music therapist Helen Bonnie and her associates.

In the early 1980s, a small group of musicians from the New England area, including this author, began a series of monthly informal meetings to share our interest in music healing. One of the participants, Jonathan Goldman, foresaw the need for a more structured organization through which people could communicate their shared interests and activities. Now located in Lexington, Massachusetts, the New England Sound Healers was founded in 1983 and was incorporated as an educational foundation in 1985. Now meeting in the greater Boston area — they have long since outgrown Jon's living room — plans are being developed for a school with a full curriculum in sound and music healing.

Two events which promise to be of special significance are unfolding simultaneously. In July 1986, Boulder College, an alternative college in Colorado, announced its intention to develop a curriculum in music healing at both the graduate and undergraduate level as part of its Department of Expressive Arts Therapies. Concurrently in Louisville, Kentucky, approval for the establishment of the Center for the Study of Music and Medicine has been granted under the auspices of the Department of Psychiatry of the University of Louisville Medical School. If both of these intentions become realities, they may well be seen in the future as the beginning of a new era in the history of music and sound healing.

With the promise of recent events in mind, we can trace a line of development from the earliest shamanist traditions to the ancient mystery schools, from the mystery schools of Pythagoras, and from Pythagoras to Louis Roger and Hans Jenny to the anticipated events of the future. In that future young musicians may, as a matter of course, receive scientifically valid training in the creation of music for specific healing purposes.

CHAPTER NINE

Music Cosmology and the Inner Sound

Musical Cosmology, seemingly a by-product of mathematical speculation, serves as an interesting background to developments in the therapeutic application of music. Although generally associated with Greece, the concept of the harmony of the spheres may have originated in Babylonia before the sixth century B.C.[1] The idea that celestial bodies create sounds as they move through the heavens is not exclusive to the Mesopotamian area, but it reached its most elaborate expression in Greece when Pythagorean philosophy connected the harmonic unity of stars and planets to the inner harmony of body and soul as a central principle of human health.

Pythagoras of Samos (560-480 B.C.) was the first Greek to state that the universe is founded and governed by the laws of music, a concept that was further developed by Socrates and Plato but denied by Aristotle. Years later, the philosopher Aristides Quintillionus, a disciple of Pythagoras, wrote ". . .every solid body creates in flight a certain sound. Thus also the stars make the ether to vibrate although our ears are too incomplete to hear these sounds."[2]

Pythagoras' belief in the interrelationship of all numbers and their functions included the movement of the heavenly bodies and the practice of music. He calculated the musical intervals of the planets between the earth and the fixed stars as:

Earth-Moon	1 tone
Moon-Mercury	1 semi-tone
Mercury-Venus	1 semi-tone
Venus-Sun	1 minor third
Sun-Mars	1 tone
Mars-Jupiter	1 semi-tone
Jupiter-Saturn	1 semi-tone
Saturn and Sphere of Fixed Stars	1 minor third

It was through the writings of Plato and Clement of Alexander that the concept of the harmony of the spheres was transmitted to the early Christian Philosophers and reached philosophical elaboration in Boethius, a Roman philosopher and mathematician who died in 524 A.D. In his treatise, *De Institutione Musica, Book I*, he designated three kinds of music: Music of the Universe, Human Music — that which unites the incorporeal activity of reason with the body and instrumental music. The Music of the Universe, he stated,

> is especially to be studied in the combining of the elements and the variety of the seasons which are observed in the heavens. . . .The extremely rapid motion of such great bodies [planets and stars — remember that Earth travels around the sun at the rate of 67,000 miles per hour!] could not be altogether without sound . . . We perceive that in the music of the universe nothing can be excessive and destroy some other part by its own excess, but each part brings its own contribution or aids others to bring theirs.[3] . . .The Pythagoreans used to free themselves from the cares of the day by certain melodies which caused a gentle and quiet slumber to steal upon them. Similarly, upon arising, they dispelled the stupor and confusion of sleep by certain other melodies, knowing that the whole structure of soul and body is united by musical harmony. *For the impulses of the soul are stirred by emotions corresponding to the state of the body.*[4]

That the belief in the harmony of the spheres was still firmly planted in the Western medieval mind a hundred years later can be confirmed in the following words of Isidore of Seville (d. 636):

> Thus without music no discipline can be perfect for there is nothing without it. For the very universe, it is said, is held together by a certain harmony of sounds, and the heavens themselves are made to revolve by the modulation of harmony. . .every word we speak, every pulsation of our veins, is related by musical rhythms of the powers of harmony.[5]

It took, however, another thousand years before these "certain sounds" were mathematically calculated by the astronomer Johannes Kepler. In the meantime, music had become infinitely more complex, a tribute to the intellectual achievements of the Renaissance mind.

In 1619, Johannes Kepler (1571-1630), a mathematician and astronomer, published his final work, *The Harmonies of the World*. In it Kepler presented his discovery that when Saturn is farthest from the sun it moves at a rate of 106 seconds of arc in a day; when closest to the sun it moves at a rate 135 seconds of arc per day. The ratio between these extremes differs by just two degrees from the ratio of 4:5, which equals the musical interval of a major third. He then calculated the musical intervals for the remaining five planets and the moon, (Uranus, Neptune and Pluto had not been discovered at that time), and worked out a system for determining the proper pitch, the proper octave for each planet, and the speed at which each planet would slowly change from its fundamental pitch to the indicated interval pitch and back again according to the planet's distance from the sun. In the case of Saturn, for example, its pitch would be Sub-Contra "G" (a major second below the lowest pitch on the piano); the major third above this pitch would be Sub-Contra "B". Since Saturn takes thirty years to revolve around the sun, it would take fifteen years for the fundamental pitch of "G" to slowly reach "B", and another fifteen years for it to return to "G" once more. Here are Kepler's ratios:

FIGURE 1

Planet	Ratio of Arc	Intervallic Ratio	Music Interval	Pitch Name	Time of One Revolution
Saturn	1'48":2'15"	4:5	M 3rd	Sub-contra G-B-G	29.5 years
Jupiter	4'35":5'30"	5:6	m 3rd	Contra B-D-D	11.9 years
Mars	26'14":38'1"	2:3	p 5th	$F^1C^2\text{-}F^1$	687.5 days
Earth	57'3":61'18"	15:16	m 2nd	$G^2\text{-}A^{b2}\text{-}G^2$	365.25 days
Venus	94'50":98'47"	24:25	unison	unison $E^3\text{-}E^3$	224.7 days
Mercury	164'0":384'0"	5:12	m 10th	$C^4\text{-}E^5\text{-}C^4$	88 days
Moon	26'26":35'12"	3:4	p 4th	$G^5\text{-}C^6\text{-}G^5$	28 days

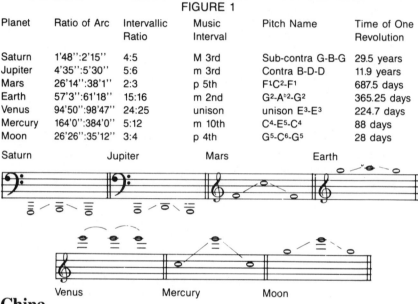

China

Whereas Western theorists expended a great amount of energy, time and paper in a literal interpretation of the harmony of the spheres, either in calculating the exact intervals or in "proving" its existence, civilizations to the East were content with the metaphysical concept. We find these words in *The Inner Chapters*, by Chuang Tsu (c. 400 B.C.), a disciple of Laotzu, the first writer of Taoism:

> Perhaps you have heard the music of men but not the music of earth. You may have heard the music of earth but not the music of heaven.
>
> The universe has a cosmic breath. Its name is wind. Sometimes it is not active; but when it is, angry howls rise from ten thousand openings.
>
> In the mountain forest, deep and fearsome, there are huge trees a hundred arm-spans around, with gaps and hollows like nostrils, mouths and ears... the sounds rush out like water, whistle like arrows, scold, suck, shout, wail, moan and howl. The leading notes are hissing sounds followed by a roaring chorus. Gentle breezes make a small harmony, fierce winds a great one. When the violent gusts subside, all the hollows become quiet.

The earth's music is the sound from these hollows. Man's music comes from the hollow reed. May I ask about the music of heaven?

When the wind blows through the ten thousand different hollows, they all make their own sounds. Why should there be anything else that causes the sound?[6]

In ancient China, music was regarded as the image of the order of the universe. The *Yueh-Chi*, an original source of Chinese musical practice, states that music is the harmony of heaven and earth and belongs to the higher spiritual realms. The early sages composed music in order that it might correspond to heaven, both philosophically and actually. Out of the marriage of these two aspects are created all things between heaven and earth. Yang is heaven — male, light, heat and odd numbers; Yin is earth — female, dark, cold and even numbers. The cyclic nature of the universe and the interplay of Yin/Yang are the basis of Chinese music theory. Writings on music theory are most commonly found in the writings on the calendar, astrology, and topology.

As early as the third century B.C., a system relating musical sounds to the order of the universe was worked out and a theory was devised by which the notes of the Chinese musical scale could be derived from a fundamental pitch pipe by simple arithmetical calculations, literally putting music in tune with the various forces of the universe. Throughout Chinese history one of the first orders of the new emperor was to call together his musicians and astrologers to collaborate in re-calculating the length of the imperial pitch pipes to insure that all music played during his reign would harmonize with all elements of nature, the earth and the heavens and therefore insure peace and harmony throughout the empire. In this context, a single sound was considered to have the power to influence other souls for good or for evil.

Under the Hahn emperor Wuudih (141-87 B.C.), the Imperial Bureau of Music was founded and charged with the responsibility of supervising all rites, ceremonies, and music; of preparing archives of all national melodies; and of establishing and maintaining the correct pitch of the imperial pipes. This bureau was incorporated into the Imperial Bureau of Weights and Measures.

In traditional Chinese numerology two is Earth (Yin) and three is Heaven (Yang); therefore, the intervals of the five tone scale were calculated by successive projections of the ratio of 2:3, producing a series of perfect fifths, five being the number of Heaven and Earth since it combines Yang and Yin.

FIGURE 2

To the resulting five-tone scale was attributed the extra-musical meanings:

Pitch:	D	E	F#	A	B
Element:	Earth	Metal	Wood	Fire	Water
Name:	Kung	Shang	Chio	Chih	Yü
Season:	Center*	Autumn	Spring	Summer	Winter
Direction:	Center	West	East	South	North

*Center was a fifth season of eighteen days commencing nine days before the winter solstice and lasting until nine days after.

Taking each pitch in turn as a new tone, the five principal modes are generated:

Kung mode:	D	E	F#	A	B	Center
Shang mode:	E	F#	A	B	B	Autumn
Chio mode:	F#	A	B	D	E	Spring
Chih mode:	A	B	B	E	F#	Summer
Yu mode:	B	D	E	F#	A	Winter

Each mode corresponds to one of the five seasons and is played during that season. Continuing the projections of fifths to twelve generations,

FIGURE 3

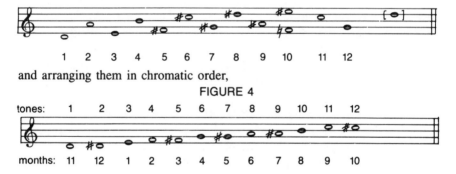

1   2   3   4   5   6   7   8   9   10   11   12

and arranging them in chromatic order,

FIGURE 4

tones: 1   2   3   4   5   6   7   8   9   10   11   12

months: 11   12   1   2   3   4   5   6   7   8   9   10

we arrive at the corresponding key note for each month of the year. Beginning with December as the eleventh month, the odd numbered months are Yang. The five modes are transposed to each of the corresponding monthly key notes resulting in sixty modes for the five voices. Melodies are played in one of the keys according to the month and the hour, and each melody belongs to one of the five modes.

The eleventh month begins with the month of the winter solstice which was considered the meeting place of Yang and Yin. Beginning with the winter solstice, Yang waxes and Yin wanes until the turning point of the summer solstice wherein Yang wanes and Yin waxes. The year is divided into five seasons to correlate with the five elements: wood, fire, earth, metal and water.

This highly complex system was a dominating factor in Chinese attitudes and

practice of music for almost four-thousand years. If it appears to be a overly in-
tellectualized and pragmatic system, it should be recognized that its foundation
lay in the firm belief in the power of sound to influence the heavens, the earth
and the minds of human beings, as well as the conviction that through the organ
of hearing lies the best means of perfection and the quickest path of enlightment.

India

In India it is said that the god **Siva** created earthly music and dance from the cosmic music and taught it to his wife, the goddess Sri, who then passed them on
to other heavenly beings. Music then sounded throughout the heavens but did not
reach Earth until Brahma, looking down upon the drudgery and toil of human
life, took pity and gave music to Earth as the fifth Veda — the Sama Veda. Nara-
da, half human and half God, invented the *Vina*, a lute-like instrument, and Bharata
transcribed the *ragas* and their theory in the classic *Natyosastra*. To this day
Saraswati, consort of Brahma, is worshipped as Goddess of Music, Knowledge,
Dance and Speech, while Lady Nada is ready to assist all aspiring musicians.

In Hindu philosophy, vibration is the root of all creation and music is a mirror
of the cosmic music. Thus through the performance of earthly music one may
experience the unheard cosmic music which is its source. In experiencing the cosmic music one can find liberation from the karmic cycle of birth and rebirth. There
is no separation between music and the sacred, for through every musical utterance one may experience union with the creative source itself.

> "What we call music in our everyday language is only a miniature, which
> our intelligence has grasped from that music or harmony of the whole universe
> which is working behind everything, and which is the source and origin of na-
> ture. It is because of this that the wise of all ages have considered music to be
> a sacred art. For in music the seer can see the picture of the whole universe;
> and the wise can interpret the secret and the nature of the working of the whole
> universe in the realm of music.[7]

Central to the practice of music is the ancient concept of "Nada" which has
a musical meaning, a physical meaning and a metaphysical meaning. The syllable
"na" represents the vital force (prana) and "da" is the fire principle; the interaction
of these two creates *Nada*. In traditional teachings, *Nada* manifests as two kinds
of sound. "Anahata nad" — an "unstruck sound" — is a vibration of ether, is
not produced by physical impact and can be heard only by inner listening through
contemplation. "Ahata nad" or "struck sound" — is the vibration of air set into
motion by physical force and is heard by our physical ears. Total immersion in
"Ahata nad" through the vehicle of music can lead to the experience of "anahata
nad", the primordial sound of the universe. In passing from the *ahata-nad* to the
experience of *anahata-nad* one must first pass through seven layers of sound as

described in *The Book of the Golden Precepts,* an ancient collection of knowledge, parts of which date from pre-Buddhist times.[8]

> Before those sett'st thy foot upon the ladder's upper rung, the ladder of the mystic sounds, thou hast to hear the voice of thy inner God in Seven manners.
>
> The first is like the nightingale's sweet voice chanting a song of parting to its mate.
>
> The second comes as the sound of a silver cymbal of the Dhyanis, awakening the twinkling stars.
>
> The next is as the plaint melodious of the ocean-sprite imprisoned in its shell. And this is followed by the chant of the vina.
>
> The fifth, like sound of bamboo-flute, shrills in thine ear.
>
> It changes next into a trumpet blast.
>
> The last vibrates like the dull rumbling of a thunder cloud.
>
> The seventh swallows all the other sounds. They die, and then are heard no more.

Nada also resides within the human body and its process of manifestation is described in the following way:

> Desirous of speech the individuated being impels the mind, and the mind activates the battery of power (fire) stationed in the body, which in turn stimulates the vital force *(prana).* The vital force stationed around the root of the navel [solar plexus], rising upwards, gradually manifests nada in the navel, the heart, the throat, the cerebrum and the cavity of the mouth as it passes through them. Stationed in these five places, *nada* takes on five different names as associated with them respectively, extremely subtle, subtle, loud, not so loud, and artificial."[9]

Just as *Nada* permeates the heavens and the individual human body, so too is human society dependent on sound, for by sound the letter is formed — the original fifty letters of the Sanskrit language — by letters the syllable, by syllables the word, by words this daily life. Thus our human world depends on sound for its regulation, for that which is found within the human body, governs society and the universe, and is the "silent" partner of the practice of music as well. That force, Nada, is the universal creative force that brings all things into manifestation. To Indian belief, music has the power to influence the course of human life in this world and can lead to ultimate bliss by merging the individual self with the divine principle of the universe and in so doing breaking the cycle of existence. In the Sanskrit texts music is therefore given the epithet *vimiktida,* which means "bestowing liberation".

A Newly Emerging Cosmology

"All the universe is alive, vibrating and pulsating with life and energy and motion. There is nothing dead in the universe."[10]

Cosmologies develop through our need to understand the unifying principle of the universe in which we live. As such, cosmologies commonly share several features:

- — they attempt to define Man's place in the universe;
- — they represent the leading edge of a culture's science;
- — they are described in terms of the culture's syntax and value system;
- — they contain religious and/or spiritual implications;
- — the foundation of the vast majority of cosmologies is the principle of vibration.

Cosmologies may be found in most of the world's cultures — both past and present — and a continual striving for refinement of the concept of cosmology attests to the culture's intellectual vitality. From its origin in pre-Sumarian societies to the most current speculations in quantum physics and in holographic models of consciousness, our search for understanding of the nature of the universe has led to ever smaller units of physical vibration.[11]

When we first discovered the atom we thought it to be a microscopic solid particle that combined with similar atoms to form physical matter. But, our advancing technology revealed that the atom was a unit of high velocity energy, a bubbling nucleus surrounded by an orbit of whirling electrons , and between them there was space. The latest development in our search for the unifying principle of the universe is now taking shape in the theories of physicists John Schwarz of California Tech and Michael Green of Queen Mary College in London; the fundamental particles of the universe are not pointlike objects as previously supposed but rather, tiny snips of subatomic vibrating particle strings 100 billion times shorter than the diameter of the nucleus of an atom. These particle strings vibrate in pre-determined ways and interact with one another to create the properties of the particles of matter. Matter, then, emerges as a kind of subatomic music unifying all the forces of nature, including gravitational force, in one simple theory.[12]

Moreover, in contrast to our present belief in a universe of four dimensions — three of space and one of time — the theories of Green and Schwartz imply a ten-dimensional universe with nine dimensions of space and one of time. If we combine this concept with that of a holographic model of consciousness, what emerges is the possibility of multi-dimensional interlocking universes that co-exist simultaneously in both time and space. If, as seems plausible, they are interconnected by vibration — consciousness itself being an aspect of vibration, then music may well be the unifying energy force between them.

So we come full-circle — returning again to the ancient philosophical belief that all the universe is held together by sound.

INTERLUDE

PART I

In India, time is traditionally measured in cycles. As described in the *Bhagavat Puana*, an ancient sacred treatise, each complete cosmic cycle consists of four successive ages each of which is called a "Yuga". At the close of each cosmic cycle the universe ceases to exist for a period of time equal to the preceding cycle after which the universe is once again brought into manifestation for a new cosmic cycle.

— One day in the life of the Hindu god, Brahma, is equal to 4,320,000,000 solar years.

— One night in the life of Brahma is equal to 4,320,000,000 solar years. During this night Brahma, the creator of the universe sleeps. At the end of the night he awakens and the creation of the universe begins again.

— One complete cosmic cycle is equal to 4,320,000 solar years and consists of four successive ages (*yugas*) whose lengths vary in the ration of 4:3:2:1.

— The present age, *Kali Yuga*, is the last in succession and is equal to 432,000 solar years.

— At the rate of 7.2 breaths per minute, the average rate during meditation, we breathe 432 times in one hour.

— Our normal breathing rate at rest is about 18 breaths per minute, or 25,920 times in twenty-four hours. The time required for our sun to complete one revolution in the galaxy is 25,920 solar years.

— At the rate of 18 times per minute, we breathe 1080 times per hour.

— At the average rate of 72 beats per minute, our heart beats 4,320 times in one hour.

— Four times eighteen equals 72, which means that our heart beats four times for every breath — a ratio of 4:1, the same ratio as the ratio between the first *yuga* and the last.

PART II

In music's harmonic series, 4th, 3rd, and 2nd partials create the ratio 4:3:2 and give us the tonic, the fifth and the octave above the fundamental tone.

FIGURE 5

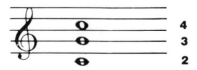

This sonority, with its fundamental an octave below create the ratio 4:3:2:1, serves as the principle accompanying drone for India's music and remains the most common vertical sound throughout the world's musics. It has also served as the harmonic basis for the development of Western harmony, wherein it is still called a Perfect Consonance, and it is the guiding principle of scale projection of all our musical structures and forms.

FIGURE 6
**The Western Major Scale
of the harmonic series.**

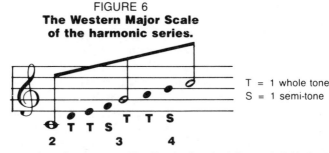

T = 1 whole tone
S = 1 semi-tone

Suite Form (Baroque and pre-Baroque)

Tonic- - - - - Dominant- - - Tonic

Key: Begins in the tonic key, modulates to the dominant a fifth higher, returns to the tonic, a ratio of 2:3:2 of the harmonic series.

First Rondo (Classical, Romantic & Modern)

Theme A | Theme B | Theme A

2 _____ to 3 _____ to 2 _____
Tonic   Dominant   Tonic

Key: The rondo is built from 2 contrasting themes, "A" and "B", and returns to the first theme for the third section. The key of Section A is tonic (I) while the key of Section B is dominant, a fifth higher. Again 2:3:2 of the harmonic series.

In Addition: The frequency of 432 cycles per second produces a tone that is slightly under our current "concert" pitch of "A" at 440 cycles per second. Previous to the twentieth century "A" at 432 cycles was the normal concert-tuning pitch for European orchestras.

PART III

If we construct a triangle in which the three sides are in proportion to each other at the ratio of 4:3:2, and extend a line from the resulting apex of the triangle to its base, the line will intersect the base at the point of the Golden ratio:

FIGURE 7

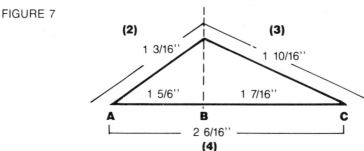

(2)   (3)
1 3/16"   1 10/16"
1 5/6"   1 7/16"
A   B   C
2 6/16"
(4)

The Golden Ratio (also referred to as Golden Mean) is a mathematical proportion numerically approximated at 1.68034, and may be found by dividing a line at a specific point to yield two unequal sections in which the smaller section (A to B) is proportionate to the larger one (B to C), as the larger section (B to C) is to the entire line (A to C). The ratio can be expressed

as $\dfrac{AB}{BC} = \dfrac{BC}{AC}.$

Considered by the Egyptians to express the creative process and by Plato to be the key to the physics of the Cosmos, evidence of the Golden Ratio can be observed in a tiny spiraled seashell and in the spiral nebulae forty-million times the size of the sun; the petal arrangement of a daisy or rose, the spatial constructions of Renaissance paintings and the underlying structure of the Greek Parthenon of Athens. The Golden Ratio describes the universal formula for growth and represents, therefore, the foundation of organic harmony. Music that takes the 4:3:2 ratio as the basis for its harmonic material is music that mirrors the natural order of the universe, and as an expression of the Golden Ratio, connects to the natural internal biological rhythms of our physical bodies as well. If music is the Reflection of the natural order of the universe, then to understand and achieve harmony with its laws, one must study the laws of music.

CHAPTER TEN

How Music Affects Us
Physically and Emotionally

Music is a dynamic multi-layered matrix of constantly shifting tonal relationships unfolding within time, through which we may experience intensified emotions and an alternation of our state of consciousness. Because of its dynamic quality, our primary attraction to music is both physical and emotional — physical because music travels through the air by means of molecular pressure waves that can be felt bodily, emotional because music creates mood environments to which we respond on a subconscious and non-verbal level. It is through our physical and emotional response to music that mental and spiritual attitudes develop which create, in turn, the basis for our aesthetic enjoyment. Ideally, the creation of music is an expression of biological, affective, cognitive and spiritual processes within a cultural context. That is, music reflects the biological processes of breath and pulse, conveys an emotional attitude, is logically ordered according to its unique musical material, and gives expression to transpersonal communion within parameters that are culturally defined. By the same token, a complete response to music should be physical, should give expression to emotional experience, should engage and stimulate the mind, and should be enriching and uplifting to the spirit. Music reflects human activity and process for it is through music that spirit, mind and body attain a unity of experience.

As organisms complete and whole within ourselves, we are the sum of our physical bodies, our emotions, our mental processes and our spiritual life. One of these cannot be affected without influencing the others in some way. Whereas psychologists do not agree on the question of whether our emotions affect our mental state or whether our mind affects our emotional life, there is general consensus that both influence our physical health and that our physical health, in turn, affects our mental and emotional life, these two influences tend to create an internal loop system whereby cause elicits response which becomes cause which then intensifies the original cause. Generally speaking, we tend to respond to our emotions more than to ideas *per se*, but here we must be cautious for many psychologists believe that an emotion is preceded by a thought to which we respond emotionally.

Although music has the power to elicit mental, emotional, physical and spiritual responses in us, beyond a few generalizations we don't completely understand how and in what way different types of music will affect us. Not everyone responds to music in the same way and an individual does not necessarily respond to one composition the same way twice. Whether we like or dislike a certain style of music, a particular composer and/or performer will affect our response, and our responses can be extremely intense. Likewise, those more sensitive to music will be affected to a greater degree than those who are less so. In summarizing a lengthy discussion of this subject, Paul Farnsworth, Professor Emeritus of Psychology at Stanford University, concluded:

> Most research shows the effects [of music] to be greater the more the music has meaning for the listener. That is, a given composition may call forth one set of effects in a musical person and quite different changes in one not musically inclined. Or the effect may differ from one time to another in the same person . . . no composition will be found which can be guaranteed to produce identical or even nearly identical physiological changes among the members of any sizable population.[1]

Farnsworth's conclusion leads us to a more fundamental observation however, for although music may be as old as the human species — older, if you are metaphysically inclined — no one has as yet been able to determine exactly *why* we respond to music in the first place. Perhaps we have overlooked the obvious. Because music is energy made audible, a composition manifests a quality of aliveness as it emerges from silence, develops through events that shape its personality and re-emerges into silence once again. If the state of aliveness manifests in soundfulness, then to be alive is to be soundful. As music gives coherence to successions of sounds, it satisfies the need to find a coherence and a sense of purpose in the events of our own lives.

As philosopher Robert Meagher has written:

> Each time a piece of music is played it is born again to a somehow new life and each time it yields once more to silence it dies another death. And each time we listen to a piece of music we rise and die again with it; for our music like ourselves is mortal and dies in the end, always awaiting rebirth.[2]

How Music Affects Us Physically

Once music enters our ears its sounds are converted to impulses that travel the auditory nerves to the thalamus, which is the relay station of emotions, sensations and feelings. When the thalamus is stimulated the cortex is engaged and it in turn, sends responsive impulses back to the thalamus to create a reverberating circuit that intensifies as the music continues. As we continue to listen, we may experience what has been termed the "thalamic reflex", the outward physical manifestation of which may take the form of foot tapping, swaying, nodding of the head or rhythmic movements of the arms and hands.[3] Within the brain the thalamus, hypothalamus, cerebellum and cerebral hemispheres of the cortex all play an active role in processing the stream of tones and rhythms into recognizable musical structures and give those tones and rhythms mental and emotional meaning.[4] The hypothalamus, connected by nerve pathways to the thalamus, influences our metabolism, our sleeping and waking patterns and other bodily functions. Through it, musical impulses are transmitted to the other brain centers. Wrapped around the thalamus is the limbic system which interacts with the endocrine gland system which in turn influences respiration, pulse, blood circulation and the release of secretions from the various glands.[5]

That music does influence our internal processes has been validated through scientific research, however the influence is not as great as had previously been believed. Experiments to measure the effect of music on breathing rate, heart rate, blood pressure, galvanic skin resistance and electrical conductivity of the body began in the late 1920's[6] and have continued over a thirty year period. Thus far the results appear to be fairly consistent. For example, one study published in 1938[7] concluded that there was no tendency for synchrony between musical pulse and heart rate. This conclusion was verified by another study published in 1952.[8] In a more comprehensive study published in 1939, C. M. Diserens and H. Fine found that:

> Music ... increases bodily metabolisms ... increases or decreases muscular energy ... accelerates respiration and decreases its regularity ... produces marked but variable effect on volume, pulse and blood pressure ... lowers the threshold for sensory stimuli of different modes ... influences the internal secretions.[9]

In addition, they concluded that music reduces or delays fatigue, increases muscular endurance and influences the electrical conductivity of the human body as manifested by increased fluctuations in the psychogalvanic reflex. All studies of the effect of music on respiration have concluded that respiration rates do increase and, not surprisingly, a study published in 1935 found that a change in tempo is the primary cause of the change.[10] Yet closer examination of the study conducted by Ellis and Brighouse reveals that only thirty-six college students were tested and that the results were based on these music compositions: Hall's *Blue Interval*, Franz Listzt's *Hungarian Rhapsody No.1*, and Claude Debussy's *Prelude to the Afternoon of a Faun*. Significantly, the increase in respiration rate occurred only during the playing of *Blue Interval* and the *Hungarian Rhapsody*. No change was observed during the Debussy composition which is tranquil and restrained by comparison.

Most studies of this type conducted between 1925 and 1955 appear to have the following characteristics in common:

1. Monitoring devices in use during this period were probably much less sensitive and accurate than more recent instruments.

2. Most of the experiments were short-term and involved a small number of people, each of whom was tested only once.

3. The selection of music for these experiments was surprisingly narrow — being confined to late romantic Western classical music, popular music of the day and the milder forms of jazz — and the selections tended to exhibit similar musical and emotional characteristics.

4. One may assume that recorded rather than live music was used. Therefore, it is feasible that the quality of recordings at that time could have influenced the outcome of the experiment. Even today, with our "state of the art" digital recording, no recorded hearing of a composition can compare favorably with a live performance in terms of the music's effect on human physiology.

It should be obvious that the physiological effect of music is related directly to the characteristics of each musical selection. One may assume that a highly dynamic and emotionally charged composition — characterized by faster tempos, shifting levels of dynamics, textural and rhythmic complexity, rich harmonic structures and frequent modulation, and melodies that encompass wide pitch ranges with frequent changes of direction — will affect our bodily processes differently than one displaying none of these qualities.

With these qualifications in mind, then, we may conclude, at least tentatively, that music:

— produces no significant changes in heart rate;

— alters breathing rate — in some cases increasing the rate and in others decreasing the rate;

— when designated as "exciting", produces a decrease in galvanic skin response while calming music produces either an increase or no change;

— produces a decrease in blood pressure;

— increases or decreases bodily metabolism depending on the tempo of the music;

— alters muscular energy and can reduce or delay physical fatigue and stress;

— lowers the threshold of sensory stimuli and either reduces or induces visualization

— can facilitate the flow of bodily energy by means of the thalamic reflex.

Some Further Speculations

Two additional aspects of the effect of music on our physiological processes still await serious investigation. They are offered here for the sake of completeness and because, as interesting theories, they may reward the researcher with potent new insights in our quest to more fully understand the physiological effect of music.

Still awaiting investigation is the question concerning the effect of music on the distinctly contrasting thought modes of the two hemispheres of the cerebral cortex and how these hemispheres may interact as we listen to music. According to present theory, the left hemisphere predominates in verbal and cognitive skills which we use in linear thinking and memorization, language skills and the intellectual organization of artistic creativity. The right hemisphere predominates in intuitive insight, non-linear organization, imagining and subconscious development of creative ideas. Whereas the left hemisphere gathers and releases information in step-by-step fashion — it is the hemisphere you are using to read and assimilate these words — the right hemisphere gathers and releases information in spurts of holistic insights.[11]

It is feasible that music integrates both functions since the two hemispheres are involved whenever we create, perform and listen to music. If, in listening to music, we find that we are concentrating analytically on the harmonic movement, the melodic development or the unfoldment of the structure, we are probably relying more on our cognitive, or left hemisphere, process. But when we passively allow the sounds to flow through us as we get a "feel" for the music, we are probably listening with our intuitive, or right hemisphere, process. To state it differently, when we *listen* to music by focused concentration, that is cognitive; when we *hear* through relaxation, that is intuitive. The influence that music may have on us — physically, mentally,emotionally and spiritually — may depend on which of the two predominates in experiencing the music and therefore shapes our associations with that particular composition.

Few people listen to music exclusively with either process, although there may be a tendency to favor one of them. It is more likely that while listening we alternate between cognitive and intuitive processes, each of which enriches the other and therefore enables us to more fully experience the music. However, for purposes of relaxation and for healing, *hearing* music predominantly with the right hemisphere — which can be facilitated by slowing the breath — should be encouraged since this seems to quiet the verbal activity of the left hemisphere and encourages visual imagery.

The Resonating Effect of Music on the Human Body

As music is heard through the action of our ears, it can also be felt by our physical bodies. For when sound moves through the air, pressure waves resembling ripples are created by the motion of the air molecules. When these pressure waves reach a surface as elastic as our skin we may, if we are resting quietly and sufficiently sensitive, experience minute sensations of vibrational movement on the outer surface of our bodies even as our attention is focused on the stimulation of our auditory nerves. Since our skin is highly porous so that heat, air, and perspiration can be released from within our bodies, it is feasible that the vibrations created by music can enter the body on a molecular, atomic or even subatomic level. If this is so, then what kind of patterns are created? If, as practitioners of *Tantra* (or *Shabd*), *Mantra* and *Nada Yoga* claim, all structure is created by sound — however ethereal that sound may be — what structural changes take place within us as we listen to, perform or even think music? If we are surrounded by an essentially vibrational electro-magnetic energy field extending from two inches to as much as eight feet from our bodies, as researchers such as Harold Saxon Burr, Christopher Hill, Peter Guy Manners and Stanley Krippner claim, and if both sound and music create coherent geometrical patterns in inert material such as sand and water, as Hans Jenny's research demonstrates, what possible effect might the patterns created in the air molecules by music have upon the vibratory activity of our electro-magnetic field? How much greater would that effect be if we were submerged in the greater density of water through which music is traveling? If there is a tendency for the vibrational patterns created in air molecules by music to interact with our electro-magnetic field, what effect might this effect differ in a slow moving, almost static music such as in an *alap* of North Indian music as compared to a fast paced Beethoven *scherzo*? If, in recording on magnetic tape, the vibrational patterns of music are converted to electro-magnetic impulses that cause the minute metal particles on the recording tape to arrange themselves into fixed patterns, might a similar pattern occur within us as we listen to music? If so, how deeply do these patterns penetrate us and how long might they last? Would repeated hearings of the same music have a cumulative effect? If wood and metal can be made to resonate, can a human body, less dense, more elastic and containing soft tissue, also be made to resonate? If water is a far more efficient carrier of sound waves, and if our bodies consist of seventy percent water, what happens within us when we sing or speak, and how much of what happens within travels through our skin, affects our electro-magnetic field and that of those who may be near us? Is it feasible that we may wear an environment of sound around us just as we wear clothing, and can this environment shield us from emotional-mental negativity just as clothes shield us from heat and cold?

Questions such as these occupy the thoughts of increasing numbers of people who are involved in developing the use of music for healing. Yet, amid the speculation and presumptions, little valid research has been undertaken, with the possible exception of the experiments devised by composer Stephen Halprin.[12] My personal belief is that there is validity to the hypothesis that music creates vibrational patterns that interact with our electro-magnetic field and influence our physical bodies in some way by means of the principle of resonance.

Summary

Changes take place within our physical bodies as a result of being exposed to both sound and music; these changes may take place whether we are consciously aware of them or not. Significantly, it may not be necessary that we maintain consciousness for these changes to occur or even that we give permission for those changes to take place. Because of this, considerable responsibility for the physical effect of music may rest with performers of music, for music does not require conscious permission from the listener in order for it to affect us on the physical level. During any musical performance, musicians should understand that what they create physically resonates each audience member and that the level of resonance may be intensified according to the number of people present. Therefore, musicians must be constantly sensitive to the effects of their music and be clear about their intentions.

The Effect of Music on the Emotions

Our primary attraction to music is most likely through its power to create moods and to elicit emotional responses from within us. Not surprisingly, it is the relationship of music, moods and emotions that has occupied our attention since ancient times, particularly in India, China and in Greece from which the following incident serves as an interesting illustration:

> A Sicilian youth, who had become intoxicated and had been inflamed by music played in the Phrygian mode, was rushing to the home of his mistress on a certain night with the avowed intention of destroying it by fire, because he had learned that she had received a rival. Accordingly, as the music continued, he became more and more enraged when Pythagoras. . . realizing what was happening, ordered the flute player to cease playing in the Phrygian mode and change his strain to the spondaic measure. Immediately the youth became calm and returned home completely healed.[13]

Although emotions have been studied intensely by physicians, psychiatrists, psychologists, philosophers, spiritual teachers, aestheticians, anthropologists, sociologists, artists and musicians, in truth we do not yet fully understand why we have emotions, how emotions are caused or why emotions seem to govern our perceptions and actions to the extent they do. Most researchers who have devoted considerable time to the study of emotions seem to agree that they are specific and object-oriented, in contrast to moods which are thought to be non-specified. For example, anger is an emotion because it is always directed toward something or someone regardless of whether we can identify the object of the anger whereas a mood, such as depression, can be the result of an unidentified emotion. In addition, emotions may be "outer-directed", "inner-directed", or both simultaneously, depending on the situation. "Outer-directed" emotions typically focus on some object, situation or person outside of oneself; "inner-directed" emotions take one's self as their focal point. For example, fear is an "outer-directed" emotion, shame is an "inner-directed" emotion, while anger can be either or both.

Psychologist Robert Solomon has identified and described forty-two emotions.[14]

Anger	Dread	Frustration
Anxiety	Duty	Guilt
Anguish	Embarassment	Hate
Contempt	Envy	Indifference
Despair	Fear	Indignation
Jealousy	Grief	Terror
Pity	Vanity	Faith
Pride	Self-Contempt	Friendship
Regret	Self-Hatred	Hope
Remorse	Self-Pity	Innocence
Resentment	Self-Love	Love
Sadness	Joy	Respect
Shame	Self-Respect	Contentment
Spite	Worship	Rage

By contrast, Gerald Jompaulski identifies only two primary emotions, love and fear, from which all other emotional qualities are derived.[15]

What increases the complexity of understanding our emotions is the fact that we do not always react emotionally to an event or situation in the same way. Indeed, the same person might respond emotionally to the same situation in different ways on separate occasions. Since every state of emotion arises from within ourselves, the same situation may provoke one person to laughter, another to tears, while a third may remain completely indifferent because each is outwardly projecting his or her personal inward attitude. It is the inward attitude that provokes one's response.

Whereas emotions result from our response to specifically identifiable objects, situations or person, *moods* have been called "metaphysical generalizations of the emotions" which create feelings. In the context of our subject of music and emotions, this is an important distinction which is often overlooked, for in music particularly, emotion and mood are not interchangeable terms. Contrary to popular belief, music cannot express emotions with any degree of success but, rather, creates moods to which we may respond on an emotional level.[16] Composer Igor Stravinski took a stronger stand on this subject when he expressed the belief that "music is, by its very nature, essentially powerless to *express* anything at all, whether a feeling, an attitude of mind, a psychological mood, a phenomenon of nature. . ."[17] The nineteenth-century composer, Felix Mendelssohn, opposes this view. "The thoughts which are expressed to me by a piece of music which I love are not too indefinite to be put into words, but on the contrary too definite."[18] The truth is most likely to be found somewhere between these two extremes.[19]

Music, by its very nature, is non-specific and expresses generalized mood qualities upon which we may project a more specific emotional meaning. The emotion with which we respond comes from within us, and the way we respond often depends on such variables as the kind of day we have had prior to hearing music, worries and cares that might influence our hearing, whether we are physically comfortable during the experience, our familiarity with the music idiom that the composition represents, past associations, and personal likes and dislikes. This explains, in part, why music is such a powerful therapeutic tool in the healing process. Music can express a mood quality that may draw forth either a corresponding mood or a specific emotion from the listener if full attention is given to the music.

One of the earliest attempts to categorize mood qualities for use in artistic expression originated in India, where the arts of music, dance, drama, poetry, painting and sculpture are founded on the concept of the "nine sentiments," or *nava rasa*. Each creation of the artist expressed one of these sentiments:

Shringara — erotic, romantic
Hasya — comic, humorous
Karuna — pathetic, sad, tearful, lonely
Raudra — furious, excited anger
Veera — heroic, brave, majestic
Bhayanaka — frightening, fearful
Vibhatsa — disgusting
Adbhuta — wonderous, exhilarated
Shanta — peaceful, tranquil, relaxed

The famous Indian musician, Ravi Shankar, has stated that of these nine *rasas*, only three are especially suited to musical expression: *Shanta*, *Karuna*, and *Shringara*. The two *rasas* least suitable for musical expression are *Bhayanaka* and *Vibhatsa*, these being more suitable in drama.[20]

In our own century, two of the earliest and most substantial studies of the mood effects of music were conducted separately by Max Schoen and Esther Gatewood.[21] These studies were followed a decade later by Kate Hevner's arrangement of sixty-six adjectives in a format that related them directly to music.[22] These adjectives, selected for their appropriateness to musical interpretation, were grouped according to eight principal mood qualities. The eight groups were then arranged in a circle whereby adjectives of one mood quality are related to but differ slightly from the immediately adjacent mood group while mood groups placed diagonally across from each other express opposite mood qualities. Music which best expresses each mood quality was selected and the results were tested over a ten-year period. In constructing her Mood Wheel, Hevner's purpose was to systematize the relationship of moods to music and to facilitate smooth transitions from one mood quality to its adjacent mood in sequence around the circle. In its therapeutic application, an emotionally disturbed patient in a state of melancholy, for example, could be led away from the mood gradually through the careful selection of music corresponding first to melancholy followed by music from each adjacent mood group in sequence.

Hevner's work, which over the years has proved its effectiveness, has been refined and expanded by Helen Bonny, a music therapist and founder of the Institute For Consciousness and Music, as an integral part of her development of Guided Affective Imagery with Music.[23] Ms. Bonny, in recognizing the value of music to enhance, prolong and therefore to experience one's personal moods on a deeper level, selected a wide variety of compositions (drawn primarily but not exclusively from the Western classical tradition) and catalogued her selections according to their compatibility to the eight mood groups. For example, music relating to Mood Group 1 (Solemn) includes: Brahms' Fourth Symphony, third movement; Palestrina's *Stabat Mater*; Hovhaness' Mysterious Mountain, third movement; and Gounod's *Ave Maria*. The opposite Mood Group 5 (Humerous) includes: Bach's Brandenberg Concerto No. 2, third movement; Elgar's *Enigma Variations*, eighth movement; Mozart's Overture to *The Magic Flute*; and Strauss' *Till Eulenspeigal*. Whereas Hevner's work is intended for therapeutic application in clinical settings, Helen Bonny has been concerned primarily with the relief of day-to-day emotional stress and for personal creative enrichment.

The two charts that follow demonstrate Hevner's arrangement of the mood adjectives and their possible correlations with the forty-two emotions and the nine *Rasas* of India.

Arrangement of Adjectives
for the Mood Effect of Music

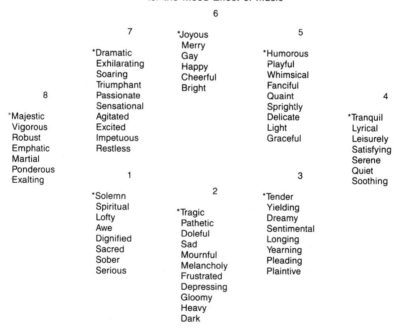

The Ten Rasas

3 Shringara — romantic, erotic, longing
5 Hasya — comic, humerous
2 Karuna — pathetic, sad
7 Raudra — fury, angry
8 Veera — bravery, majesty
7 Bhayanka — frightening
- Vibhatsa — disgusting
1 Adhatsa — wonderment
4 Shanta — peace, tranquility
1 Bhakti — devotional

* = The 8 Principle Mood Qualities

Arrangement of the 42 Emotions as Listed in
Solomon, "The Passion" with Corresponding Indian Rasas

6

Joy
Ecstacy
Euphoria
7 Friendship 5

Anxiety   Hasya
Anguish   comic—humor
Fear   amusement
8 Anger   4
Raudra
Indignation   fury—anger   Contentment
Pride   Bhayanaka   Gratitude
Respect   frightening   Shanta
Duty   peace-
Veera   tranquility
  majesty
                 1   3

Worship   Hope
Faith   Innocence
Love   Love
Devotion   2   Shringara
Adbhuta   romance—
  wonderment Frustration   longing
Bhakti   Jealousy   eroticism
  devotional   Pity
                Regret
                Remorse
                Sadness
                Shame
                Karuna
                  pity—sadness

Emotions Not Categorized

Contempt   Hatred   Self-Contempt
Despise   Indifference Self-Hatred
Embarrassment Resentment   Self-Love
Envy   Spite   Self-Pity
Guilt   Vanity   Self-Respect

Rasa Not Used

Vibhatsa — disgusting

Possible Correlations Between Mood Qualities and Music

The assignment of music to any specific mood has been, for the most part, a subjective process whereby one's affective response to a specific composition is matched to one of the eight principal mood qualities. Although it is fairly easy to differentiate between solemn music (Mood Quality 1) and its opposite, humerous music (Mood Quality 5), it is more difficult to differentiate between music for any two adjacent mood qualities. For example, in what basis might we designate a composition as being *humorous* rather than *joyous* which, according to the Mood Wheel, are adjacent mood qualities? Few of us would classify the opening movement of Beethoven's Fifth Symphony as being tranquil or humerous. The music is agitated, restless and dramatic in its opening, we would agree. But why? The movement changes mood quality for a more lyrical (tender?) second theme. What changes take place in the music that create the change of mood, even if the change is slight and lasts but a short time?

With questions such as these we are led, inevitably, to a consideration of the contrasting traits of the various separate components that combine in a musical composition. The components, or parameters, of music include: melody, harmony, time and rhythm, texture (the number of voices and their relationship to each other), dynamics (loudness levels), timbre (characteristics of the sound sources), range and placement of the sounds (high, low, middle), and layering of musical activity (foreground, background). Two aspects of each of these parameters should be taken into consideration: the quality of each parameter at any given moment and the way in which each parameter changes as the music progresses. These two elements create the flow of movement through time and space, and the movement may be slow and static, dynamic or, at the extreme, chaotic and frenetic. It is the combination of these parameters and the movements created by them that produces the mood qualities to which we respond emotionally. To illustrate this point let us examine the parameter of dynamics, the relative loudness or the softness of the music.

The dynamic levels used in music range from silence to very quiet (*pianissimo*) to moderately quiet (*mezzo piano*) to moderately loud (*mezzo forte*) to loud (*forte*) to very loud (*fortissimo*) to painfully loud. These are the steady states of the dynamic levels and they are relative to the number of musicians who are playing at any given moment. For example, a single violinist playing very softly will produce a sound that is quieter than an entire violin section of an orchestra playing at the same dynamic level. Music that is predominantly in the very quiet to moderately quiet dynamic range elicits an emotional reaction in us that is very different from louder dynamic levels. Quiet music may imply a sense of intimacy, secrecy, mystery, awe, melancholy, delicacy, whimsy, or restless agitation depending on its context and the qualities of other musical parameters such as tempo and rhythm. Yet dynamic levels do change and the way in which they change and the frequency with which they change influences our emotional response. Thus, we may experience gradual changes of dynamic levels or sharp and frequent contrasts of dynamic levels.

A music composition cannot be assigned to a particular mood quality of the basis of dynamic level alone, however. By way of example, in adding the parameter of tempo — determined by the number of beats per minute — to our consideration of dynamic levels, we are able to become more specific in assigning a mood quality to a music composition. Therefore, music of a quiet dynamic level and a slow tempo could express the mood of Tragic (2), Tender (3), Tranquil (4) or Solemn (1), whereas quiet music in a faster tempo could express the mood quality of Humerous (5), Joyous (6), or even Dramatic (7, agitated, restless, excited), but would probably not be assigned to Majestic (8). If our music composition exhibits the qualities of quiet dynamic level, slow tempo *and* is in a minor key, we are likely to assign it to the mood quality Tragic (2, mournful, melancholy); if the key is a major one, it will probably express the mood qualities of Tender (3) or Tranquil (4), and so forth. Proceeding in this way, as each parameter is considered separately, our assignment of music to the various mood qualities becomes easier and the use of the Mood Wheel becomes more accurate. Eventually, in classifying music by taking each separate parameter into account, an entirely new and more objective system of classification may evolve, thereby minimizing or eliminating mood qualities as a means of categorizing music. To this end, a list of music parameters can serve as an objective reference when used in conjunction with the subjective process of selecting music for each mood quality. The following procedure is suggested:

1. Find music of a least six minutes duration that is expressive of one mood quality.
2. Assign this composition to one of the eight mood qualities according to your subjective response.
3. Repeat steps 1 and 2 for music which expresses the opposite mood quality.
4. Taking each music parameter in turn, make a list of the musical differences between the two selections. Several hearings of each composition may be required.

This procedure may be required for each pair of contrasting moodhqualities until one music selection is assigned to each. Then proceed to the first mood quality and, in the same manner, begin to select a second music composition for each mood. When you have two or three compositions for each, you can begin to make comparisons of the music parameters for each mood quality. As similarities begin to emerge, common characteristics will be more evident and this will eventually allow for a greater predictability of mood response.

The Parameters of Music

Dynamics

Silence - Very Quiet - Moderately Quiet - Moderately Loud - Loud - Very Loud - Painfully Loud

Change of Dynamic Levels

Steady State	Gradual Change of Dynamic Level	Sharp and Frequent Contrast of Dynamic Level
One Dynamic Level Predominates	(Tapered)	

Tempo—number of beats per minute

No Regular Beats - Very Slow - Slow - Moderately Slow - Moderately Fast - Fast - Very Fast

Change of Tempo

Steady State	Gradual Change of Tempo	Sharp and Frequent Change of Tempo
One Tempo Predominates	Increase Decrease	

Melody (Theme, Subject)

Static	Dynamic	Frenetic
Centered Around One or Two Pitches	Wider Pitch Range, Conjunct Movement Predominatly by Step	Wide Leaps, Frequent Change of Direction, Disjunct

Melodic Motion

Stepwise, skipping, leaping, articulated, continuous, rising, falling, level, chromatic, diatonic, atonal.

Rhythm

Unmetered	Metered	Frenetic frequent stops and starts — metered or unmetered
	symetrical, asymetrical syncopated, additive	

Rhythmic Growth

cellular	motivic	subphrase	phrase	larger phrase groupings

Movement - Growth

Static	dynamic (moderate)	Very Dynamic
• slow development • ornamental motion	• smooth, transitional • directional motion	• rapid development • frequent shifts

Texture

Monophonic	Heterophonic	Homophonic	Polyphonic
Simple	to		Complex
• unaccom-panied melody	• several voices in unison	• melody with chordal accompaniment	• many independent voices
melody over single held tone (drone)	all voices move in same rhythm (homo rhythmic)	many rhythms at same time (polyrhythmic)	

Spacial Levels of Musical Activity

Foreground • melody alone 1 layer of activity	Foreground (melody) and Backgroung (harmony) 2 layers of activity	Foreground Middleground Background multilayered

Tone Quality (Timbre)

Strings, Woodwinds, Brass, Percussion, Electronic, Human voices, Earth sounds, Combinations

Single Voice	Small Ensemble (2-16 players)	Medium Ensemble (17-40 players)	Large Ensemble (over 40 players)

— Range of Pitches

Very Small Range

—Placement of Range   Total Musical Pitch Spectrum

Low	Middle	High
Split	Balanced	

—Degree and Frequency of Timbral Contrast

One Timbre (no contrast)	Contrast of 2 or 3 Timbres	Contrasts of Many Timbres
Gradual Change of Timbre	Terraced Change of Timbres	Frequent and Sharp Contrast

Note: The four parameters common to all music and implicit in every music are: Sound, Silence, Time and Space.

Sound and Silence are interrelated.
Time and Space are interrelated.
Silence is given articulation through the element of Time.
Sound creates Space.
Space gives dimension to Sound.

The interaction of Sound, Time and Space creates motion.

Applications

Most medical doctors, psychologists, psychic and holistic healers acknowledge the relationship between emotions and health, and many seem to be reaching agreement that emotions are a major factor in the development of illness. Emotions that are not expressed when they are felt may be turned inward where they can add stress to weakened parts of the body. When the stress is prolonged our natural ability to resist disease is impaired and illness may ensue. By the same token, the most prevalent type of music in our culture is that which lends itself to the expression of personalized emotions, feelings and moods. When used regularly, music is an effective vehicle for the dissipation of normal day-to-day emotional stress. But in times of intense emotional crisis, music can focus and guide emotional release by bringing the emotion to catharsis and providing it with the means of expression.

In a study published in 1958, authors I.A. Taylor and F. Paperte concluded that:

> Music, because of its abstract nature, detours the ego and intellectual controls and, contacting the lower centers directly, stirs up latent conflicts and emotions which may then be expressed and activated through music; . . .that music, acting *through* the ego controls, produces a rapid development of the fantasy world, thus increasing the speed at which therapy may proceed; . . .if the structural dynamics of the music impinging on the sensorium is similar to the prevalent structure the two will unite and thus fusion will allow music to affect emotions directly.[24]

The authors' third conclusion points directly to the principle known as the "iso" or "equal" principle and simply means that the mood quality of the music should match the mood or emotion of the person for whom it is played. Therefore, if you wish to give full expression to an emotion or mood, select music that most closely corresponds to it. However, if you wish to alter the mood, this may be accomplished by choosing music that most effectively contrasts with the mood being changed. When attempting to exorcise a highly charged emotion, first play music that most closely expresses that emotion and then, by choosing music for each adjacent mood quality in sequence, gradually change the character of the music to facilitate a gradual transformation of your emotional state. In this context, Hevner's Mood Wheel can serve as a valuable aid, for each of the eight mood qualities may be translated into more specific emotional responses which can be experienced in a personal self-healing way.

Our emotions are in constant flux, often from moment to moment. Most often they are fleeting and invested with little energy. Sometimes they are barely perceptible to our conscious minds. But when an emotion begins to dominate our psyche, it can throw us off balance. Before we can regain our balance and return to emotional equilibrium, it must be addressed and expressed in a healthful way and the issues which were its cause must be resolved. Then, through music, we may experience the deeper levels of tranquillity that lie beneath the influence of the ripples and upheavals of our emotional life.

CHAPTER ELEVEN

How Music Effects Us Mentally and Spiritually

Whereas the influence of music on our physical bodies can be measured, the moods created by music and our emotional responses can be observed, and ample literature exists which indicates the influence of music on spiritual and aesthetic life, the effect of music on our mind is, perhaps, the least understood. We are not limited by the three-trillion cells of our brain nor confined to the space within our skull. The world as perceived by our senses forms a part of our mind, yet all conscious awareness — from that of a single atom of one body cell to the vastness of the universe itself — is encompassed by our mind and is therefore available to us. The mind is limited only by the constraints which we place on it. These constraints may be defined by the value systems of our cultural tradition and by personal conditions derived by the limitations we place on our sensory perceptions, both qualitatively and quantitatively.

The level of mind with which we are most familiar is that of cognitive, or linear, thought. Greatly influenced by sensory input, emotional response and concern for personal survival and comfort, this level of mental activity can dominate our mental processes with an almost endless stream of verbal chatter — thoughts upon thoughts with which we mesmerize ourselves. Yet this is only one aspect of our mental capacity, albeit the most familiar, because it has received the most consistent attention by our educational systems. We also possess an intuitive, holistic and symbolic thought process that is associated with the right hemisphere of the brain.[1] It is in this thought process that artistic concepts and intuitive insights have their origins. The intuitive and the cognitive aspects of our thinking process are interconnected through relay systems in the brain. Ideally, both should be readily available.

Any active involvement with music, whether composing, performing or listening, engages both hemispheres and therefore balances both aspects of our mental processes. This might be more obvious with regard to creating music have, for the much heralded benefits to be gained from creating and playing music been generously documented in educational and music therapy journals. But what actually takes place within the mind while one is fully engaged in the act of listening to music is far more difficult to observe since it is a highly personal and internal process that does not easily lend itself to external monitoring. What we do know thus far is that it is reasonable to assume that no two people hear an identical performance of music in the same way, nor is it likely, that one will hear a recorded version of a music composition in the same way on each occasion. If this were not so, then we would tire of our records rather quickly.

What follows, then, is purely theoretical speculation of what occurs in the mind as we listen to music.

To begin, when we listen to music, we might notice that the steady stream of internal verbal chatter abates as we follow the linear unfolding of the melodic line. As the additional components of the composition — i.e., harmonic movement, rhythmic development, counter melodies, shifting textures — come to our conscious attention, we continually relate the melodic lines to the supporting music around them, separating the various components from the general matrix and then re-integrating each separate part into the emerging structural patterns. This information is then stored in our memory which constantly relates to and influences our perception of each new piece of musical information as it is presented. Each new piece of information, in turn, influences our memory and therefore changes our perception of each new musical event. To accomplish this, we must continually shift back and forth from our more familiar cognitive linear perception to a wholistic intuitive perception in order to integrate the emerging patterns. A balance of both aspects of our mental process is absolutely essential to the activity of hearing music, and the entire process is instantaneous, non-verbal and automatic.

Recently, the following simple experiment was conducted with a class of music theory students. It can easily be duplicated. Beginning with one metronome, I asked the students to group the beats into units of two beats, then three beats, four beats, five beats, and then patterns of alternating groups of two plus three beats by hearing an accent on the first beat of each grouping. This they could do with little effort even though it was their perception and expectation that enabled them to hear the groups.

Next, I set a second metronome in motion at a slightly faster tempo. We were able to perceive the two different tempos simultaneously as well as a composite rhythmic pattern created by the two metronomes. Finally, I set a third metronome in motion with some rather interesting results. We discovered that when we concentrated on one of the metronomes, it seemed to become louder; when we shifted our attention to the second metronome, it seemed to become louder while the first metronome seemed to diminish in loudness. When we shifted our attention to the rhythmic patterns created by the three metronomes in combination, we perceived them as being of equal loudness. From this brief experiment we theorized that when we concentrated on one metronome we were using our linear-oriented left hemisphere, and when we listened to the evolving rhythmic patterns precluded by the interaction of the three metronomes, we shifted to our right hemisphere. The majority of the students found it nearly impossible to listen to these emerging patterns for a protracted length of time without shifting their attention to one of the metronomes. When confronted with the complexities of an actual music composition, it can be assumed that the same two-sided process of hearing takes place.

Thus far we have briefly examined the conscious level of our mental activity and the way in which music affects us at this level. In recent years, psychologists have identified several levels of consciousness within this general category which they refer to as "altered states of consciousness" and their relationship to music in due course, but let us first summarize the effect of music on the conscious mind in general terms and then consider other levels of the mind and how they may be influenced by music.

Music engages the conscious mind through its power of attraction. As we become involved with the music, internal discourse diminishes and visual imagery may be released. This is the level of concentration during which we are involved with the music on an intellectual and aesthetic level. The fuller our level of involvement, the less consciously aware of our individualized personalities we may become. When our involvement approaches the stage of complete immersion, we may have reached the transpersonal level of the super-conscious mind during which the state of focused concentration gives way to a state of expanded awareness. Visual imagery may be left behind as we begin to experience music as waves of alternating patterns that create motion.

Beyond consciousness of individuality and personal emotion, we reach the philosophical level of hearing. Beyond even the philosophical level we may attain a level at which all sounds are heard as complementary parts of absolute infinity. At this level all music expression, all sounds, gestures, and silences communicate the essence of timelessness and of deep joy. Beyond this lies the infinity of absolute silence where even music falls away.

Beneath the surface level of the conscious mind lies the vast, mostly uncharted region of the unconscious. By general agreement, the unconscious is the repository of forgotten memories, emotions, fears and feelings that influence our daily actions, and the emotional responses, thoughts, habits, needs and judgments, that spawn our personal mythologies. According to some theories, there are two levels of the unconscious, the individual centered personal unconscious and the nonpersonal collective unconscious. The collective unconscious is an essentially nonverbal repository of our shared human experience, a species memory beyond racial, ideological and national identities. Music can evoke these forgotten memories to conscious awareness as it encourages unconscious mental activity and decreases cognitive thought processes. Here our involvement with music is the social and feeling level of personal-collective emotions and is the experience of direct sensation.

Various writers on the aesthetics of music have endeavored to understand why we are attracted to certain styles of music and to specific composers within a style of music. Many theories have been presented. One of these states that there is a direct communication between the unconscious mind of the composer and of the listener, which is conveyed through the music. According to this theory, we are attracted to the music by composers whose unconscious memories convey emotional life experiences and feelings similar to, or in some way relating to, our own.[2] If this is plausible, then it follows that our musical preferences are often not simply the result of purely intellectual or aesthetic considerations alone. On the level of the collective unconscious this theory may explain the communal nature of audience participation in the presentation of music in a concert situation, as well as the importance of music in religious and national rituals. From this perspective, music has a much more powerful effect than words alone, rendering musicians with the potential for greater influence over other than most political leaders or national ideologies.

In our investigation thus far we have given consideration to four levels of mental activity, three levels of involvement and seven levels of listening. By way of summary and in an effort to simplify the concepts that have been presented, the following diagram may be helpful as a suggested hypothesis for further exploration and refinement. The reader is invited to make his/her own variations.

A note of caution is necessary, however, where such charts are concerned: the experience of music is never as simple as this or any other diagram might imply for music operates on many levels at once. Likewise, our experience of music takes place at all levels, sometimes alternating, sometimes simultaneously. Although some music may be more conducive to one or more levels of involvement, of mental activity or of musical understanding, we are capable of experiencing all levels with any musical composition regardless of its idiom or style. Many people differentiate between "good" music and "bad" music. Most often this judgement reflects personal prejudice. No such judgement is implied here. It is certainly true that the kind of music we listen to influences who we are and how we perceive ourselves, each other and the world around us. But it must be emphasized again that we should cultivate the ability to respond to music on a physical, emotional, mental and aesthetic level. Condemnation of music categories and styles is counterproductive and limiting. Rather, let us seek the best examples of every type of music, for they are all valuable resources.

Altered States of Consciousness

Taken as a whole, the five levels of mind constitute what is referred to as our consciousness. As such they are available to every human being. In recent years, however, research psychologists have felt the need for further refinement in categorizing the many levels of awareness that we may experience in daily life. These have become known as "states of consciousness" of which twenty have been

Summary of Music Effects

MIND LEVEL

Super Conscious
—transpersonal

Conscious Level
—Individual centered
—cognitive thought
—intuitive thought

Personal Unconscious Level
—individual centered
—storehouse of forgotten memories, feelings, emotions

Collective Unconscious Level
—social centered
—experience of shared human experiences
—species memory

INVOLVEMENT LEVEL

Level of Total Involvment
—becoming identical with the object of concentration
—complete union — no separation

Intellectual Involvement
—thinking about the characteristics of the object of identification

Involvement in Terms of Feeling
—experience of direct sensation

MEANING LEVEL

Supreme Level
—search for union with a higher force

Philosophic Level
—search for meaning beyond the music
—metaphysical connections
—emotional music identified with composer's personality

Aesthetic Level
—search for beauty
Intellectual Level
—musical characteristics and logic

Intellectual Level
—musical characteristics and logic

Sensory Level
—emotional identification
—bodily sensations and feelings

Social Level
—universal communication
—shared ritual
—shared concern

identified — one that has been designated as our "normal waking" state of consciousness, and nineteen additional states of consciousness. An altered state of consciousness constitutes a qualitative shift in mental functioning and may be defined as "a mental state which can be subjectively recognized by an individual as representing a difference in psychological functioning from that individual's normal alert, working state."[3]

One psychologist, Dr. Stanley Krippner, has been a pioneer in the identification of the various altered states of consciousness. He has designated the levels of consciousness as: normal waking state, sleeping, dreaming during sleep, hypnogogic, hypnopompic, hyperalert, lethargic, rapture, hysteria, fragmentation, regressive, meditative, trance, reverie, daydreaming, internal scanning, stupor, coma, stored memory, and expanded. Within the "expanded state" he identified four additional levels: sensory level, recollective level, symbolic level, integral level.[4]

Some of these consciousness levels can be considered as negative states and result from a breakdown of a healthful body/mind balance or from severe emotional trauma. These include: coma, stupor, lethargic, regressive, hyperalert, hysteria and fragmentation. A sensitive use of music may be able to overcome some of these states.

A second group constitutes what we tend to experience daily: sleep, dreaming during sleep, hypnogogic, hypnopompic, normal waking state, daydreaming. Certain types of music can change some of these states. In this regard, the sleep state is a special category. One kind of music can induce a sleep state either through boredom or realization while another can terminate this level of consciousness either slowly and gracefully or rather abruptly.

The third group consists of those positive states of consciousness which we occasionally experience under special circumstances. They can be induced or aided by music. They are: meditative, trance, rapture, reverie, internal scanning, stored memory, and the four levels of the expanded state that lead to a peak experience.

Common to all states of consciousness, other than our normal waking state, is that they are either caused by or create an alteration in time perception that differs from what is characteristic of the normal waking state. A special feature of music, and one of its primary attractions, is that it can alter our sense of time as we listen — a process that we shall examine in detail later. Therefore, music can be a very effective means of altering our state of consciousness and has been used for such purposes from very ancient times to the present day. Indeed, this has been one of its principal uses particularly with regard to altered states listed in Group Three which includes religious ceremonies and healing rituals. The connection between music, therapy and the alteration of mind states is obvious, affecting therapists, patients, and observers alike. Yet, in our society, few have made that connection. To my knowledge, there has not been a convincing study of the role that music plays in altering consciousness, while the use of specific types of music for the purpose of altering consciousness states to facilitate the

States of Consciousness

Consciousness State	Characteristics:	Relationship to Music	Additional comments
1. The Dream State	Occurs periodically as part of the sleep cycle.	Music's influence on the dream cycle has never been explored.	
2. the Sleep State	Tests indicate that there is some mental activity during sleep.	Music can induce sleep, prevent sleep, or terminate sleep.	
3. Hypnogogic State	Occurs between wakefulness and sleep. Presence of visual and auditory imagery.	Effect of music never explored.	
4. Hypnopompic State	Occurs between sleep and wakefulness at end of dream-sleep cycle. Presence of visual and auditory imagery.	Effect of music never explored.	
5. Hyperalert State	Prolonged increased vigilance while one is awake resulting from activities demanding intense concentration or by measures necessary for survival.	Effect on music never explored. Hypothetically music could prevent, interfere with or aid this state, may keep this state from developing into hysteria.	Depends on the music and the circumstances.
6. Lethargic State	Dulled, sluggish mental activity. Can be induced by fatigue, sleep deprivation, malnutrition or by despondent moods and feelings.	Music can relax the individual into sleep or, when caused by depression, help to lift the individual out of this state.	Music applications have been used in traditional music therapy.
7. States of Rapture	Intense feeling and overpowering emotion, usually pleasurable and positive. Induced by sexual stimulation, franzied dances, orgiastic rituals and religious activities.	Music can induce or intensify this state.	One of the principal uses of music throughout history.

Consciousness State	Characteristics:	Relationship to Music	Additional Comments
8. States of Hysteria	Intense feeling and overpowering emotion usually negative and destructive. Induced by rage, fear, terror, violent mob activity, and psychoneurotic anxiety.	Music can calm hysteria.	This use of music was advocated by Pythagoras.
9. States of Fragmentation	Lack of integration among important segments, aspects or themes of the total personality. Similar to condition of psychosis, dissociation, amnesia. Induced by physical trauma to the brain, psychological stress, hypnosis and sensory deprivation.	Music can help prevent the state from occurring, or can help to lift the individual out of it.	Certain types of music may actually cause or intensify fragmentation.
10. Regressive States	Behavior that is clearly inappropriate in terms of the individual's physiological status and chronological age. Induced by "age regression" manipulation or by senility.	Effect of music never fully explored	In experimental "age regression" manipulation for therapeutic purposes, certain kinds of music, such as lullabies and children's songs, can be used as background to the therapist's voice.
11. Meditative States	Minimal cognitive mental activity, lack of visual imagery and the presence of continuous Alpha brain waves. Induced by massage, meditative disciplines, floating in water and music.	This is a primary use of music in many cultures where music is practiced as a spiritual discipline. Music can lead to the meditative state.	Cultures where music is practiced as a spiritual discipline are non-Western cultures with ancient origins. There is not continuous tradition of meditation music in Western cultures.

Consciousness State	Characteristics	Relationship to Music	Additional Comments
12. Trance States	Alertness, concentration of attention on a single stimulus and by the absence of continuous Alpha waves. Induced by voice of hypnotist, listening to one's heartbeat, trance-inducing rituals, repetitive grilling, prolonged watching of revolving object, watching a dramatic presentation, performing a task that requires attentiveness but which involves little variation in response, chants or music.	One of the oldest musical traditions and found in virtually every culture. Music does induce trance under certain conditions. Cultures with strong traditions of trance music include Bali, Indonesia, Africa, Turkey, Pakistan, most Shamanistic cultures. In these music is used for the specific purpose of inducing trance for healing and religious purposes.	In our own culture examples of trance music include rock music, disco music, gospel music and avant-garde minimalist music.
13. Reverie	Rapid eye movements, but also occurs during trance. Experimentally induced by a hypnotist who suggests that the individual will have a dream like experience.	Music can induce reverie.	
14. Daydreaming States	Rapidly occurring thoughts which bear little relation to the external environment. Induced by boredom, social isolation, sensory deprivation, psychodynamic needs and night time dream deprivation.	In our culture this is a major use of music. Almost everyone daydreams with music.	Daydreaming to music is considered to be inappropriate by most music educators and is actively discouraged in "music appreciation" classes.
15. Internal Scanning	Awareness of bodily feelings in organs, tissues, muscles, etc. on a non-reflective level. Induced by athletic activity, sensory awareness work or by the presence of intense pain.	Effect of music has never been explored.	

Consciousness State	Characteristics	Relationship to Music	Additional Comments
16. stupor	Suspended or greatly reduced ability to perceive incoming stimuli. There is little motor activity and little use of language. Induced by certain types of psychosis, drugs and large quantities of alcohol.	Music appears to have no effect in inducing or terminating this state.	
17. Coma	Inability to perceive incoming stimulii. Little motor activity and no use of language. Induced by illness, toxic agents, epileptic seizures, trauma to the brain or glandular dysfunctin.	Music has no effect in either inducing this state or in arousing an indivudual out of it.	
18. Stored Memory	Memory Trances (or engrams) of past events that are not immediately available to an individual's reflective awareness but which exist on some level of the individual's consciousness. May be recalled by conscious effort, may emerge spontaneously, may be evoked by electrical or chemical stimulation of the cortex, or by psychoanalytic free association.	Music can release stored memory under certain conditions as a part of the environment.	Music used to enhance commercials may be operating on this level of consciousness through the process of association and recall.
19. "Expanded" States	Lowered sensory threshold and an abandonment of habitual ways of perceiving the external and/or internal environment. Induced through hypnosis, sensory bombardment, psychedelic drugs or may occur spontane-	Music can facilitate expanded states of consciousness on all four levels.	

Consciousness State	Characteristics	Relationship to Music	Additional Comments
	ously. Progresses along four different levels: *Sensory level*—subjective reports of alterations in space, time, body image and sensory impressions. *Recollective-Analytic level*—novel ideas and thoughts emerge concerning the individual's psychodynamics or conception of the world. *Symbolic level*—identification with historical or legendary persons, with evolutionary recapitulation, or with mythical symbols. *Integral level*—a religious and/or mystical experience in which the individual has the subjective impression of dissolving into the energy field of the universe.	*Sensory level*—Music subjectively alters time-space perceptions and sensory impressions. *Recollective-Analytic level*—Music aids in releasing intuitive thought processes. *Symbolic level*—Music has its own level of symbolic meaning that can be transferred into mythilogical symbolism. *Integral level*—deep involvement with music can induce a religious or mystical experience.	One of the basic principles of Guided Affective Imagery with Music as developed by Helen Bonny. It is the goal of every serious musician to experience this level of consciousness at least once. It is the basis of the philosophy of music in India.
20. "Normal" State	Logic, rationality, cause and effect thinking, goal directedness, reflective thinking.	Music can either cause a return to the normal waking state, help an individual to remain in the normal state, or lift one out of the normal waking state, depending on the type of music, the circumstances in which it is heard and the intention of the listener.	Heard at this level, music is aesthetically appreciated for the unfoldment of its musical content or for the expression of personalized emotions.

healing process is virtually unexplored. It seems to have been thoroughly understood by the shamans of primal cultures, both ancient and contemporary.

All music can alter our state of consciousness in some way. As yet undetermined is what kind of music effects our consciousness in what way and, particularly, what kind of music is most useful for bringing about those states most desirable for healing purposes. The following chart, then, lists the twenty states of consciousness and their characteristics as described by Dr. Krippner, with additional comments on how music may relate to them.

Applications

At present there appear to be three ways in which music can be used in conjunction with mind states. The first of these is to maintain a "normal waking state" when a condition of restful alertness is desired and when the states of sleep, daydreaming, trance, hyperalertness or fragmentation are to be avoided. Certain types of music may be used while studying, driving a vehicle, or when one is engaged in repetitive actions over long periods of time. When used for these purposes, music helps increase mental concentration and may diminish the risk of accidents. Its applications are found in the business and industrial world where it is used to provide a relaxed working atmosphere.

A second application of music is to aid in the termination of negative consciousness states such as lethargy, hysteria, regression and fragmentation, or in changing consciousness states that are inappropriate in a given situation. For example, music can be effective in restoring to a "normal waking state" an individual who has gone into a state of trance, or it can encourage relaxation in an individual who is in a hyperalert state.

The third application of music is to provide a safe environment in which an individual may experience levels of consciousness that are perceived as conducive to mental health and a creative, enriching life. In recent years this use of music has developed into a new form of music therapy and a professional career for its growing number of practitioners. It is called "Guided Affective Imagery with Music" by its developer, Helen Bonny.[5] Bonny and her associates founded the "Institute for Consciousness and Music" in Baltimore, Maryland (1973) for further research and for the training of facilitators in its methodology. Guided Affective Imagery (GAI) was originally developed by Hanscarl Leuner as a method of evoking visual imagery. Its procedure involves relaxation of the body, concentration of the mind and the visualization of a scene, such as a meadow, by a facilitator. GAI was initially used without music, but it was soon discovered that music enhanced the experience considerably. Originally developed as a therapeutic tool for psychiatric patients, it became evident that GAI with Music could be an enriching experience for mentally healthy people, the objective being to gain an understanding of "non-ordinary" levels of consciousness by experiencing them in a safe environment. As Helen Bonny has stated, the purpose of Guided Affective Imagery with Music is to:

 — explore one's inner self,
 — develop self awareness,
 — clarify personal values,
 — release blocked-up psychic energy sources,
 — enrich group spirit,
 — bring about deep relaxation,
 — foster religious experience.

Through this experience one enters "avenues of insight and creativity, centers of self-realization and self-evaluation, layers of memory and dreams, realms of religious and transpersonal experience."[6]

The method is characterized by a four-step procedure that begins with an induction consisting of physical relation. The induction terminates with a countdown. The exercise begins with the description of a visual setting, usually pastoral, which is described by the facilitator, and is followed by a selection of music that supports the visualization. When the music stops, the exercise is terminated by a count-out during which the individual returns to ordinary consciousness. The final step is a period of self-reflection or group-sharing of the visual imagery. The facilitator (or therapist) often helps process the imagery for personal or archetypal meaning.

Typically, the music is selected from Western European classical literature with orchestral and choral music of the Classical and Romantic eras predominating. The music is carefully chosen and ordered sequentially to match the experience being evoked. In order to elicit a religious experience for example, sacred choral music is very often used. The music selections are usually from fifteen to thirty minutes in length.

Guided Affective Imagery with Music is intended to bring an individual from the "normal waking state" to the richness of the "expanded state of consciousness" in its four levels: sensory, recollective-analytic, symbolic and integral. As a general rule, altered states of consciousness tend to remain ego centered. That is, both the outer perceived world and the inner experienced world are evaluated according to their relationship to the individualized self. To the extent that this is so, the experience of listening to music with Guided Affective Imagery remains primarily a physical, emotional and mental activity in which the individual remains the center of attention. Accordingly, participants in this experience are assured that listening to music in an altered state of consciousness will involve their total awareness, the fullest participation of their multi-dimensional self, and that they will normally never entirely leave ordinary consciousness."[7] The purpose is to strengthen one's self image and this, in itself, can have a positive healing value in a society that all too often effectively devalues one's self-esteem and one's sense of control over one's personal destiny and growth.

It is only at the integral level of the "expanded" state of consciousness that the individualized self begins to surrender its personal identity. Ultimately the "self" must be relinquished, for as long as there is an experiencing of the "I" one has not reached the highest state within which even experiencing falls away. The paradox is that the vehicle which facilitates the experience of "expanded" states is also the vehicle that keeps one at that level as long as imagery is present, *because it is always the self that is imagining*. Only when visual imagery falls away is one ready to go beyond even this level of consciousness. Visual images are, in fact, constructions of the unconscious mind and may actually manifest from the ego's effort to protect itself from being dissolved into, through and beyond the music. To go beyond consciousness of the self, to touch the timelessness of eternity, is the ultimate purpose of the experience of music.

How Music Affects Us Spiritually

Just as music affects us physically, emotionally and mentally, so it also influences us on a spiritual level. But unlike the first three, the spiritual effect of music is a cumulative one. As we listen to music our internal body rhythms may be changed as the vibrations of the sounds resonate our physical organism. We know too, that our response to music is an emotional one and that as we listen our moods and feelings respond. Likewise, the two hemispheres of our brain are involved in processing the music and interpreting its meaning. At the very least, our mental concentration is focused. However, these effects may last but a short time after the music has ended generally within half an hour we have returned to our normal physical, emotional and mental activity.

Even so, something of the music remains with us. Its memory certainly, but beyond this there remains an undefinable essence that permeates our inner world as it influences our perceptions of the outer. Repeated listening to one type of music or active involvement through its creation and performance strengthens this effect and may ultimately result in a permanent change within us that influences our relationship to the outer world — its events, its people and its natural environment. After an extended period of time we may begin to mirror the quality of the music in our movements, our speech, and our sense of time perception as it reflects the internal space created by the music with which we are involved.

Like the physical food that sustains our bodies, music influences the state of our spiritual health and the vitality of our soul's energy. If spirit and soul are in harmony and in balance, if they are strong and vital with life energy, we are less susceptible to illness and the negative thought forms and emotional energies that surround us. If in a physical sense we are what we eat, then it is equally true that in terms of the spirit, we are what we hear. Yet we may be unmindful of the cumulative effect of what we eat and are insensitive to the influence of sound upon our internal vibratory patterns. Beneath the surface rhythms and changing pitches of music lies a subtler level of vibration that is the music's essence. It is this inner level of vibration, created by the energy of the music, that harmonizes us spiritually and is, therefore, the deepest source of music's healing potential.

It is this element that remains within us after the music has ceased to sound. As mentioned earlier, all music possesses physical, emotional, mental and spiritual qualities, any one of which may dominate a composition according to its individual content and structure. But there is a realm of music that is beyond individualized emotion and whose essence lies beyond the mental plane, a music that transcends its intellectual content, the techniques of its construction and even its aesthetic beauty. Such music calls forth a response from us that transcends the realm of human activity and concern. Entering this purer world of sound, awareness of ourselves as separate, self-contained and self-sufficient entities may vanish. At this point we experience the essential unity of the manifested universe as a reflection of unmanifested creation bound together by the ceaseless movement of vibrational energy. Beyond even this, we may experience absolute stillness, the source from which both manifested and unmanifested creation originate.

In many world cultures, the practice of music is a highly developed spiritual discipline that may lead to the liberation of the soul. Nowhere is the practice of music as a spiritual discipline more highly developed than in India where the practice of *Mantra Yoga* and *Nada Yoga* is pursued as a form of meditation. In *Mantra Yoga* the meditator develops "one pointedness" and inner tranquility by fixing the mind on a single sound object. *Nada Yoga* is a form of process meditation during which one's attention is focused on changing sound objects. By its very nature, music allows for both processes at the same time. Each single sound can be an object of attention through concentration, and one's attention can be focused on the changing process of the moment-by-moment unfoldment of successions of sounds.

Two types of music are used for spiritual purposes throughout the world; one leads to the trance state while the other leads to the meditative state. Trance most commonly results when repetitive rhythmic patterns are sounded simultaneously over a long period of time. Trance music is utilized for spiritual and healing purposes in Turkey, Africa, Indonesia, in some cultures of the United States and Caribbean areas, and in those parts of the world where shamanistic societies are still intact. However, music that is capable of producing trance is found in all cultures, including our own. In many cases trance music relies heavily on the use of drums. This observation resulted in several significant investigations between 1937 and 1958[8] and produced the hypothesis that the state of trance, with its accompanying behavior characteristics, results from the effect of rhythmic drumming on the central nervous system. In 1934 experiments demonstrated that flashing a bright light at a frequency corresponding to that of the alpha brain wave resulted in the strengthening of brain wave production and that a slight shift in the light frequency resulted in a corresponding shift in brain wave frequency.[9] Subsequent investigations of ritual ceremonies employing drums demonstrated a predominance of rhythms that combined to produce a resultant frequency of seven to thirteen cycles per second, corresponding to the alpha wave output. The resulting stimulation affects many sensory and motor areas of the brain not otherwise affected in ordinary circumstances and effected some of the following behavioral changes in the participants of such rituals:

1. Visual and aural sensations of color, movement and sound.
2. Physical movement such as swaying, spinning, jumping, shaking and twitching.
3. Unusual perceptions or hallucinations.
4. Increase of breathing rate, very rapid heartrate, profuse sweating and rolling of the eyes.[10]

As a result, some participants were compelled to dance. The music of these dances almost always contains a combination of different drumming rhythms which accompany the main drum rhythm and which are mirrored in the movements of the dancers. Such sensory stimulation results in the state of trance which is the desired goal of such ceremonies. Clairvoyancy often accompanies the ecstasy of the dancers; during this time those who are in deep trance may foretell the future, advise others on personal questions and become instruments for healing.

In most trance ceremonies the drumming, dancing and singing is soft and slow in the beginning and gradually increases in tempo and loudness until the state of trance is achieved. At this point the tempo and loudness levels are maintained. Such ceremonies are an important part of the spiritual life of the community and they are always communal activities. Their purpose is communion with the spirit world by facilitating the loss of awareness of the self as an individualized and separate entity. In achieving the trance state individuals often display the movement and vocal characteristics of the spirits with whom they are trying to communicate, and for the time that they are in trance, they are regarded as the physical manifestation of the spirits themselves. Trance music, then, affects the body first by altering brain wave frequency and by flooding the sensory areas of the brain. As a result, the glandular system increases hormone production which, in turn, affects the emotions and mind. Trance is a state of consciousness that is induced by the physical body for spiritual purposes and therefore the music that is used for these ceremonies is selected for its ability to affect the necessary physical changes.

Music for meditation, by contrast, affects the mind first and the body second by creating an atmosphere that is conducive to stillness and inner contemplation. Music used as a prelude to meditation has a number of characteristics that appear to be common to spiritual practices that employ either meditation or some other form of quiet contemplation. It is first of all quieter and slower moving; a melodic phrase may last the length of one exhalation and about half of an inhalation with silence during the remainder of the inhalation. When the music is sung or played on a wind instrument, the breath exhalation may be as much as four times as long as the inhalation. Whether one is singing or listening, the purpose is not hyperventilation but, rather, its opposite — to slow and deepen breath, to reduce tension and to dramatically alter our normal perception of time by focusing on the present moment. The slower the rate in which individual sound events pass through our consciousness, and the greater the periods of silence between them, the slower our sense of time becomes. At some point we may "drop through" the spaces of silence and, no longer concentrating on the sounds, we may experience the state of timelessness. But here I must be cautious with my words, for at this moment there is no "I" that experiences; there is only silence and timelessness. By passing through the narrow silence between the sounds "we" enter the universal expansiveness of creation, the birthplace of the manifested universe and of "our selves". Upon re-entry into our time-oriented environment, we may bring the memory of that stillness and tranquility.

All music, of course, has its spiritual component and we can respond to all music in a spiritual way, for all music alters our perception of time. When our perception of time is changed, we are affected both emotionally, mentally and spiritually. Music that is used specifically for meditative purposes possesses some of the following characteristics:

> Melody: is of two types. The first (and probably the older) types uses only three different tones, the main tone plus one tone immediately below it and the other immediately above it. Example: Hindu Vedic Chanting. The second type uses up to seven diatonic tones, and the melody progresses mostly by steps with few skips. Skips are often followed by steps in a direction opposite to the leap. For example:

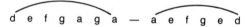

d e f g a g a — a e f g e d

This melodic type is found in Gregorian Chant of the Roman Catholic Church

> Duration of Phrase: equal to one breath.

> Loudness Level: moderately soft to very soft. No violent contrast of loudness level.

> Rhythm: smooth and flowing rhythm with no sudden rhythmic changes. Often there is no perceivable steady pulse from phrase to phrase. When words are employed, their natural rhythm determines the length of the pitches.

> Tempo: The rate at which the pitches change is moderately slow to very slow. Meditational music, in contrast to trance music, is almost never fast because music for meditation is not body oriented. Rather, its intent is to calm bodily energies so they may be utilized in the meditation process.

> Silence: Silence, either implied or actual, is a major component in much meditational music. Periods of silence are often found between phrases or even between individual notes. When they occur between phrases the length of silence is often governed by the breath.

> Tonal Quality: Although meditational music comes in many varieties of instrumental and vocal combinations, preference or the quieter instruments prevails.

Of these the most common for meditation and for healing are combinations of flutes, strings and voices. This combination is found in almost all musical cultures.

Texture: Meditational music is most often found to be of a simple texture. Monophony, a single instrument or one voice, and hetrophony, a single melody line supported by an accompaniment that follows the contour of the melody, seem to prevail over counterpoint, two independent melodies sounded at the same time, or melodies with harmonic support. For this reason classical Western art music is usually not effective for meditational purposes. It is intellectually too complex and tends to arouse the emotions.

Emotional Content: Both meditational music and music for chanting are not intended to express personal emotions. Therefore labels such as "sad" or "happy" are not applicable. The predominant quality of meditational music is of trans-personal peacefulness and inner joyousness.

Potentially, the experience of listening to music serves as preparation for inner hearing as we move from the world of audible vibration to the subtler world of inner vibration experienced as pure consciousness. In describing the seven levels of this subtle world,[11] the Sufi mystic Meher Baba states that

Sound exists throughout all the seven planes, differing in its expression of feeling, ecstasy and bliss. The sound, sight or smell of the higher planes can with no stretch of the imagination be likened to what we are used to on the physical plane... Our physical organs of Hearing, seeing, and smelling are useless for experiencing and enjoying the higher planes. Therein it is a different eye that sees, a different ear that hears and a different nose that smells. You know already that these are inner senses, counterparts of the external senses in man, and it is with the former that one experiences the higher planes.

Avoid the mistake of likening the sound of the higher planes to something different in intensity and frequency of vibrations to the sound of the physical plane; know it for a certainty that there is actually what may be called sound in the first three planes. The form, beauty, music and bliss of this sound are beyond description.

As stated above, although there is sound in all the seven planes, it is smell that is peculiar to the second and third planes, while sight belongs to the fifth and sixth planes...

The seventh plane stands unique. Here the sound, sight and smell are divine in essence and have no comparison to those emanating from the lower planes. In this plane one does not hear, smell or see but one *becomes* sound, smell and sight simultaneously, and is divinely conscious of it.[12]

It is reported in the *Surangama Sutra*, a sacred Buddhist teaching written before 700 A.D., that the Buddha assembled 26 of his disciples and commanded them to speak of their methods of practice and of their personal experiences in achieving enlightenment. After the first 24 had spoken the twenty-fifth, Avalokitesvara, described his method of realization in the following way:

> At first by directing the hearing ear into the stream of meditation this organ
> from its object was detached. By wiping out the concept of both sound and stream
> entry, both disturbance and stillness were clearly non-existent. Thus advancing
> step by step, both hearing and its object ceased . . . As the Buddha now asks about
> the best means of perfection, according to my own experience, the best consists
> in employing the organ of hearing for an all-embracing concentration to ease the
> conditioned mind for its entry into the stream of meditation, thereby achieving
> the state of samadhi (i.e., perfect enlightenment). . .[13]

When Avelokitesvara completed his explanation, the Buddha commanded the
disciple, Manjusri, to select the one most suitable for the benefit of living beings
who wished to attain enlightenment. Manjusri then rose from his seat and, after
comparing the 25 methods, selected Avalokitesvara's method of meditation on the
organ of hearing as the perfect vehicle.

When one dwells in quietude,
Rolls of drums from ten directions
Simultaneously are heard,
So hearing is complete and perfect.
The eyes cannot pierce a screen,
But neither can mouth or nose.
Body only feels when it is touched.
Mind's thoughts are confused and unconnected,
But voice whether near or far
At all times can be heard.
The five other organs are not perfect,
But hearing is all pervasive.
The presence or absence of sound and voice
Is registered by the ear as "is" or "is not".
Absence of sound means nothing heard,
Not hearing devoid of nature.
Absence of sound is not the end of hearing,
And sound when present is not its beginning.
The faculty of hearing, beyond creation
And annihilation, truly is permanent
Even when isolated thoughts in a dream arise,
Though the thinking process stops, hearing does not end,
For the faculty of hearing is beyond
All thought, beyond both mind and body. . .
Ananda and all of you who listen here
Should turn your faculty
Of hearing to hear your own nature
Which alone achieves Supreme Bodhih
That is how enlightenment is won.[14]

Avalokitsvara's method of disengaging the organ of hearing from its object-sound and then directing that organ into the stream of concentration was, therefore, praised by Manjusri as the most convenient for people on this earth. This was the method to which the Buddha gave his approval as being the most consistent with his teachings. In his approval, the Buddha reaffirmed one of the oldest methods of realization known to us. In the *Malini Vijaya*, a text that contains a comprehensive listing of various spiritual practices and is said to be five thousand years old, we find a number of instructions pertaining to sound. In this ancient document we are advised; "Bathe in the center of sound, as in the continuous sound of a waterfall. Or, by putting fingers in ears, hear the sound of sounds. Intone a sound audibly, then less and less audibly as feeling deepens into this silent harmony."[15]

If music affects us in a spiritual way — at a level that transcends the realm of personalized emotions — then the music we ingest daily may influence the healthfulness of soul and spirit alike. For the music that is our steady diet resonates within our spirit longer than its effect upon our body, mind and emotions. It is in this sense that, on the spiritual level, the effects of music are cumulative and can, over time, either strengthen or weaken us. Likewise the music we hear within our minds can be every bit as powerful as thehmusic we experience through our physical ears. For even though the actual music may have ceased, its influence on us may continue to resonate within and therefore permeate our mind, direct our emotional life, regulate our bodily energies and ultimately influence our spiritual aspirations and overall healthfulness.

CHAPTER TWELVE

Systematic Approaches
to Music Healing

Although there are many systematic approaches to the use of tones for healing purposes — some very old and some being developed today — the same cannot be said with regard to the application of music for healing purposes. A complete system includes a theoretical foundation, a diagnostic procedure, a methodology of application that evolves from the theoretical principles, and a predictability of results. There is a rudimentary systematic approach in traditional music therapy and many colleges offer a course of study in its applications. Yet music therapy is closely aligned with behavioral psychologies and uses the same approaches and terminology. As such, music therapy is limited to emotional and physical behavior applications as adjunct to psychology. Music healing implies a much more comprehensive approach that addresses the needs of the whole person on all levels: physical, emotional, mental and spiritual. Within the developing practice of music healing, the foundations of a theoretical approach to treatment on the emotional, mental and spiritual levels is beginning to evolve within Western practices. But thus far, a theoretical foundation for treatment of physical illness continues to elude us. At the present moment applications of music for healing continue to concentrate on the emotions, spirit, mind and electro-magnetic field as a way of influencing the physical body. The reverse procedure has not yet provided satisfying results.

Some recent practitioners have taken the assigned pitches for each of the seven energy centers of the body *(chakras)* and have created short compositions that use the assigned pitch as the tonic or key-note. For example, in music for the first energy center, the composition is in the key of "C" major, for the second, the composition is in the key of "D" major. Music for the third energy center is in "E" major; for the fourth, "F" major; the fifthe, "G" major; the sixth, "A" major and finally, B major is utilized for the crown of the head. The historical justification and a clear theoretical basis for this practice remains obscure, however, and physical benefits have not been tested and published.

Similarly, some attempt has been made to assign pitches to astrological signs, yet the source of this theoretical foundation and its methodology remains a mystery. Additionally, there seem to be several views as to which key-note belongs to what sign. In my own case, for example, my astrological sign (Taurus) has been assigned to the keys of C#, D flat, E and A flat by as many different writers. The fact that one of the most respected writers on astrology who is, in addition, an important composer, philosopher and author of several books on music aesthetics — Dane Rudhyar — has never related music to astrology during his fifty years involvement with both, is a significant comment in itself.

A search on non-Western and ancient music offers some enticing hints of a theoretical basis for healing with music, but so far that search has produced frustratingly little that we can use today, particularly with regard to the use of music in the treatment of our internal structures: organs, glands and the like. We find hints in writings on music from India, Tibet, China and enough references from Greece and the Hebrews to warrant continued research with these musical and healing traditions.

One ray of hope has recently emerged, however, in the efforts of Robert McClellen, a resident of Western Massachusetts. In addition to being an accomplished musician, McClellan is a scholar, a practitioner of traditional Chinese healing methods and an expert accupressurist. He is developing a healing method, complete with a theoretical foundation and verifiable results, by combining music with Chinese medical philosophy that focuses on the internal body structures by means of the ancient accupuncture energy meridians. The fact that his work draws upon the most ancient continuous healing and musical tradition still extant in the world makes his approach all the more respectable, not to mention sublime

The Principles of Yin/Yang

All traditional Chinese medical practice[1] is founded upon two primary concepts, the philosophy of Yin/Yang and the concept of the Five Elements. One of the most relevant hypotheses of Yin/Yang philosophy is the concept that any state of being implies the existence of its opposite, or contrasting, state of being. Since everything in our universe is in a state of motion at all times, anything that is characterized as exhibiting the quality of Yin has a tendency to move toward Yang; anything that is Yang has a tendency to move toward Yin. Therefore all things and all states of being are engaged in a dynamic interplay or oscillation between two states. The concept is referred to as "dualistic monism" since the two states of Yin/Yang constitute a whole. At the most basic level, if a state of being exists then its opposite, the state of non-being, also exists because of the dynamic interplay between the two.

According to Chinese philosophy Yin manifests the qualities of the feminine, moisture, coolness, smallness, darkness, exhaustion, separation, conservation, responsiveness and contraction. The emotional qualities of Yin include passivity, sympathy, sorrow.

Since Yin manifests the movement toward expansion from the contracted state — energy is dispersed in the process of expansion — the release of Yin energy ultimately leads toward expansion when the creative energy of Yin is depleted.

The qualities of Yang are characterized as: expansion, the masculine, dryness, heat, centralization, the active, the gathering of energy, and aggressiveness. The emotional qualities of Yang are the more active and volatile ones of anger, excitement and frustration. Since Yang manifests movement toward contraction from the expanded state—energy is collected in the process of contraction — the gathering of energy ultimately leads toward contraction when the gathering energy of Yang is fully compacted.

FIGURE 12-1

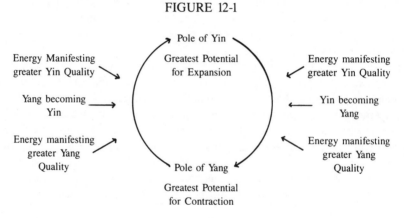

All illustrations in this chapter are copyright 1981 by Sam McClellan. Used by permission.

The Five Elements

The concept of the Five Elements — or transformations, as they are more accurately translated — is a further elaboration of the concept of Yin/Yang. The five elements consist of wood, fire, earth, metal and water. In traditional Chinese medicine they describe the interactions of all processes and states of being and as a way of understanding the cyclic movement between Yin and Yang.

Wood represents the creative aspect, when energy is expended to create something, such as in germination or the season of Spring.

Fire (Expansion) represents the aspect of maturation. Energy is expended for growth as found in the season of Summer.

Earth (Balance) relates to balance when energy is in equilibrium, such as during late Summer or early Autumn.

Metal (Contraction) represents the gathering of energy, as when a tree draws sap into its roots during late Autumn as Winter approaches.

Water (Conservation) represents the storage of energy, or return to potential and is manifested as death or the season of Winter.

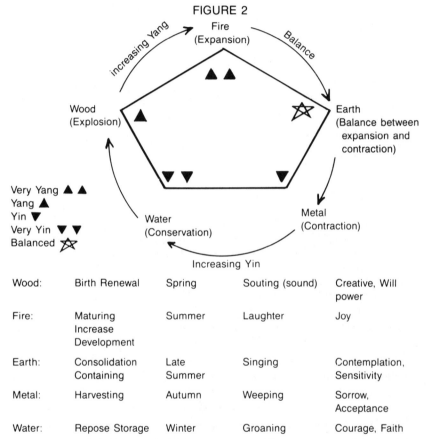

FIGURE 2

Wood:	Birth Renewal	Spring	Souting (sound)	Creative, Will power
Fire:	Maturing Increase Development	Summer	Laughter	Joy
Earth:	Consolidation Containing	Late Summer	Singing	Contemplation, Sensitivity
Metal:	Harvesting	Autumn	Weeping	Sorrow, Acceptance
Water:	Repose Storage	Winter	Groaning	Courage, Faith

Moving clockwise through each successive phase produces the Creative cycle or the generative mode. Moving clockwise but skipping every other phase produces the control cycle, or destructive mode. By way of simple illustration: Wood feeds Fire but Fire is controlled by Water. Therefore the fire element, being controlled by the water element, never depletes the element of wood. Thus all phases are kept in balance with all interaction to each other to insure a free flow of energy throughout the entire cycle. Should the cycle become unbalanced, then certain elements have become overly active, while others, being depleted, become underactive. The pattern of imbalance generally involves two adjacent elements manifesting either under-activity or over-activity while the element directly opposite on the diagram produces the opposite extreme of activity.

A further development of this ancient medical practice has been to associate the five elements with the corresponding body meridians of traditional acupuncture.

FIGURE 3
The five elements and their corresponding meridians

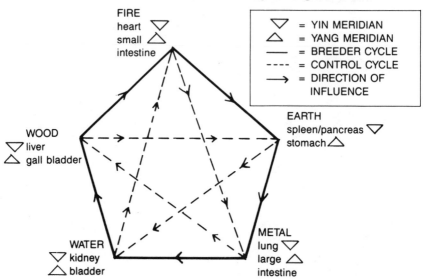

Each organ represents a complete system whose meridian lines can be traced throughout the body. Each element is associated with two organ meridians, one Yin and one Yang. Together they form an interactive relationship with each other that follows the same creative and controlling cycle as the Five Elements. When each system functions in harmony with all of the other systems, a state of balance is said to exist. Through diagnostic procedures it is possible to determine the causes of imbalance in each system, the degree of each imbalance, whether the imbalance manifests as overactivity or underactivity, and how to restore balance in all systems.

One of the diagnostic indicators of imbalance in the organ meridians is the association between five emotional spectra, the five Yin organ meridians, and the five elements since, in the holistic approach of Chinese healing philosophy, there is no separation between the mental/emotional and the physical aspects of the self. By assessing the predominant emotional characteristics of the patient's personality it is possible to determine imbalances in the corresponding organ meridian.

Element	Yin Meridan	Emotion
Wood	Liver	Anger
Fire	Heart	Over excitement
Earth	Spleen/Pancreas	Sympathy, Over Sensitivity
Metal	Lung	Excessive Grief
Water	Kidney/Adrenals	Fear

In preparation for his work with music and the Five Elements, Robert McClellan constructed a set of five spectra which correlate to relative activity of any meridan, in imbalanced or balanced state with the emotions.

Element	Underactive	Balanced	Overactive
Wood	Lack of Will	Will Power	Anger
	Lethargy	Creativity	Frustration
Fire	Sadness	Balance	Overexcitement
	Lack of Joy	Joy	"Overjoyed"
Earth	Obsessions	Empathy	Over sensitivity
	Intellectualization	Compassion	Poor Memory
	Lack of Appreciation		
Metal	Aversion to Change	Letting Go	Over Sorrowfulness
	"Holding" Worry	Acceptance	Letting go too Much
Water	Anxiety	Courage	Foolhardiness
	Fearfulness	Appropriate Caution	Destructiveness

As demonstrated in Illustration 5, any imbalance in one organ meridian will affect other organ meridians and will therefore also influence emotional states. This imbalance is explained through the Creative Cycle — sometimes referred to as the "Breeder" Cycle — and the control cycles of the Five Elements. Let us say, for example, that Wood is the overactive element. This condition will cause Fire to be overactive (Creative Cycle) and Earth to be underactive (Control Cycle). Earth element will pass its underactive condition to Metal (Creative Cycle) and also cause Water to be overactive (Control Cycle). Water will pass its overactive condition back to Wood. On an emotional level, a person who is caught in this imbalanced cycle may exhibit frustration (overactive Wood), overexcitement (overactive Fire), obsessiveness (underactive Earth), emotional "holding" (underactive Metal), and destructiveness (overactiveness Water) which, in completing the cycle, increases frustration (overactive Wood).[2]

The remedy for this deteriorating situation might include balancing the Wood element by calming the liver meridian, balancing the Fire element by calming the heart meridian, and balancing the Earth element by energizing the spleen/pancreas meridian. The remaining two elements will return to balance without additional assistance. In this way, by examining oneself and observing which emotions one most easily expresses and those which one most often suppresses, one can determine which organ meridians are overactive and which are underactive. Treatment, however, requires a thorough knowledge of the corresponding meridian placement and other skills of acupuncture and accupressure. At the body level, diagnostic tests can be performed by means of the technique of Applied Kinesiology to determine the corresponding weaknesses in the organs that would be affected.

Music, the Five Elements and the Emotional Spectra

With these principles in mind, Robert McClellan began a series of experiments using the five forms of the five-note pentatonic scale of traditional Chinese music.[3] As a first step he related each of the notes to one of the Five Elements and constructed a series of five scales. Each scale was then assigned to one of the elements according to its intervalic relationship and emotional effect. He did the same with tempo, beat, pitch duration and sound quality.

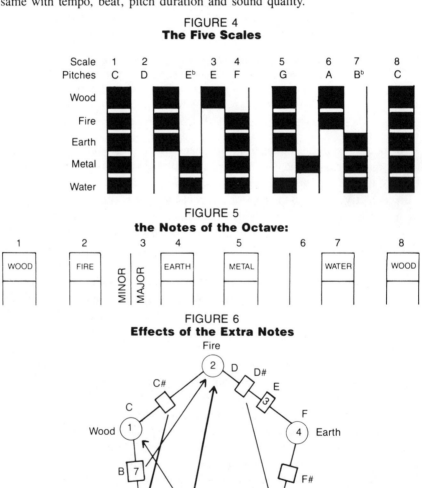

FIGURE 4
The Five Scales

FIGURE 5
the Notes of the Octave:

FIGURE 6
Effects of the Extra Notes

From this procedure the resulting scales for each Element were produced.[3]

	Tonic					
Wood:	C	D	F	G	A	C
Fire:	C	D	E	G	A	C
Earth:	C	D	F	G	B$^\flat$	C
Metal:	C	E$^\flat$	F	G	B$^\flat$	C
Water:	C	E$^\flat$	F	A$^\flat$	B$^\flat$	C

McClellan's working hypothesis with regard to the scales was that by balancing the emotional qualities of the music that is composed from them, one could balance the emotions and therefore assist in balancing the meridians associated with each element. He describes his process as follows:[5]

> I have created these ideas through the application of both intellect and intuition, seeing which patterns fit into the larger patterns of the Five Elements cycle and the Yin/Yang concept. I realized that the Earth scale should be the basic scale since it is a balance of both Yin and Yang. Each scale has an associated element and an emotional character that is related to that element. There are two Yang scales which emphasize the lower frequencies — Metal and Water — , and a balanced scale — Earth — that has the same intervallic spacing throughout. The Earth scale is neither carefree (more Yang) nor especially tense (more Yin). It provides reflection and awareness, from which comes compassion and empathy.
>
> The Yang scales of Wood and Fire are the same except for the third note of each. Together they create our Western major scale without the seventh tone. The major scale, often used for joyful or triumphant music, tends to dissipate stored energy. This is consistent with the qualities associated with Yang. The Metal and Water scales are Yin scales and are the same except for each of their fourth scale degrees. Together they create our Western natural minor scale minus the second scale degree. This is the scale most often associated with more melancholic, sadder or more anguished music. These are the less volatile emotions and lend themselves to energy storage. This is consistent with the qualities associated with Yin.
>
> The conclusions I have come to were originally determined by examining the effects of each note of the octave compared with the tonic, or bottom, note. These results were tested using [the muscle testing techniques] of applied Kinesiology as well as the emotional reactions of various individuals. I found that playing a note with the tonic loudly and quickly was energizing for certain elements and calming for others in the exact fashion of the pressure points of acupuncture treatment. If, however, the same notes were played for a longer time they will have the opposite effect. If the tone continues it becomes a drone, producing a hypnotic effect. These same reactions are apparent in acupuncture therapy where quick, intense stimulation of a point will produce tonification

(energizing). Prolonged stimulation will cause a calming effect while continuous stimulation produces lack of sensation in an area. This is known as acupuncture anaesthesia or analgesia.

Following these preliminary conclusions, ten short music selections were composed, two for each element, with five designated to energize the elements and five designated to sedate. For testing purposes McClellan then used the methods of Oriental diagnosis to determine the energy imbalance in several volunteers and played five selections for them in an order that was determined by the results of the testing which, in theory, would balance the elements within them. In this way, the music affected them on both a mental/emotional level and on a physical/energy level. Through use of Applied Kinesiology and Oriental Pulse Diagnosis, each person was retested at the end of the session for verification of the theory. The results of four such sessions are given in Illustration 9.

Illustration 9

Person No. 1

Underactive Element - Water
Overactive Elemtne - fire and Earth

Muscle Test

Meridian	Before	After	Comments
Liver (Wood)	4:4	4:4	"Second test felt
Heart (Fire)	2:3	4:5	easier. Body felt more
Spleen (Earth)	3:3	4:5	relaxed."
Lung (Metal)	4:4	4:4	
Kidney (Water)	2:2	3.5:4	
	left right		
	side side		

Person No. 2

Underactive Element - Water and Metal
Overactive Element - Fire

Muscle Test

Meridian	Before	After	Comments
Liver (Wood)	5	5	"Seemed a little
Heart (Fire)	5	5	strange."
Spleen (Earth)	5	5	
Lung (Metal)	3	4.5	
Kidney (Water)	3.5	4	

Person No. 3

Underactive Element - Water
Overactive Element - Fire and Earth

Muscle Test

Meridian	Before	After	Comments
Liver (Wood)	2:1	2.5:2.5	Person was sick. Day
Heart (Fire)	2:1	3:4	before she had a fever
Spleen (Eart)h	2:2	3:4	and slept all day. She
Lung (Metal)	2:2	3.5:3.5	was in a weakened
Kidney (Water)	2:2	3:3	condition.

Person No. 4

Underactive Element - Wood
Overactive Element - Earth and Metal

Muscle Test

Meridian	Before	After	Comments
Liver (Wood)	2	4	"Definitely felt
Heart (Fire)	5	5	stronger."
Spleen (Earth)	5	5	
Lung (Metal)	2	4	
Kidney (Water)	3	4	

In these experimental sessions all of the music selections maintained the same tonic note throughout. Hence the effects of changing keys was not explored. Also, the effect of introducing pitches not found in the five tone scale is being more fully considered and a hypothesis is being developed. In terms of rhythm, McClellan discovered that slow tempos are energy gathering; fast tempos are energy dispersive. Likewise triple meters seem to be energy gatherers and duple meters are energy dispersive. This deduction is consistent with the philosophy of Yin/Yang where in numerological terms, two is Yang and three is Yin.

Finally, McClellan has made some observations about the general characteristics of Western music as a reflection of our culture's values.

Most Western music is based on notes of short duration, especially popular music. I believe this is a retention from a time when music was used to tonify, energize and 'raise spirits'. In many Eastern cultures music was used more to calm and often to create a meditative state. Rhythmically, the opposite appears to be true. Western music is notoriously tied to the multiples of two and three, whereas Eastern music tends to divide a musical space into alternating combinations of twos and threes. In this way, a group of African drummers may reflect the interactions of the rhythms of life — heart beat, breath, footsteps, work with hands — into a holistic framework that creates a larger rhythm. Western rhythms are linear, perhaps following the heart or the lungs but seldom both. This has begun to change because of a growing movement to perceive holistically.

Most music compositions are composed of two or three elements in our cul-ture. These elements seem to be always adjoining. There are certain pieces, es-pecially the longer classical pieces, which move through four or five elements. . . Most importantly, it should be obvious that given the complexity of most music, one will not be able to determine the effects of a piece without a good deal of work and calculation. In my composition I try to intellectually set the frame-work much of the time, determining the effect I want and possibly the notes I wish to include. For example, if I want to energize metal and sedate fire I will include a drone of the fire note, the second, and include notes for the scale that will tonify metal.. Once these areas of concentration are set, often the creative takes over and creates a piece with the desired effect. Many times my knowledge of the effects of the notes and rhythms has increased by examining the composi-tion afterwards.

The person who uses this way of seeing music will also come to see how our society creates imbalances in order to fuel itself. Most of the work done in this culture is done not from a sense of joy and purpose, with a conscious under-standing, but from an anxious perspective, constantly insecure. Depletive music fuels this anxiety. Music can be used, though, as a tool for increasing awareness and Music can be used, though, as a tool for increasing awareness and helping to move through the emotional constraints we have placed upon ourselves.

If our emotions are a part of the landscape in which we live then it is possible to change the landscape by relinquishing those emotions that are not beneficial to our state of being. McClellan's work is only a few years old but, in this short time he has managed to show us a new and unexplored dimension of music and healing. With further development and refinement his work can become the basis for an increased understanding of our culture, ourselves and the healing process as it is manifested through music.

CHAPTER THIRTEEN

Characteristics of Healing Music

What constitutes the most effective music for therapeutic purposes depends less on objective traits and more on subjective preference. Keeping in mind that currently the most prominent use of healing music is for reduction of emotional and physical stress, the effectiveness of the music depends on intention, providing an environment that will enhance the listening process. This is an attitude of focused concentration while listening, and a willingness to allow one's breathing to become slower, deeper and fuller. Within these considerations, however, some common factors do emerge that will enable one to make effective choices. These will be discussed in detail for the remainder of this chapter.

At the most basic level of differentiation there are two forms of music that possess therapeutic values, each with its own particular characteristics. The first of these is by far the more prominent, containing within it all of the styles and forms that are indigenous to the culture. In Western culture, for example, the list may include folk music, church music, "art" music, national music, commercial popular music, and the various musical styles that have been derived from the African-American tradition. The meanings, associations and emotions that we experience in listening to this music are shared by the members of our own culture; people from other cultures may learn to appreciate the music from Western musical traditions, but it is unlikely that they will have the same associations.

The primary therapeutic use of the music in this category is a vehicle for the expression of emotion and the release of physical energy. Most of the music used by music therapists in clinical settings falls into this category with emphasis placed on our folk and classical traditions.

Almost all Western music from this category shares these common characteristics:

— its rhythms are structured over a steady pulse that is commonly grouped into meter;

— its tempo may fluctuate radically within one composition;
— dynamic levels shift frequently, sometimes with violent contrasts of loud and soft sections;
— both its melodies and structural forms are built on and evolve from its harmonic structures;
— its larger forms such as symphonies and sonatas evolve from the development of one or more principle themes which are treated to continuous variation.

These characteristics create in the music a dynamic energy in which a sense of pressing forward encourages anticipation and creates a feeling of going somewhere. The energy that is created intensifies through a series of increasingly intense climactic plateaus which sweep us along to the inevitable resolution and release.

Because of our familiarity with the music of our own culture and the inevitable preferences and biases that result, its effectiveness as a healing agent is governed by personal likes and dislikes. Music that is to be used for healing or for therapeutic benefits must do so on the basis of attraction first, for if the recipient is not attracted to the music, it will have either no effect or it will only aggravate the condition.

Therefore it is necessary to possess a fairly extensive record or tape library containing a wide variety of music and, perhaps, organized according to the Mood Wheel illustrated in Chapter 10.[1] Fortunately, much of the work of cataloging has been accomplished by music therapists already. An extensive listing is available in Helen Bonny's valuable book, *Music and Your Mind* although the selections are heavily weighted in favor of Western classical music. A similar catalogue of other types of Western music would be a most valuable addition.

Beyond the culturally defined, however, is another level of music whose characteristics are more similar than they are different. This is the music that possesses the greatest potential for healing on a deep level, for it appears to be more related to the rhythms of the natural world than to human cultures. Its roots may lie in the most ancient of music traditions and in its many variations, and it has resonated the earth and all beings on it ever since. It was heard in the pyramids of Egypt and the temples of Greece, in the pine groves of ancient China, in the courts of India, and Persia, and in the early Christian cathedrals of twelfth century France. Today it can be heard in the sounds of the Japanese Koto and Shakuhachi, in the Muslim call to prayer, in the Gamelans of Indonesia, Onhevery area of Earth it continually invites us to be still, to listen, to feel its resonance within, and to experience the stillness where spirit may speak to us in a language that is beyond words. Technically, it is a more primal music devoid of over-intellectualization, and seeks a form of expression beyond the limitations of personalized emotions as well as the affectations of cultural aesthetics. It echoes the sounds of Earth which have been its inspiration. Its quality is tranquility; its emotion is joy of spirit.

The most common sounds of Earth are the continuous timbre of wind and water in motion. Heard from a distance, both sound like a continuous roar but as wind approaches or as we approach a waterfall, we begin to discover the infinite number of individual sounds that create the composite sound. This most ancient of sounds is mirrored in music by the *drone*, a continuously sounding tone, which in some form, is found in every musical culture of the world.

As life evolved, the second most prevalent Earth-sound began to emerge: the rhythmic sounds of insects, frogs and birds that in music are mirrored by the use of *ostinatos*, continuously repeated melodic and/or rhythmic patterns, also found in every musical culture. Within the ocean, the universal symbol of the unconscious and of the security of our pre-birth life within the womb, are found both in the drone of the ocean's roar and the ostinato of the surf as it reaches the shores. And we find both drone and ostinato in the spiritual chants of our religions. Perhaps, on an unconscious level, the drones and ostinatos foundhin all music represent two elements necessary to life, water and air. The use of drones and ostinatos is, in any case, an important component of healing music. In this context it is interesting to observe that in cultures where trance is used as a regular part of spiritual practice, ostinatos predominate in the accompanying music whereas in cultures where meditation is used as a regular part of spiritual practice, uninterrupted drones seem to predominate. Within the religions of the Western world, neither trance nor meditation has been a predominant factor, and the presence of drones and ostinatos is less obvious.

The melodies of this form of music are simple and sustained, evolving continuously over drones and ostinatos. Their quality is quiet and contemplative, inviting us to the peace of introspection. Being of a preharmonic nature, the tones of these melodies evolve from the various modal scales found throughout the world, unencumbered by the richness of harmony that we associate with Western classical music. Because of its simplicity we enter a world of textural sparseness within which we may savor each new tone as it emerges. The rising and falling of the phrases is gentle and leisurely, allowing us the space to breathe slower with less constriction. As we begin to be aware of the spaces between the tones, the restrictions of cultural time surrender to the internal time of our inner world — unhurried and comfortable because the tones do not urge us onward.

Rhythmic ostinatos, when present, are leisurely and serve to regulate the even balance of inspiration and expiration of our breath. There are no sudden changes of tempo nor violent contrasts of loud and soft dynamics. The music is not sectioned into a series of contrasting themes separated by transitions and other cultural trappings generally associated with Western music. Rather, each phrase evolves organically from the one that preceded it so that the completion of one becomes the beginning of the next. Our impression is of one continuous evolving melody from beginning to end. When the last notes have been swallowed into silence, we may sense that beneath the silence, the music continues to unfold in movement that mirror the eternally evolving universe, Within the gentle security of this womb of sound our bodies can relax in a state of repose, the fluctuations of our emotions are calmed, our intellectual activity is stilled. Our spirit is now free to follow the tones into that universe whose harmonious movements we now recognize as identical to those within.

Time, musical tempo and rhythm are all invariably related to motion and space. Rhythm results from the movement of kinetic energy and is measured against the constant of space. The state of being that is motion has no fixed absolute meaning. Rather, motion is always related to perception, i.e., an object may appear to be stationary because we fail to perceive its motion. For example, a star observed night after night appears stationary even though it and the earth are moving through space, the earth at the rate of 66,000 miles per hour. Likewise, that the sun appears to move across the sky is the result of the rotation of the earth, which we do not perceive.[4]

All processes move at their own rhythm and, with other processes, create a multi-layered composite rhythm that, in its total motion, never returns to its original point. All motion, therefore, is spiral-like rather than circular, coiling in constantly changing planes. Time results from our awareness of processes in motion and how we measure time is a product of culture and reflects its value system.

Music, too, is kinetic energy in motion. That is, what gives music its sense of motion is the build-up of kinetic energy that connects each melodic tone in sequence.[5] When the tones vary in duration, the increase of kinetic energy becomes significant. Kinesthetic process, then, is the basis of the dynamic force that provides rhythm with the spark of life. Beat, a steady and evenly placed pulse, and meter, the division of beats into units of strong-weak or strong-weak-weak pulses, are not synonymous with rhythm. Rhythm can, and does, exist without beat or meter, yet we often confuse them with rhythm just as we often confuse time with our method of measuring time. By way of example, it is like watching the movement of clouds across the sky from behind a transparent grid and mistaking the grid for the movement.

On one level, beat and meter[6] are the means by which we measure music, but they should not be confused with rhythm itself. They are somewhat analogous to a clock. The division of time into hours, minutes and seconds is the result of our attempt to objectify the passage of time and should not be mistaken for our deeply personal experiential time. There is no "single" time as implied by clocks; rather, there are many layers of time which co-exist simultaneously. The same is true of rhythm. It is no accident that the Western procedure of dividing rhythm into meters and notating it in measures developed alongside the widespread use of clocks. Both are characteristic of Western culture; we organize our daily activities according to the clock and our music is seldom without pulse and meter.

Music without meter and an easily perceived pulse, and time without clocks with which to measure it, opens us to the possibility of chaos. Our obsession with both may reflect a discomfort with what is perceived as a lack of form and order. However, many non-Western cultures provide both musical and non-musical vehicles, such as meditational practices, as a way of moving from a normal day-to-day state of consciousness to an altered state, or from a culturally defined reality to one that is more universally shared. The ability to alter one's perceptual reality and a culturally defined method of doing so are critical factors in the processes of healing that recognize the importance of soul and spirit in the healing process. Traditionally, these vehicles have been provided through spiritual practices and the arts particularly music and dance.

In order for music to be an effective agent for the integration of body-mind-emotions-spirit and for deeper levels of healing it must be calming and provide the opportunity to release us from our cultural bonds. In other words, our ordinary perception of time — which in Western culture means "clock time" — must be suspended so that we may experience our internal time as the product of our natural metabolism. We must also develop a music which lacks measures and the phrase structures that are defined by them in order to create a sense of timelessness and spaciousness. This may be accomplished in four ways.

First, the length of each composition there should be long sections of music in which pulse and meter are missing. Third, symmetrical phrases and phrases of equal duration that close with clearly defined cadences should be avoided and fourth, cadences (i.e., stopping places where all movement ceases) should be avoided until the final cadence at the close of the composition.

In an attempt to summarize the characteristics of healing music, the following chart is offered. By creating music that uses these characteristics one may produce a pan-cultural music that will be effective regardless of personal or cultural biases.

A Musician's Summary of
Healing Music Characteristics — Pan-Cultural

Pulse (when present):	At or below heart rate (72 per minute) for calming and reducing tension.
	Slightly above heart rate for energizing (72-92 per minute).
	Triple meters slow the breath more effectively than duple meters.
Rhythm:	Smooth and flowing at all times for integrating internal body rhythms with energy flows.
Drones:	When used without ostinatos, have a meditational and calming effect. Pitches of drones: root and fifth, root, fourth, octave; root, fifth, major seventh, octave; root, fifth, minor seventh, octave; root, fourth, fifth, octave.
Ostinatos:	When at slow pulse rates, harmonize and integrate internal body rhythms, breath and heart rate. At fast rates can lead to a frenetic state. Ostinatos can produce a trance state in the listener.

Melodies:	Slow and sustained for meditational purposes; pitch sequences primarily by step; at heart pulse rate or slightly faster for energizing purposes; tones drawn from the modes of five, six and seven tones. Predominantly diatonic and asymmetrical. Too many cadences should be avoided.
Dynamics:	Very soft to moderately loud depending on the composer's intent; no violent contrasts of loud and soft; changes in dynamic levels should be slow and gradual, never sudden.
Harmony:	Used sparingly if at all; when used, harmony should be modal and diatonic; harmony should be restricted to triads, avoid sevenths and ninths as they are too thick; movement of chord changes should be extremely slow.
Duration:	Minimum of fifteen minutes of steady music; 20 to 45 minutes optimum duration.
Texture:	Drone plus maximum of two other voices for calming purposes. Voices should be widely spaced from each other. When using ostinatos for energizing purpose, up to four layers of ostinatos.
Tone Quality:	Generally the softer quality instruments; most common ensemble, flute, string and voice; others, pure organ tones (no vibrato), synthesizer when made to sound like organs, or other acoustic string and wood instruments.
Resonance:	Time should be sustained from four to eight seconds using either natural or electronic reverberation for calming purposes. Minimum reverberation for faster tempos when intention is to energize.
Phrase Structure:	Smooth and flowing; one phrase should last for the duration of one slow expiration of the breath as a minimum length when the intention is to calm.

It should be clearly stated that in listing these characteristics for an effective healing music, there is no intention to make value judgments on music that does not possess some of all these qualities. There are many forms of music on our universe and all are of value for the enjoyment they provide. Different music may have different intentions and all may have healing potential according to the kind of healing that is needed in any given situation.

Applications of Music for
Long Term Maintenance of Health

Music alone cannot assure healthfulness if other aspects of our lifestyle are detrimental to our health. But when combined with proper diet, proper sleep, fulfilling work, an active life of the mind, nurturing relationships, recreation and spiritual aspirations, a sense of wholeness will permeate our being and insure minimal disruption because of sickness.

The effect of music on health is cumulative over extended time periods. Therefore the type of music we hear, the time of day that we hear it, the environment we create for ourselves before, during and after listening, and what we do as we listen, determines the benefits we receive. When these are carefully attended to, the music will balance our body/mind/emotion energies by means of resonance. For through resonance, the vibrational patterns created in space by music can impose similar patterns in our electro-magnetic field resulting in a resiliency that is centered within the stillness of equilibrium.

When we are centered in this way, the winds of tumult cannot unbalance us for long. Rather, we hum like a finely tuned tuning fork which, through resonance, gains in strength and deflects the negative emotions and thought patterns that originate in the fearfulness of others.[3]

The music that is listened to or played should be carefully selected for daily balancing. Time should be set aside every day for the music and the same music listened to every day for at least a month in order to feel its cumulative effect. Music that is chaotic or repressive should be avoided. One type of music for energizing should be selected and another for stress reduction. Throughout the day awareness should be focused on the music that is provided in the work place, in restaurants and in places where people congregate. Avoid environments where the music feels detrimental to your state of being. The music selected in the morning is especially important, for what is heard first may permeate the mind and resonate throughout the day. Over time these considerations should lead to a more centered existence, enabling you to maintain an attitude of personal inner spaciousness that will influence thought processes, physical movement characteristics, speaking voice quality, emotional stability and interpersonal relationships. These manifestations of personal stillness will change one's relationship to the environment and, through resonance, will have a positive effect on those around one.

Finally, the value of any composition is dependent on the level of awareness, both spiritual and technical, and the motivation of the composer/performer of the music. The creation of music for the purpose of healing must always be motivated by service, never for material gain or glorification of the ego. *The healer in sound must first of all aspire to dwell within the Inner Sound* and know it as the source of all manifested creation and as a channel for the healing process. He/She must work in a high vibration of spiritual purity in order to reflect the healing power of music with clarity, compassion and non-attachment.

EPILOGUE

The employment of sound and music for healing is a science/art that is still in its early stages of development. For even though music has been used therapeutically for centuries, its theories, methods and procedures have yet to be fully investigated, revised and validated. Until this is accomplished, music healing will continue to be regarded as folklore and superstition founded on hazy platitudes and unsubstantiated assumptions. When we claim that music is a healing art and are met with skepticism, we may wish to withdraw from dialogue and seek, instead, the comfort of support from other believers. Yet nothing is more antithetical to progress than agreement based on presumption. If we are to deepen our understanding, then it is our skeptical friends who are our greatest teachers. Their sincere questions deserve thoughtful consideration and we, in turn, must be willing to admit honestly to them and to each other when we do not know the answers. For in defining more accurately what we do not know, we begin to lay a solid foundation upon which this healing art/science can develop.

Presently, it is the use of specific tones and ultrasonic frequencies that has received the greatest attention. Because the application of tones and ultrasound frequencies are directed at the physical body, they are the least complex and the most easily tested. By contrast, the application of music for healing is at a much less developed stage. Its complexity in combining rhythm, tones, and all the other characteristics associated with a musical composition render it more difficult to test under laboratory conditions. To overcome some of these difficulties it may be necessary to devise a series of experiments with specific procedures and objectives, applicable to a wide variety of musical styles, that test each of the components of music in turn — no easy task. Based on the results, we may then be able to create a type of music that will be relatively unfamiliar to those who might participate in further experiments in order to divert personal aesthetic biases and past associations.

At present no verifiable system of music healing exists with the possible exception of the pioneering work of Robert McCLellan. Even in his work, which shows great promise, it is premature to draw conclusions. Further testing and refinement must be done, and Robert is the first to agree. Meanwhile, several non-Western cultures appear to have long traditions of music healing practices: India, China, Tibet, Africa, and those areas where shamanism is still prevalent. They await investigation.

If music and sound are to become useful healing therapies, then we must broaden our scope and enlist the aid of experts in related fields. These might include: anthropologists and ethnomusicologists to study cultures that traditionally connect music with therapeutic applications, cultural historians to collect and catalog the mythologies and legends pertaining to the use of music within a healing context, medical researchers to examine the effect of sound on the physical body and neurologists to study the effect of music within the brain, psychologists to study the relationship of music to emotions and states of consciousness, medical doctors and homeopathic healers who can contribute their understanding of the causes and treatment of disease and to assess various theories that might be formulated.

There are four progressive stages in the task before us. The first stage is the critical and difficult one of historical research and experimentation. During this stage we might concentrate on collecting and cataloging the mythologies and legends that pertain to past usage of music within healing contexts. Other researchers could investigate cultures whose healing methods traditionally include the use of music. These studies should be cross-referenced in order to formulate substantive hypotheses for testing.

The second stage is the establishment of research centers that combine those therapies which use various aspects of vibration. Here music researchers might collaborate with specialists in color therapy, ultrasonics, cymatics, flower essences, polarity therapy, and bio-acoustics. The work of these specialists could be enhanced by psychologists, nutritionists, psychophysical practitioners and spiritual advisors to develop a holistic approach to health that addresses all aspects of the human condition.

The third stage would encompass the development of a new form of pan-cultural music that combines rhythms, melody, tempo, drones and ostinatos for specific therapeutic purposes. Perhaps a new ritual of performance will emerge within specially designed environments where music, color, scents and movements might be co-ordinated for purposes of healing, relaxation, meditation and aesthetic enjoyment.

The fourth stage will encompass the development of a curriculum for the training of music healing practitioners. Such a curriculum will develop naturally with the realization that music has a powerful influence on the quality of our daily lives and that the study of music without regard for its affect on people is no longer appropriate at this critical time in human history. Perhaps in the future, as a result of our efforts we will witness the emergence of a music by prescription, where music creators are employed in the past by medical and other healing centers as they have been employed by churches, courts of royalty and universities. From the diagnosis of healing practitioners, composers could create music to assist the recovery process or prevent the manifestation of illness. Doctors might prescribe a series of vocal toning exercises or a listening diet of music just as they now prescribe other remedies.

The nineteenth century philosopher, Friedrich Nietzche (1844-1900), once said that life without music would be a mistake. I would take that thought one step further by expressing the view that life without music would be impossible. This whole universe is one great symphony and around us everything and every creature of this Earth continually resonates to that symphony, adding its own voice according to natural harmonic law. It is only we confused humans who add the cacaphony and create the dissonance. We shall continue to do so until we relearn how to hear the silence within and how to once again manifest our life in harmony with the greater whole.

The source of our confusion lies in the attempt to impose human concepts of order onto a universe that is a dynamic process of emerging energetic and ordered patterns of which we are but one manifestation. We have, then, mistaken these concepts of the perceived universe for the true state of reality. In our frantic search for a world in which things are clearly defined, we have confused our self-created illusions of stability for the essential repose that lies at the center of all manifested creation. In the process we have mistaken rigidity for repose. When one rigidity comes into conflict with other rigidities, we assume that one must dominate the others and in our illusion, we are prepared to defend our particular form of rigidity unto death, whether on an individual or international level.

Yet beneath the rigidities which we construct lies the fluidity of a universe in motion, and beneath this fluidity lies the true repose referred to by T.S. Eliot as "The still point of the turning world."[1] In those rare moments when we experience true peacefulness, we are reminded of our awareness that the "still point" lies somewhere deep within. But because we have forgotten how to search for it we compensate by constructing boundaries around ourselves and regard the similarly constructed boundaries of others as threats to the repose we all seek. Ultimately, the fear that we won't find repose prevents us from recognizing it within ourselves, within each other, and within the universe. What hinders the search for true repose is our unwillingness to relinquish our illusion of dominance over the universe that sustains us, and our suspicion of forces we do not understand.

The power of music as a healing force is that through it we may re-experience the fluidity of the world in which we live. From its teaching we may be led through the layers of movement within music and within ourselves to progressively deeper layers until we reach the point of stillness at its center and our own. Having reached the repose of perfect equilibrium around which the vibrational patterns swirl, we will come to experience the peace of divine unity and, recognizing it within ourselves and each other, we are once again returned to wholeness.

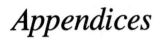

Appendices

APPENDIX A

Thoughts on Correlations of Color and Sound

Color healing, or "Chromotherapy" as it is now called, is not a new concept in human history; it is mentioned in the healing procedures of ancient China, Egypt, Greece, Tibet and India. In the West interest in the therapeutic uses of color was revived in the early twentieth century in England when it was discovered that by painting the recovery rooms of hospitals green the healing process of patients following surgery was greatly enhanced. Chromotherapy is now used in some English hospitals where selection of room colors is done with great care.

In America the introduction of color therapy has met with much skepticism and resistance. In some cases, American advocates of color therapy have encountered considerable harassment by the Food and Drug Administration, the medical establishment and even the postal department. As of 1974 only between twenty and thirty physicians had incorporated color as a part of their therapeutic systems.[1]

The association of tones and color has an equally long history that begins with ancient Chinese medical concepts. Yet, until the middle of the twentieth century the process of relating a specific tone to a specific color has been a psychological and intuitive process that has produced a dizzying and confusing array of opinions with seemingly little consensus among its exponents. Compounding this confusion, there appears to be little agreement as to which "yellow" is the "true yellow", which "red" is "true red", and when precisely does "red" become "orange". But most confusing, perhaps, is the attempt to arrive at a point of separation for each color as we have with musical pitches.

The frequency range of our piano is from 27½ cycles per second to 4,186 c.p.s. — although musicians name both the same "pitch". Within this range we have designated specific frequencies as named pitches such a "A,B,C" is a stepping stone manner with the implication that anything in between is not a pitch.[2] We have done the same with color. Just as we have given the "C" to a specific frequency in the audio range, so we have given the name "red" to a certain range of light frequencies. Consequently, we recognize seven principal colors within the color octave: red, orange, yellow, green, blue, indigo, violet. We also recognize seven principal pitch names within an audio octave: A,B,C,D,E,F,G.[3] One would hope that the two would conveniently correspond to each other. Alas, not so. The charts that follow are the result of an arduous and sometimes giddy attempt to make sense of the relationship of color-to-pitch as others have designated them.

Source: Ancient China

Name	Pitch Equivelent	Color	Elements	Direction	Season
Kung	C	Yellow	Earth	Center	Late Summer
Shang	D	White	Metal	West	Autumn
Kyo	E	Blue	Wood	East	Spring
Chi	G	Red	Fire	South	Summer
Yu	A	Black	Water	North	Winter

Source: Bali

Name	Scale Degree	Color	Diety	Direction
ding	1	5-colored	Shiva	Center
dong	2	White	Iswara	East
deng	3	Yellow	Mahadewa	West
dung	4	Red	Brahman	South
dang	5	Black	Vishnu	North

Source: India

Name	Scale Degree	Color[a]	Color[b]
Sa	1	Lotus	Pink
Re (Ri)	2	Green or Orange	Pale Green with Red
Ga	3	Gold	Orange with Crimson
Ma	4	Jasmine	Pale Pink
Pa	5	Dark	Red with Yellow
Dha	6	Yellow	Yellow
Ni	7	All Colors	Dark

a. Alain Danielou, *North Indian Music* (New York, Praeger, 1968).
b. Shahinda, *Indian Music* Delhi, India, 1923).

Source: Alexander Scriabin — Russian Composer (d. 1915)

C	Red	G	Rosy Orange
C#	Violet	G#	Purple
D	Yellow	A	Glint of Steel
D#	Glint of Steel	A#	Soft Blue
E	Pearly Blue and Shimmer of Moonlight	B	
F	Dark Red		

Source: Dyhani Ywahoo — Public Lecture

A	Green	Eyes
C	Red	Heart-Ears
D	Yellow	Flesh
E	Metal White	Skin, Mouth, Intestines
G	Blue Black	Bones, Anus

Source: Rolland Hunt — Rosicrucian Fellowship — Steven Halprin

C	Red	261.2
D	Orange	292.1
E	Yellow	329.1
F	Green	349.2
G	Blue	392.0
A	Indigo	440.0
B	Violet	493.0

Some Key Colors:

C major	White	Red
D major	Yellow	Yellow
F	Green	Red
F#	Grayish-Green	Bright Blue
A	Rosy	Green

B minor — "the Black key" — Beethoven
E minor — "unto a maiden robed in white with a rose-red bow upon her breast" — Schubert

Summary of Color-Pitch Relationships
  (numbers refer to number of sources)

Pitch	Color
C	Red (7), Purple, Green, Yellow (2), Lotus
C#	Red, Turquiose, Green, Violet
D	Orange (6), Yellow (3), Blue, White, Green, Greenish Blue
D#	Yellow, Indigo, Blue, Glint of Steel
E	Yellow (5), Metal White, Crimson Red, Violet, Blue, Gold, Indigo
F	Blue (2), Green (4), Ultraviolet, Violet, Dark Red
F#	Violet (2), Infrared, Bright Blue
G	Green, Blue (4), Blue Black, Black and White, Red (2), Rosy Orange, White, Jasmine
A	Indigo (4), Green (2), Amythist, Orange, Blue, Red, Black (2)
A#	Orange, Yellow, Orange Red, Glint of Steel
B	Violet (4), Purple, Azure Blue, Lemon, Soft Blue, Yellow

Light, like sound, is a frequency. The frequency of light occupies the forty-ninth octave of vibration; sound, by contrast, occupies the fourth to the fourteenth octaves — a total of ten octaves from 16 c.p.s. to about 17,000 c.p.s. (430 x 10^{12}). An octave, remember, is a two-to-one ratio. When we "see" light we are actually perceiving the total frequency spectrum of theforty-ninth octave — sort of like hearing all of the frequencies of sound — from 16 to 17,000 c.p.s. at once.[4] However, when the light rays are split, as when they are sent through a glass prism or when we see a rainbow, we perceive the individual bands of color that are contained within light. The seven principal colors, each with their own frequency range within the octave and arranged in order from lowest to highest frequency, correspond to the seven pitch classes — a, b, c, d, e, f, g — designated for musical notation. Once the actual frequencies of the colors are know it should be a fairly simple mathematical procedure to match the frequencies of the various pitches with them by reducing the color frequency downward by forty octaves to bring it within the sound spectrum. For example: taking the frequency of the lowest color — a very dark red — 430 x 10^{12}, we reduce it by forty octaves and we arrive at the frequency 391.3 c.p.s. using the standard concept of pitch tuning in which 440 c.p.s. equals "A", we find that the closest corresponding pitch is "G", below "A", at 392 c.p.s. This is a perfect match, of course, but we will discover that not all the pitch frequencies match exactly because of the nature of our equal tempered system of tuning. Here then is our chart of correspondences.[5]

Color Frequency	Color Name	Frequency down 40 Octaves[6]	Pitch Name	Pitch Frequency	Difference
430($\times 10^{12}$)	Red	391.3	G	392	.7
460($\times 10^{12}$)	Red/Orange	418.6	G#	415	3.6
490($\times 10^{12}$)	Orange	445.9	A	440	5.9
520($\times 10^{12}$)	Yellow	473.2	A#	466	7.2
550($\times 10^{12}$)	Lemon	500.5	B	494	6.5
580($\times 10^{12}$)	Green	527.8	C	524	3.8
610($\times 10^{12}$)	Turquoise	555.1	C#	555	.1
640($\times 10^{12}$)	Blue	582.3	D	588	5.7
680($\times 10^{12}$)	Indigo	618.7	D#	623	4.3
720($\times 10^{12}$)	Dark Violet	655.1	E	669	13.9
760($\times 10^{12}$)	Darker Violet	691.5	F	700	8.5
800($\times 10^{12}$)	Ultra Violet	727.9	F#	742	14.1

By now it has become clear that before any meaningful progress with sound and color correlations can be achieved, we will need to relinquish our attachment to pitch names and the equal-tempered scale (which is, after all, human-made), and adopt numerical frequencies in both color and sound. When there is a discrepancy between color and sound frequency relationships, even if only a few cycles per second, the two may neutralize any potential therapeutic effect. When we read that the pitch A-sharp corresponds to the color "yellow" we must know the frequency of both the yellow and

PART-SCALE OF COSMIC VIBRATIONS
Some of whose effects are recognized and studied by Science

Number of Vibrations per Second

62nd	Octave	4,	611,	686,	618,	427,	389,	904	Unkonwn
61st	"	2,	305,	843,	009,	213,	693,	952	
60th	"	1,	152,	921,	504,	606,	846,	976	X-Rays
59th	"	. .	576,	460,	752,	303,	423,	488	
58th	"	. .	288,	230,	376,	151,	711,	744	
57th	"	. .	144,	115,	188,	075,	855,	872	Perfumes
51st	"	. .	2,	251,	799,	813,	685,	248	
50th	"	. .	1,	125,	899,	906,	842,	625	Chemical Rays
49th	"	. .		562,	949,	953,	421,	312	Light (Physical Color)
48th	"	. .		281,	474,	976,	710,	656	
47th	"	. .		140,	737,	488,	355,	328	Heat
46th	"	. .		70,	368,	744,	177,	664	
45th	"	. .		35,	184,	372,	088,	832	
40th	"	. .		1,	099,	511,	627,	776	Unknown
35th	"	. .		. .	34,	359,	738,	368	
30th	"	. .		. .	1,	073,	741,	824	Electricity
25th	"	. .		. .		33,	554,	432	
20th	"	. .		. .		1,	048,	576	
15th	"	. .		. .		. .	32,	768	
10th	"	. .		. .		. .	1,	024	
9th	"	. .		. .		. .		512	
8th	"	. .		. .		. .		256	
7th	"	. .		. .		. .		128	Physical
6th	"	. .		. .		. .		64	Sound
5th	"	. .		. .		. .		32	
4th	"	. .		. .		. .		16	
3rd	"	. .		. .		. .		8	
2nd	"	. .		. .		. .		4	
1st	"	. .		. .		. .		2	

Reproduced from Roland Hunt, *Fragrant & Radiant Healing Symphony* (London, H.G. White Publishing, 1937).

the A-sharp. Then, in producing both frequencies simultaneously we must possess equipment that is accurate and stable so that the frequencies will not fluctuate when sustained for a long period of time.

One of the earliest books devoted to the relationship of sound and color to appear in the English language was authored by the Englishman, Roland Hunt.[7] His book, *Fragrant and Radiant Healing Symphony*, was first published in1937 and carried the following explanatory subtitle: "An enquiry into the wondrous correlation of the healing virtues of Colour, Sound, and Perfume and a consideration of their influence and purpose." In it Hunt quotes Harriet I. Childe-Pemberton who, in speaking of a book supposedly written by Bernadine de St. Pierre in the late eighteenth century, may have uncovered the origin of the idea of seven colors and seven corresponding pitches. In commenting on St. Pierre she writes, "The ideas propounded by the author, though admittedly fascinating, were held in the nineteenth century to be fantastic and unscientific, especially the idea that treats of analogies, such as the relationship between the seven colours of the rainbow, and the seven tones of the music-scale".[8]

Mr. Hunt bases his theories of the relationship of pitch, colorhand scent on a "Scale of Cosmic Vibrations" which he presents later in his book.[9] His scale consists of sixty-two octaves of vibration in which sound occupies the fourth to fifteenth octaves, color the forty-ninth octave, and "perfumes" the fifty-first to fifty-seventh octaves.

The underlying principle of the scale of vibrations, and therefore the foundation of all theories pertaining to correlations of pitch and color, is referred to as the "Periodic Law", or the "Law of Octaves". Mr. Hunt claims that the Periodic Law was independently applied to the classifications of chemical elements by Mendeleeff and Newlands in the latter part of the nineteenth century and that the same law "can be applied to everything in Nature, not to materiality alone,"[10] since life is manifested under four guises — matter, form, energy and intelligence — and is periodic, i.e., vibrational. The Periodic Law demonstrates the principle of periodicty — the recurrence of similar properties at regular reoccuring intervals. In terms of sound, this means that every frequency will display similar characteristics when it is doubled according to the two-to-one ratio of octave. By doubling a frequency of, let us say, 200 c.p.s. we produce a frequency of 400 c.p.s.; doubling this frequency results in a frequency of 800 c.p.s. which will bear a likeness to the previous two. According to the Law of Octaves, then, if the frequency of 200 c.p.s. is doubled forty times wehwill arrive at the octave frequency of the color spectrum. It is from this theory that the idea of correlation is, however, far too simplistic and mechanical, for it does not take into account an important physical law. In taking a sound frequency and doubling it forty times, one does not produce light. Sound depends on pressure waves of the molecular motion of air and molecular motion is slower that the motions of atoms or of particles of atoms. Light, because of its greater frequency, involves the vibratory motion of atomic particles since light waves are infinitely shorter than sound waves.[11] In the words of Dane Rudhyar,

"To think of sound, radio waves, light, and X-rays as different levels (or 'octaves') of frequencies adequately defined by mere numbers may be intellectually and analytically justifiable, but it makes sense in terms of human consciousness and vital responses. Ultrasounds exist beyond the range of perception of our ears or auditory centers, but even if their frequencies were greatly increased, they would never become colors. The connection some people perceive between sounds and colors stems from their subjective psychic responses to sound and color, but it does not refer to objective periodical motions transmitted to the consciousness by two entirely different means of perception, each related to particular kinds of nerve activity and organic responses."[12]

It would appear, then, that perceived correlations between light and sound, or color and pitch, is an entirely subjective and therefore personal matter which explains why there seems tohbe so little agreement among various sources. The belief in the correlation of sounds, colors, and perfumes has been around for a long time and shows no sign of going away. Yet to this day, there seems to be no scientific evidence to either sustain or negate it.

This is not to imply, however, that there is no merit in the idea. In fact, there is no reason to assume that the creation of a healing procedure that coordinates a specific sound frequency with a corresponding light and perfume frequency according to the periodic law of octaves, would not produce powerful healing potential. Such a procedure must be the result of valid scientific experimentation under controlled conditions with verifiable results. This could be easily accomplished and could result in an entirely new field of healing. The first step necessary is to gather all existing data from Radionics, Cymatics, Ultra-Sound therapy, Polarity therapy, Color therapy, the perfume industry, and Bach and California Flower Essence therapies.[13]

APPENDIX B

Bibliography

Pundit Acharya, *Breath, Sleep, the Heart and Life* Clearlake Highlands, CA: Dawn Horse Press, 1975.

Pundit Usherbudh Arya, *Mantra and Meditation* Honesdale, PA: Himalayan International Institute of Yoga Science and Philosophy, 1981.

Meher Baba, *God Speaks* New York: Dodd, Mead and Co., 1970

Alice Bailey, *A Treatise on Cosmic Fire* New York: Lucis Press, 1977.

_____, *A Treatise on White Magic* New York: Lucis Trust, 1951.

_____, *Esoteric Healing* New York: Lucis Trust, 1953

R. Ballentine, M.D., *The Science of Breath* Honesdale, PA: Himalayan International Institute of Yoga Science and Philosophy, 1976.

Wilmer Batholomew, *Acoutics of Music* Englewood Cliffs, N.J.: Prentice Hall, 1942.

Christopher Ballantine, *Music and its Social Meaning* London: Harwood Academic Publishers, 1985.

Victor Beasley, *Your Electro-Vibratory Body* Boulder Creek, CA, University of the Trees Press, 1978.

Itzhak Bentov, *Stalking the Wild Pendulum* New York: Bantam Books, 1979.

John Blacking, *How Musical Is Man?* Seattle, WA: University of Seattle Press, 1974.

Lawrence Blair, *Rhythms of Vision* New York: Schocken Books, 1976.

H.P. Blavatsky, *The Voice of the Silence* Wheaton Ill.: Quest Books, 1970.

John Blofeld, *Mantras: Sacred Words of Power* New York: Dutton Books, 1977.

Helen Bonny, *Music and Your Mind; Listening with a New Consciousness* New York: Harper and Row, 1975. Out of Print.

Malcolm Budd, *Music and the Emotions* London: Routledge & Kegan Paul, 1985.

Harold Saxon Burr, *Blue for Immorality* London: Neville Spearman, 1976.

Thomas Clifton, *Music as Heard: A Study in Applied Phenomenology* New Haven, CN: Yale University Press, 1983,

MacDonald Critchley, *Music and the Brain* New York: Charles C. Thomas, 1977.

Baba Hari Das, *Silence Speaks* Santa Cruz, CA: Sri Lama Foundation, 1977.

William Davis, *The Harmonies of Sound, Color and Vibration* Marina del Ray, CA: DeVorss, 1980.

John Diamond, *Life Energy in Music: Notes on Music and Sound* Hollywood, CA: Zeppelin, 1983.

Nevill Drury, *Music for Inner Space; Techniques for Meditation & Visualization* Lindfield, Australia: Unity Press, 1985.

Anton Ehrenzweig, *The Hidden Order of Art* Los Angeles: University of California Press, 1968. Out of Print.

Gordon Epperson, *The Music Symbol* Ames, Iowa: Iowa Stat University Press, 1967. Out of Print.

Paul R. Farnsworth, *The Social Psychology of Music* Ames, Iowa: Iowa State University Press, 1969.

Theo Gimbel, *Healing Through Color* Essex, England: C.W. Daniel Company Limited, 1980.

P. Gouldron, *Ancient and Oriental Music* New York: Stuttman Co., 1968.

Lama Anagarika Govinda, *Creative Meditation and Multi-Dimensional Consciousness* Wheaton, IL: Quest Books, 1976.

_____, *Foundations of Tibetan Mysticism* New York: Weiser Books, 1969.

F. Lanier Graham, ed., *The Rainbow Book* New York: Vintage Press, 1979.

Donald J. Grout, *A History of Western Music* New York, Norton Books, 1960.

Elizabeth Haich, *Initiation* Garberville, CA: Seed Center Publications, 1974.

Manly Hall, *The Therapeutic Value of Music* Los Angeles: Philosophical Research, 1955.

Peter Hamel, *Through Music to the Self* Boulder, CO: Shambhala Press, 1980.

Steven Halpern, *Tuning the Human Instrument* Belmont, CA: Halpren Sounds, 1980.

Max Heindel, *The Musical Scale and the Scheme of Evolution* Oceanside, CA: The Rosicrucian Fellowship, 1973.

Corinne Helene, *Color and Music in the New Age* La Canada, CA: New Age Press, 1964.

_____, *Healing and Regeneration Through Music* La Canada, CA: New Age Press, 1976.

_____, *Music; the Keynote of Human Evolution* La Canada, CA: New Age Press, 1965.

Hermann Helmholtz, *On the Sensations of Tone* New York: Dover Books, 1954.

Roland Hunt, *Fragrant and Radiant Healing Symphony* London: H.G. White Publishing, 1937.

Walter Addison Jayne, *The Healing Gods of Ancient Civilizations* New Hyde Park, N.Y.: University Books, 1962.

W. Brugh Joy, M.D., *Joy's Way* Los Angeles: J.P. Tarcher, 1979.

Hans Jenny, *Cynatics Basle* Switzerland: Basilius Press, 1974. Two Volumes.

Sir James Jeans, *Science and Music* Cambridge, England: Cambridge University Press, 1947.

Hazrat Inayat Khan, *Healing; Mental Purification; The Mind World* Farnham, Surrey, England: Service Publishing Co., 1978.

_____, *The Music of Life* Santa Fe, NM: Omega Press, 1983.

Pir Valayat Khan, *Toward the One* New York: Harper and Row, 1974.

Madhu Khanna, *Yantra; The Tantric Symbol of Cosmic Unity* London: Thames and Hudson, 1979.

Laural Elizabeth Keys, *Toning: The Creative Power of the Voice* Marina del Rey, CA: DeVorss, 1973.

Stanley Krippner and Daniel Rubin, eds., *The Kirlian Aura: Photographing the Galaxies of Life* New York: Doubleday, 1974.

Karl D. Kryter, *The Effects of Noise on Man* New York: Academic Press, 1970.

Sandra LaForest and Virginia MacIver, *Vibrations: Healing Through Color, Homeopathy and Radionics* New York: Weiser Books, 1979.

Lucie Lamay, *Egyptian Mysteries* New York: Oxford Publishing Press, 1981.

Susanne Langer, *Problems of Art* New York: Scribers, 1957.

_____, *Reflections on Art* New York: Oxford University Press, 1961.

C.W. Leadbetter, *Man, Visible and Invisible* Wheaton, IL: Quest Books, 1969.

George Leonard, *The Silent Pulse* New York: Dutton Books, 1978.

Hal A. Lingerman, *The Healing Energies of Music* Wheaton, IL: Quest Books, 1983.

Charles Luk, *Secrets of Chinese Meditation* New York: Weiser Books, 1972.

Robert W. Lundin, *An Objective Psychology of Music* New York: Ronald Press, 1967.

David McAllester, *Douglas Mitchel — Navahoe Singer* Tempe: University of Arizona Press, 1981.

Ernest McClain, *The Myth of Invariance* New York: Nicholas Hays, Limited, 1976.

Robert Meagher, *Cave Notes* Philadelphia: Fortress Press, 1974

Alan Merriam, *The Anthropology of Music* Chicago: Northwestern University Press, 1964.

Leonard Meyer, *Emotion and Meaning in Music* Chicago: University of Chicago Press, 1961.

_____, *Explaining Music* Chicago: University of Chicago Press, 1974.

_____, *Music, the Arts and Ideas* Chicago: University of Chicago Press, 1967.

Ajit Mookerjee, *Tantric Art* New Delhi, India: Kuman Gallery, 1973.

Hiroshi Motoyam, *Theories of the Chakras* Wheaton, IL: Quest Books, 1981.

Guy Murchie, *Music of the Spheres* Boston: Houghton-Mifflin, 1961.

Lennart Nilsson, *Behold Man* Boston: Little, Brown and Co., 1973.

John N. Ott, *Health and Light* Old Greenwich, CN: Devin-Adler, 1973.

Harry Partch, *Genisis of a Music* New York: DeCapo Press, 1974.

Claire Polin, *Music of the Ancient Near East* New York: Vantage Press, 1954.

Swami Rama, *Living With the Himalayan Masters* Honesdale, PA: Himalayan Institue of Yoga Science and Philosophy, 1978.

Yogi Ramacharaka, *Raja Yoga* Chicago: Yogi Publications, 1906.

Philip Rawson, *The Art of Tantra* Greenwich, CN: New York Graphic Society Ltd., 1973.

David Reck, *Music of the Whole Earth* New York: Scribner's and Sons, 1977.

Dorothy Retallack, *The Sound of Music and Plants* Marina del Ray, CA: DeVorss, 1972.

Lewis Rowell, *Thinking About Music* Amherst, MA: University of Massachusetts Press, 1983.

Dane Rudhyar, *The Magic of Tone and the Art of Music* Boulder, CO: Shambhala Books, 1982.

Peter Russell, *The Brain Book* New York: Hawthorne Books, 1979.

Curt Sachs, *The Rise of Music in the Ancient World* New York: Norton Books, 1940.

_____, *The Wellsprings of Music* New York: McGraw-Hill, 1965.

Lee Sannella, M.D., *Kundalini-Psychosis or Transcendence?* San Francisco: H.S. Dakin Co., 1976.

Sarngadeva, *Sangitaratna*, trans. by R.K. Shringy Delhi: Motilal Banarsidass, 1978.

R. Murray Schafer, *The Tuning of the World* New York: Alfred Knopf, 1977.

Max Schoen, *The Effects of Music* Freeport, NY: Books for Libraries Press, 1927.

P.M. Schullian and M. Schoen, eds., *Music and Medicine* New York, Schuman, 1948.

Jack Schwartz, *Human Energy Systems* New York: Dutton Books, 1980.

Cyril Scott, *Music: Its Secret Influence Throughout the Ages* Wheaton, IL: Quest Books, 1960.

Sid J. Segalowitz, *The Two Sides of the Brain* Englewood Cliffs, N.J.: Prentice Hall, 1983.

Alfred Sendry, *Music in the Social and Relogious Life of Antiquity* Crabury, N.J.: Fairleigh Dickenson University Press, 1974.

Ravi Shankar, *My Music, My Life* New York: Simon and Schuster, 1968.

F. Joseph Smith, *The Experiencing of Musical Sound* London: Harwood Academic Publishers, 1985.

Robert C. Solomon, *The Passions* New York: Anchor Books, 1977. Lionel Stebbing, ed., *Music: Its Occult Basis and Healing Value London: New Knowledge Books, 1958.*

Igor Stravinski, Poetics of Music New York: Norton Books, 1950.

Oliver Strunk, *Source Readings in Music History* New York: Norton Books, 1950.

David V. Tansley, D.C., *Radionics and the Subtle Anatomy of Man* Essex, England: Health Science Press.

Charles Tate, ed., *Altered State of Consciousness* New York: Anchor Books, 1972.

William Tiller, *Radionics* Los Altos, CA: The Academy of Parapsychology, 1971.

Peter Tompkins, *Mysteries of the Mexican Pyramids* New York: Harper and Row, 1976.

Alan Walker, *A Study in Musical Analysis* New York: Glencoe Free Press, 1962.

Frank Waters, *The Book of the Hopi* New York: Penquin Books, 1977.

Lyall Watson, *Supernature* Garden City, N.Y.: Anchor Books, 1973.

Egon Wellesz, ed., *Oxford History of Music, Vol. I* London: Oxford University Press, 1957.

John White, ed., *The Highest State of Consciousness* New York: Anchor Books, 1972.

Shirley Rabb Winston, *Music as the Bridge; Edgar Cayce on Music* Virginia Beach, VA: A.R.E. Press, 1972.

Alexander Wood, *The Physics of Music* New York: Dover Books, 1961.

Paramahansa Yogananda, *Autobiography of a Yogi* Los Angeles: Self-Realization Society, 1971.

Meredith Lady Young, *Agartha: Journey to the Stars* Walpole, NH: Stillpoint Publishing, 1984.

Victor Zuckerkandl, *Man the Musician* Princeton, NJ: Princeton University Press, 1973.

_____, *Sound and Symbol* Princeton, NJ: Princeton University Press, 1956.

NOTES

Introduction

1. Clair Polin, *Music of the Ancient Near East* (N.Y., Vantage Press, 1954). P. Gouldron, *Ancient and Oriental Music* (N.Y., Stuttman Co., 1968).

2. Henry George Farmer, "The Music of Ancient Mesopotamia," in the "IThe Oxford History of Music. Vol. I, ed. by Egon Wellesz (London, Oxford University Press, 1957), pp. 229-232.

3. Ibid., Marius Schneider, "Primitive Music," pp. 42-43.

   Music is the seat of secret forces or spirits which can be evoked by song in order to give man a power which is either higher than himself or which allows him to rediscover his deeper self. . . The mystical sound-substance inherent in all things, manifesting itself now directly, now indirectly, exists everywhere, even beyond the range of the human ear.

4. Ibid., p.41

   The progressive development of the physical and metaphysical conception of the world can be clearly traced from the earliest cultures right into the Megalithic Age, and the systematic symbolism of that age underlies the religious systems of the highly developed cultures.

5. Ibid., Henry George Farmer, "Music in Ancient Egypt," p. 258.

6. Ibid., p. 258.

7. Ibid., Lawrence Picken, "Music of Far Eastern Asia," p. 87.

8. Ibid., Henry George Farmer, "Music of Islam," p. 440.

9. Ibid., p. 440.

10. Guy Marchie, *Music of the Spheres, Vol. 2* (N.Y., Dover Books, 1961), p. 382. The author gives a contemporary expression to the underlying metaphysical thought of Tibetan, Hindu and Tantric writings.

11. G. S. Kirk, *Heraclitus — The Cosmic Fragments* (Cambridge, England, Cambridge University Press, 1970), p. 14.

12. Yogi Ramacharaka, *Raja Yoga* (Chicago, Yogi Publications, 1906), p. 79.

13. Elizabeth Haich, *Initiation* (Garberville, Calif.) Seed Center Publications, 1974), p. 212.

14. *The Oxford History of Music* Arnold Blake, "Music of India," p. 198.

   The sound alluded to. . .is only the *ahatanada* (struck or manifested sound), which cannot exist without its ideal counterpart, the *anahatanada* (unstruck or unmanifested sound). It is this dual nature of sound as *ahata* and *anahata* which brings it right into the center of religious-philosophical speculations, because the unmanifested state, the *anahatanada*, is identified with the creative principle of the universe in its transcendental form of Shiva himself, as well as in its immanent form as the syllable OM which is said to reside in the heart.

15. "All music is nothing more than a succession of impulses that converge toward a definite point of repose." Igor Stravinsky, *Poetics of Music* (N.Y., Vintage Press, 1947), pp. 37-38.

16. Lama Anagarika Govinda, *Foundations of Tibetan Mysticism* (N.Y., Weiser Books, 1969), pp. 26-27.

Ibid., p. 26

17. The secret of this hidden power of sound or vibration, which forms the key to the riddles of creation and of creativeness, as it reveals the nature of things and of the phenomena of life, had been well understood by the seers of olden times: the Rishis who inhabited the slopes of the Himalayas, the Magi of Iran, the adapts of Mesopotamia, and the mystics of Greece — to mention only those of whom tradition has left some traces.

18. Frank Waters, *Book of the Hopi* (New York, Penquin Books, 1977), pp. 3-8.

19. *Oxford History of Music*, p. 47.

20. Lawrence Blair, *Rhythms of Vision* (N.Y., Schocken Books, 1976), p. 116.

21. *Oxford History of Music*, p. 48.

22. David Reck, *Music of the Whole Earth* (N.Y., Scribner's & Sons, 1977), p.7.

23. Sarngadeva, *Sangitaratnakara*, trans. by Dr. R. K. Shringy (Dehli, Motilal Banarsidass, 1978), 12.2, p.23.

Nadena Vyajyate varnah padem
Varnat padad vacah vacaso
Vyavaharo 'yam nadahinam ato jagat.

24. Paul Radin, "Music and Medicine Among Primitive Peoples," in *Music and Medicine*, ed. by P. M. M Schullian and M. Schoen (N.Y., Schuman, 1948), p. 17.

25. *Oxford History of Music*, p. 48

26. Bruno meinecke, "Music and Medicine in Classical Antiquity," in *Music and Medicine*, ed. by P. M. Schullian and M. Schoen (N.Y., Schuman, 1948), p. 48.

27. Ibid., p. 49

28. Reck, op. cit., p. 7.

29. Lawrence Picken in *Oxford History of Music*, p. 87.

A system relating musical sounds to the order of the universe had been developed by as early as the date of the compilation of the *Joulii* (The Ceremonial of the State of Jou), third century B.C. By this time the Imperial Bureau of Music had been incorporated into the Imperial Bureau of Weights and Measures.

30. *Music and Medicine*, p. 4.

31. Oliver Strunk, *Source Readings in Music History* (N.Y., Norton, 1950), p. 83.

32. Alfred Sendry, *Music in the Social and Religious Life of Antiquity* (Cranbury, N.J., Fairleigh Dickenson University Press, 1974), p. 247.

33. Fumio Koizumi, Record Liner Notes, "A Bell Ringing in the Empty Sky," (New York, Nonesuch Records, No. H-72025).

34. *Oxford History of Music*, p. 231, 259.

35. Sendry, op. cit., p. 244.

36. Ibid., p. 245.

37. Ibid., p. 244.

Chapter 1

1. Several excellent books on acoustics are listed in the bibliography.
2. The ability to read music notation is helpful throughout the chapter although it is not a necessity!
3. In instruments without fingerboards-i.e., pianos, harps, hammer dulcimers — each string produces only one fundamental pitch.
4. Pythagoras will be mentioned many times in the course of this book.
5. This composite picture would last for a very small portion of one second since the string and all its segments are in constant motion.
6. It should be clarified that elements of the harmonic series are present in almost every sound in nature as well. Also "tone" in this context means a sound with one fundamental and identifiable pitch. Many sounds used in music do not produce single pitches but rather, bands of pitch tessitures. In many ways, these are even richer in "harmonic" content but they are not necessarily "harmonious". Examples are drums, gongs, cymbals.
7. An understanding of the harmonic series is absolutely essential to the utilization of music as a healing agent.
8. It must be remembered that nothing is ever totally at rest.
9. Paraphrased from Fritjof Capra's excellent book, *The Tao of Physics* Chapter 4 (Shambhala Books, 1975). This book is "required reading" for any musician with an interest in healing.
10. Ibid., p. 73.
11. Ibid., pp. 65-66

Chapter 2

1. Case in point: If you push your ears away from your head you are able to hear sounds in front much more efficiently.
2. Many recording engineers now record music concerts in stereo by using two microphones located about eight inches from each other on a single stand in front of the performers.
3. For actual photographs of the ear, consult Lennart Nilsson's excellent *Behold Man*, Boston Little, Brown, and Company 1973 pp. 201-219.
4. Perhaps we will discover that sound regulates the functioning (i.e., secretion) of the gland system which, in turn, regulates our mental, physical and emotional condition.
5. Harry Partch *Genesis of a Music*; New York Da Capo Press; 1974.

Chapter 3

1. Peter Guy Manners, **"Public Lecture"**, (Amherst, Mass.), April 5, 1983.
2. Victor Beasley, *Your Electro-Vibratory Body*, (Boulder Creek, Calif., University of the Trees Press, 1978), pp. 19-20.
3. Manners, **"Lecture"**.
4. Beasley, op. cit., p. 34.
5. Itzhak Bentov, *Stalking the Wild Pendulum*, (New York, Bantam Books, 1979), pp. 57-58.
6. Hans Jenny, *Cymatics*, Vol. II (Basle, Switzerland, Basilius Press, 1974). pp. 95-132.

7.   Manners, "**Lecture**".

8.   Lee Sannella, M.D., *Kundaline — Psychosis or Transcendence?*, (San Francisco, H.S. Dakin Co., 1976), pp. 71-95.

9.   *Ibid.*, pp. 79-80.

10. Lyall Watson, *Supernature*, (Garden City, N.Y., Anchor Books, 1973), pp. 89-96.

11. John Miller, Ph.D., conversation with the author (Amherst, Mass., August 12, 1980).

12. Beasley, op. cit., pp. 109-113.

13. Bentov, op. cit., p. 59.

14. Manners, "**Lecture**".

15. C. W. Leadbetter, *Man, Visible and Invisible*, (Wheaton, Ill., Quest Books, 1969).

16. Alice Bailey, *Esoteric Healing*, (New York, Lucis Trust, 1953).

17. Paramahansa Yogananda, *Autobiography of a Yogi*, (Los Angeles, Self-Realization Fellowship, 1971).

18. Harold Saxon Burr, *Blueprint for Immortality*, (London, Neville Spearman, 1972).

19. For more detailed discussion on human auras: *The Rainbow Book*, ed. by F. Lanier Graham, (New York, Vintage Books, 1979); *The Kirlian Aura: Photographing the Galaxies of Life*, ed. by Stanley Krippner and Daniel Rubin, (New York, Doubleday, 1974).

20. Bailey, op. cit., p. 3.

21. Lawrence Blair, *Rhythms of Vision*, (New York, Schocken Books, 1975), p. 133.

Chapter 4

1.   Pir Vilayat Khan, *Toward the One* (New York, Harper and Row, 1974), p. 229.

2.   Swami Rama, *Living with the Himalayan Masters:R (Honesdale, Pa., Himalayan International Institute of Yoga Science and Philosophy, 1978), p. 441.*

3.   Alice Bailey, *Treatise* on White Magic (New York, Lucis Trust, 1951), p.

4.   *The Rainbow Book*, ed. F. Lanier Graham (New York, Vintage Books, 1979), p. 134.

5.   Because the body is a unit that consists of interrelated sub-units, change of condition in one or more sub-units affects the larger unit as a whole.

6.   That cells can be regenerated is a claim made by Cymatic Therapy practitioners.

7.   Walter A. Jayne, M.D., *The Healing Gods of Ancient Civilizations* (New York Hyde Park, N.Y., University Books, 1962), information on healing temples of Egypt and Greece, po 33-52, pp. 257-300.

8.   For a more complete discussion of Radionic therapy consult: Sandra LaForest and Virginia MacIvor, *Vibrations: Healing Through Color, Homoeopathy and Radionics* (New York, Samual Weiser, 1979).

9.   The work of Drs. Gallert and Massy is examined in Beasley, op. cit., pp. 172-184.

10. Jenny, op. cit., Vol. II, p. 165.

11. Ibid., p. 170.

12. Ibid., p. 173.

13. Ibid., p. 185.

14. Peter Guy Manners, "The Future of Cymatic Therapy,"

15. Manners, "**Lecture**".

16. Manners, "**Lecture**".

17. Dr. Manners' address is: Bretforton Hall near Evesham Worcestershire WR11-5JH England

18. Psychology today, (June, 1983).

19. "Ultrasonics," in *Mosby's Medical and Nursing Dictionary*, ed. by Laurence Urdaug (St. Louis, MO, C. V. Mosby Company, 1983), p. 358.

20. F. G. Sommer, et al, "Evaluation of Gynecologic Pelvis Masses by Ultrasound and Computed Tomography," *Journal of Reproductive Medicene* (Jan. 27, 1982), pp. 45-50.

21. Ibid., p. 112.

22. Ibid., p. 358.

23. Ibid., p. 358.

24. Ibid., p. 358.

25. "Ultra sonics," *Black's Medical Dictionary*, ed. by William A. R. Thomson (New York, Barnes and Noble, 1979), p. 904.

26. "Ultra Sound," *Encyclopedia Britannica* (1981 ed.), vol. 18, p. 843.

27. L. Rowe and A. Cantwell, Jr., "Hypodermitis Schlerodermiformis. Successful Treatment with Ultrasound," *Archives of Dermotology*, 118(5), (May, 1982), pp. 312-14.

28. A. S. Garrett and M. Garrett, "Ultrasound Therapy for Herpes Zoster Pain (letter)," (Nov. 1982), pp. 709, 711.

29. Black's Medical, p. 904.

30. C. A. Warfield and J. M. Stein, "Low Back Pain," *Hospital Practice*, 17(11), (Nov. 1982), pp. 50A, 50E, 50H-K.

31. V. C. Nwuga, "Ultrasound in Treatment of Back Pain Resulting from Prolapsed Intervertebral Disc," *Archives of Physical Medicine and Rehabilitation*, 64(2), (Feb. 1982), pp. 88-9.

32. P. M. Corry, et al, "Combined Ultrasound and Radiation Therapy Treatment of Human Superficial Tumors," *Radiology*, 145(1), (Oct. 1982), pp. 165-9.

33. J. G. Brockis, "Percutaneous Removal of Renal Stones," *Journal of Research*, 76(1), (Jan. 1983), pp. 4-5.

34. J. W. Segura, et al, "Percutaneous Removal of Kidney Stones, Preliminary Report," *Mayo Clinic*, 57(10), (Oct. 1982), pp. 615-9.

35. N. M. Bleehen, "Ultrasound, Microwave and Radiotherapy Radiations: The Basis for Their Potential in Cancer Therapy, Proceedings of the 10th L. H. Gray Conference, Oxford, July 13-16, 1981," *British Journal of Cancer (Supplement)*, (March 1982), pp. 1-257.

36. M. Shellshear, "Ultrasound and Mastitus," *Australian Family Physician*, 11(8), (Aug. 1982), p. 642.

37. M. McIsaac, "Ophthalmic Surgery in the Elderly," *Primary Care*. 9(1), (Mar. 1982), pp. 173-9.

38. W. J. Hodgson and A. J. McElhinney, "Ultrasonic Partial Splenectomy," *Surgery*, 91(3), (Mar. 1982), pp. 346-8).

39. N. H. Ferguson, "Ultrasound in the Treatment of Surgical Wounds," *Physiotherapy*, 67(2), (Feb. 10, 1981), p. 43.

40. *Encyclopedia Britannica*, vol. 18, p. 843.

41. The film was shown at the Boston Science Museum.

42. Unfortunately, I cannot provide publication details for this article. It appeared in the Rochester (N.Y.) Times-Union during the Spring of 1967.

43. Blair, p. 117.

44. Lyall Watson, *Supernature* (Garden City, N.Y., Anchor Press, 1973), pp. 90-96.

45. Guy Manners, **"Lecture"**.

Chapter 5

1. Sendry, op. cit., p. 37
2. Waters, op. cit., p. 4
3. Philip Rawson, Art of Tantra, (Greenwich, Conn., NY Graphics Society, 1973), p. 69.
4. Pandit Usharbudha Arya, *Mantra and Meditation* (Honesdale, PA, Himalayan International Institute of Yoga Science and Philosophy, 1981), p. 28.
5. Ibid., p. 29.
6. Lama Anagarika Govinda, *Creative Meditation and MultiDimensional Consciousness* (Wheaton, Ill., Quest Books, 1976), p. 71.
7. Baba Hari Das, *Silence Speaks* (Santa Cruz, Calif., Sri Lama Foundation, 1977), p. 157.
8. Yogi Bhajan, **"Public Lecture"** (Amherst, Mass., January 26, 1976), In my research on Mantra I have found no other authority who expressed this interpretation. — Author's note.
9. Ajit Mookerjee, Tantric Art, (New Delhi, India, Kuman Gallery, 1973), p. 11.
10. It should be noted at the outset of this discussion that Western medical concepts do not yet acknowledge these views of human anatomy. Although the concept of chakras has been a basic part of Hindu and Tantric thought for hundreds of years, no substantial evidence to verify their existence has as yet been presented. This does not necessarily mean that these aspects of esoteric anatomy are myths. Rather, it is likely that the technical means for investigation have yet to be developed. Virtually all Western psychic healers and occultist writers with who I have had contact attest to the existence of *chakras*, and researchers such as Christopher Hill of the University of the Trees are attempting to study them by means of accepted scientific method. I am included to assume their existence unless proven otherwise.
11. The four agents of distribution are: etheric system, nervous system, endocrine system and blood system.
12. Although the adrenal glands are physiologically nowhere near the base of the spine, they are associated with the *Mulkdhara Chakra* in a psychological way. The *maladhara chakra* is related to physical survival while the adrenal glands produce the hormone adrenaline, which is utilized in greater amounts when physical survival is threatened. Hence, the adrenals are sometimes referred to as the "fight or flight" glands.
13. In altering the breathing rate, presumably one alters the vibrational rates of the *Nadis*, of *Prana* and therefore of the basic metabolism. This process would alter one's mental activity.

Chapter 6

1. I am indebted to Bonnie Bainbridge Cohen, Director of the School for Body-Mind Centering (Amherst, MA) for providing much of the material in this and subconsequent sections of this chapter. Her innovative work in human physiology has yet to be fully recognized.
2. The pelvic floor (pelvic diaphragm) attaches from the tail of the spine to the pubic bone. Because in most cases it was atrophied in human cadavers, its existence was unknown until quite recently.
3. Bonnie Cohen, conversation with the author (January 24, 1984, Amherst, MA).
4. Ibid.

5. Ms. Cohen characterizes the difference between the expansion of the thoracic diaphragm before breathing and pulling the diaphragm inward before breathing as the "difference between a sigh and a gasp."

6. In hyperventilation the rest/recovery phase of breathing is eliminated; hyperventilation cannot continue for long periods of time.

7. "Vocal diaphragm" is the term given by Ms. Cohen in place of "vocal fold" as being more accurately descriptive of its action and shape. The more common term "vocal cord" is misleading. The vocal cord is, more accurately, the inner edge of each band of the vocal diaphragm.

8. Henry Gray, *Gray's Anatomy* (N.Y., Bounty Books, 1977), pp. 955-965.

9. Charles Brooks, *Sensory Awareness* (Santa Barbara, Calif., Ross-Erikson, 1984).

R. Ballentine, *The Science of Breath* (Honesdale, PA, Himalayan International Institute of Yoga Science and Philosophy, 1976).

Pundit Acharya, *Breath, Sleep, the Heart and Life* (Clearlake Highlands, CA, Dawn House Press, 1975).

Carola H.S. Read, *Breathing, the ABC's* (N.Y., Harper Colophon, 1978).

Douglas Stanley, *Your Voice: Applied Science of Vocal Art* (N.Y., Pitman, 1957).

10. Bonnie Bainbridge Cohen, *Reflections on the Voice in Terms of Spatial Relationships of Vowel Sounds and Organic Support of Effect Qualities in the Production of Vowels, Pitch and Intensity* (Amherst, MA, School for Body-Mind Centering, 1977), p. 3.

11. In courses taught at the School for Body-Mind Centering, Ms. Cohen has trained students to develop this skill.

12. Inayat Khan, *Music* (New Delhi, India, Sufi Publishing Co., 1973), p. 57.

13. Ibid., pp. 58-59.

14. My efforts to locate documentation of a systematic use of voice for toning of glands and organs has not been successful thus far. It is possible that such knowledge was in the possession of the ancient Egyptians and the Pythagoreons, but this is unprovable.

15. Cohen, op. cit., p. 3.

16. Robert Claiborne, "What Caused the Sudden Rise of Modern Man?" in *Mysteries of the Past*, ed. by Joseph J. Thorndike, Jr. (N.Y., American Heritage, 1977), p. 109.

17. Ibid., p. 108.

18. Bonnie Cohen, Conversation with the author (January 24, 1984).

19. "Palm Healing Seminar," *The Order of the Universe*, 5(6), 1975, p. 21-28.

20. Harold M. Schmeck, Jr., "As Scoffing Fades, Pineal Gland Gets Its Due," New York Times, January 31, 1984, p. C1.

21. In the case of men, place your hand over the area where, in women, the gonads are found. According to Bonnie Cohen, this is a reflex area for the testes.

22. For an explanation of the harmonic series, review Chapter 1.

Chapter 7

1. Here the analogy of a river into which a dam has been constructed is a useful visual image.

2. In this form of breathing the jaw is relaxed and the teeth do not touch. The breath is drawn up through the nostrils into the upper nasal areas, descends into the trachea by totally relaxing the front of the throat and releasing the glottis. Visualize your throat as

an unobstructed hollow pipe through which the air rushes as it is pulled into the lower lungs by the thoracic diaphram. Exhalation can be either through the nose or the mouth.

3. Points of strong resonance may not always match the designated tones of the pitch-pipe. When this is the case, simply notate the equal-tempered pitch immediately below the resonating pitch for reference purposes.

4. "Chi" is a term commonly found in Chinese medical treatises and is utilized in all martial arts. It is said to be located about three inches below the navel and is considered to be the main source of psycho-physical strength. Incidentally, a friend who is a scholar of Chinese metaphysics, herbal medicine and the martial art of "Tai Chi" says that excessive talking weakens one's "Chi" or strength.

5. If you are living south of the equator, both of you should face north.

6. The word "active" is not an accurate term since all participants are active in the healing process. Here the term is used only as a convenience.

Chapter 8

1. Inayat Khan, op. cit., p.92.
2. Frances Densmore, "The use of Music in the Treatment of the Sick by American Indians", in the *Music and Medicine* (New York, Da Capo Press, 1948), p.35.
3. Ibid, pp. 35-37.
4. In this context it should be noted that the beginnings of our notational system date from about 700 A.D.; the system has evolved through many changes and refinements.
5. Curt Sachs, *The Rise of Music in the Ancient World* (New York, W.W. Norton, 1943), p.58.
6. Walter Addison Jayne, *The Healing Gods of Ancient Civilizations* (New Hyde Park, N.Y., University Books, 1962), p. 98.
7. Lucy Lamay, *Egyptian Mysteries* (New York, Crossroad Pub., 1981), p. 86.
8. Ampere, *Essai sur la Philosophie des Sciences*, quoted by R.A. Schwaller de Lubics in The Temple Man (Brookline, MA, Autumn Press, 1977), p. 19.
9. Ibid, p. 19.
10. Henry George Farmer, "The Music of Ancient Egypt", *Oxford History of Music*, p. 259.
11. Sendry, op. cit., p. 42.
12. Ibid, p. 50.
13. Ibid, p. 244.
14. Ibid, p. 244.
15. Ibid, p. 245.
16. Ibid, p. 245.
17. Ibid, p. 245.
18. Clement of Alexandria, quoted by Oliver Strunk in Source Readings in Music History (New York, W.W. Norton, 1950), p. 59.
19. Bruno Meinecke, "Music and Medicine in Classical Antiquity" *Music and Medicine*, pp. 47-50.
20. Ibid, p. 50.
21. Ibid, p. 55.
22. Ibid, p. 57.
23. Ibid, p. 57.

24. Ibid, p. 58.
25. *Oxford History of Music*, p. 252.
26. Ibid, p. 252.
27. *Music and Medicine*, p. 68.
28. Ibid, p. 147.
29. Ibid, pp. 147-148.
30. Ibid, pp. 148-149.
31. Addresses for some of those mentioned are:

Sonic Research Institute
1775 Old Country Road
Belmont, CA 94002

Sunray Meditation Society
P.O. Box 36
Huntington, VT 05462

Naropa Institute
2130 Arapahoe Ave.
Boulder, CO 80302

Lesley College
29 Everett St.
Cambridge, MA 02238

New England Sound Healers
42 Baker Avenue
Lexington, MA 02173

Boulder College
2235 Broadway
Boulder, CO 80302

New Mexico Academy of Massage and
    Advanced Healing Arts
P.O. Box 932
Santa Fe, NM 87501

Chapter 9

1. Sendry, op.cite., p.48.
2. Ibid., p.48.
3. Strunk, op.cite., p.85.
4. Ibid., p.48. [Author's italics].
5. Ibid., p.94.
6. Chuang Tsu,*The Inner Chapters*, translated by Gia-Fu Feng (New York, Vintage Press, 1974), p.20.
7. Khan, p.7.
8. _____, *The Voice of the Silence*, translated by H.P. Blavatsky (Wheaton, Il, Quest Books, 1970), pp.27-28.
9. Sarangadeva, *Sangita Ratnakara*, translated by R.K. Shringy and Prem Lata Sharma (Delhi, India, 1978), Bk. I, 3 iii-iv. This treatise dates from the thirteenth century. Sarangdeva was both a physician and a musician.
10. Yogi Ramacharaka, *Raja Yoga*, (Chicago, Yogi Publication Society, 1906), p.56.
11. For further information on holographic models of consciousness and their inter-relatedness to quantum physics see: Micheal Talbot, *Mysticism and the New Physics* (New York, Bantam Books, 1980).
12. Michael B. Green, "Superstrings", from "Scientific American", Sept. 1986, pp.48-60.

Chapter 10

1. Paul R. Farnsworth, *The Social Psychology of Music* (Ames, Iowa, The Iowa State University Press, 1969). p. 213.

2. Robert Meagher, *Cave Notes* (Philadelphia, Pennsylvania, Fortress Press, 1985), p. 118.

3. I.M. Alt Shuler, "A Psychiatrist's Experiments with Music as a Therapeutic Agent" in Music and Medicine, ed. by P. M. Schullian and M. Schoen (New York, Schuman, 1948), p. 271.

4. Ibid, p. 270.

5. Lennart Nilson, *Behold Man* (Boston, Little, Brown and Company, 1983), pp. 201-277.

6. Ida H. Hyde, "Effects of Music Upon Electro-Cardiograms and Blood Pressure," in *The Effects of Music*, ed. by M. Schoen (Freeport, N.Y., Books for Libraries Press, 1927), pp. 184-197.

7. D.M. Johnson and M. Irawick, "Influence of Rhythmic Sensory Stimuli Upon Heart-Rate," *Journal of Psychology*, 6, (1938), pp. 303-310.

8. D.S. Ellis and G. Brighouse, "Effects of Music of Respiration and Heart-Rate," *American Journal of Psychology*, 65 (1952), pp. 39-47.

9. C.M. Diserens and H. Fine, *A Psychology of Music*, quoted by Paul Farnsworth in *The Social Psychology of Music*, p. 211.

10. J.R. Miles and C.R. Tilley, "Some Physiological Reactions to Music," *Guy's Hospital Gazzette*, 49, (1935), pp. 319-322.

11. Sid J. Segalowitz, *Two Sides of the Brain* (Englewood Cliffs, N.J., Prentice-Hall, 1983), pp. 45-60; hPeter Russell, *The Brain Book* (New York, Hawthorn Books, 1979), pp. 48-63.

12. Steven Halpern, *Tuning the Human Instrument* (Belmont, Calif.) Spectrum Research Institute, 1980), pp. 161-166.

13. *Music and Medicine* Meinecke, op.cit., p. 71.

14. Robert C. Solomon, *The Passions* (N.Y., Anchor Press, 1977), pp. 254-255 and pp. 280-371.

15. Gerald Jampolsky, *Love is Letting Go of Fear* (New York, Bantam Books, 1981).

16. In this case I am referring primarily to instrumental music. Songs do express emotions but primarily through the lyrics.

17. Igor Stravinsky, *An Autobiography* (New York, Simon and Shuster, 1936), p. 53.

18. Personal letter from Felix Mendelssohn To M.A. Souchay, Berlin, October 5, 1842, quoted in Farnsworth, op. cit., p. 72.

19. For further discussion of this subject: Farnsworth, op. cit., pp. 78-90.

20. Ravi Shankar, *My Music, My Life* (New York, Simon and Schuster, 1968). pp. 26-27.

21. M. Schoen and E.L. Gatewood, "The Mood Effects of Music," in *The Effects of Music*, ed. by Max Schoen, pp. 131-182.

22. Kate Hevner, "Expression in Music: A Discussion of Experimental Studies and Theories," *Psychological Review*, 47 (1935), pp. 246-268.

23. Helen Bonny and Lon Savary, *Music and Your Mind: Listening with a New Consciousness* (N.Y., Harper and Row, 1975).

24. I.A. Taylor and F. Paperte, "Current Theory and Research in the Effects of Music on Behaviour," *Journal of Aesthetics*, 17(2), (1958), pp. 251-258.

Chapter 11

1. Sue Tilberry, "The Right Brain", *Valley Advocate* (jan. 28, 19810, pp. 1, 12, 13, 15.

2. Allan Walker, *A Study in Musical Analysis* (New York, Glencoe Press, 1959), pp. 143-148.

3. Stanley Krippner, "Altered States of Consciousness", in *The Highest State of Cons-*

ciousness, edited by John White (Garden City, N.Y., Anchor Books, 1972), p. 1.
4. Ibid., pp. 1-5.
5. Helen Bonny and Lou Savary, *Music and Your Mind*, (New York, Harper and Row, 1975).
6. Ibid., p. 15.
7. Ibid., p. 15.
8. E.E. Evans-Pritchard, *Witchcraft, Oracles and Magic Among the Azande* (Oxford, Clarendon Press, 1937); H.H. Reese, "The Relation of Music to Diseases of the Brain", *Occupational Therapy Rehabilitation*, 27:12-18 (1948). William Sargant, *Battle for the Mind* (New York, Doubleday, 1957);
9. E.D. Adrian and B.H.C. Mathews, "The Berger Rhythm", *Brain*, 57:355-384 (1934).
10. Andrew Neher, "A Physiological Explanation of Unusual Behavior in Ceremonies Involving Drums", Reprint, journal unknown.
11. Below the first level is the gross world of desires, thoughts and emotions. When the consciousness of the soul enters the spiritual path it enters the first plane of the subtle world which it experiences with its gross consciousness. The second plane is the domain of infinite energy. At the third plane the soul consciousness is capable of performing miracles. The fourth plane is the threshold of the mental world. The fifth plane is that of full consciousness of thought. The sixth plane is the state of full consciousness of feeling. At the seventh plane the soul is fully conscious of the self as infinite and eternal and is also conscious of the source of energy and mind which is the state of God-realization.
12. Meher Baba, *God Speaks* (New York, Dodd, Mead and Company, 1970), pp. 186-187. For a detailed discussion of the seven planes, consult parts V and VI, pp. 40-63.
13. Charles Luk, *The Secrets of Chinese Meditation* (New York, Weiser Books, 1972), p. 32.
14. Ibid., pp. 37-40.
15. Paul Reps, *Zen Flesh, Zen Bones* (Garden City, N.Y., Anchor Books 1975), pp. 163-64.

Chapter 12

1. The basic principles of the Philosophy of Yin/Yang and of the Five Elements are presented here in a very simplified way strictly for the purpose of providing background for Robert McClellan's work with music. Yin/Yang and the theory of the Five Elements is extraordinarily complex and requires years to be thoroughly understood. For those who wish a more thorough understanding several books could be recommended among them; Johathan Klate's excellent book, *The Tao of Acupuncture*, is one of the clearest. It can be ordered by writing to the Pioneer Valley Center for the Healing Arts, 17 Kellogg Avenue, Amherst, MA 01002; (413) 253-2500.

2. In more recent communication with Mr. McClellan, he emphasized that "there are possible imbalances that can result from any one element going out of balance. For example, if water goes out of balance, it could imbalance mostly wood and earth, which seems to be the most probable result, or it could imbalance fire and earth or fire and metal . . . a truly holistic approach necessitates a non-centralized perspective, hence I would stress that the way to effect a rebalancing of the person must include within it not just a water cure, as in the above example, but also balancing aspects of the other two elements as well." Robert McClellan, Personal letter to author, August 24, 1983.

3. Clarification for non-musician readers: The Western equivalent of this scale consists of all the black notes on the piano. Within each octave there are five black keys, each one

of which can serve as a tonic note. The character of the scale and of the music that uses that scale changes radically when a different black note is selected as the tonic.

4. Robert McClellen stresses that the selection of exact pitch names is of less importance than the relationships of the notes of the modes. Any pitch may be selected as a basic tonic note as long as the intervallic relationships follow the pattern that he has outlined. If, for example, the pitch "G" is selected as the tonic, the modes are:

Wood:	G	A	C	D	E	G
Fire:	G	A	B	D	E	G
Earth:	G	A	C	D	F	G
Metal:	G	Bb	C	D	F	G
Water:	G	Bb	C	Eb	F	G

5. All quotes are from an unpublished manuscript and from conversations. Robert McClellan is currently writing a more detailed description of his research and results which, when available, will be far more detailed than this description can be. His "Music of the Five Elements" and "Life Patterns: Music of the Five Elements, Vol. II" are now available in both disc and tape cassette format from Spirit Records, 42 Baker Street, Lexington, MA 02173.

Chapter 13

1. This is the purpose of the Mood Wheel of Kate Herver, illustrated in Chapter Ten.

2. By way of clarification, it should be emphasized that "minimal emotional content" does not imply a music devoid of expression. Music of high emotional content relies on melodic conflict resulting from themes of a contrasting nature, rapid harmonic changes and strenuous rhythmic movement. During the course of a composition, the conflict reaches toward a dramatic catharsis that is followed by resolution. In music of minimal emotional content no such conflict occurs — no struggle, no drama. Examples include the raga styles of India, Indonesian gamelan music and music by some of the younger American composers such as Terry Riley, Phillip Glass, Meredith Monk, Barbara Benary and Steve Reich.

3. This is not merely a poetic analogy. As an experiment you might try humming one pitch to yourself throughout an entire day, stopping only when interacting with other people and when inhaling or swallowing. At the end of the day assess the cumulative effect upon you and the quality of the day you have just experienced.

4. "Motion...always implies something that does not move or that moves differently — a frame, a background, against which the motion appears as motion.", Victor Zuzkerkandl, *Sound and Symbol* (Princeton, N.J., Princeton University Press, 1956), p. 95.

5. Zuckerkandl expresses this concept in the following way:

> No musical tone is sufficient unto itself; and as each musical tone points beyond itself, reaches, as it were, a hand to the next, so we too, as these hands reach out, listen tensely and expectantly for each next tone. To be auditively in the tone now sounding means, then, always being ahead of it too, on the way to the next tone.

Ibid., p. 94.

6. Beat, or pulse, is found in music of all cultures and has a musical relationship to rhythm. However, our method of notating rhythm into measures is characteristically Western.

7. For further discussion of this concept, philosopher Susan Langer offers many valuable and convincing insights. *Feeling and Form*, Chapter 7 entitled "The Image of Time" is particularly useful. (New York, Charles Scribner's Sons, 1953), pp. 104-119.

Epilogue

1. T.S. Eliot, *Four Quartets* (New York, Harcourt, Brace and World, Inc., 1943), p. 15.

Appendix A

1. Albert C. Muller, "Theoretical and Experimental Aspects of Color Therapy," paper presented at the second annual meeting of the Color Research Center, Arlington, VA, June 19-20, 1976.
2. I recently heard a story of a young piano student who, after being introduced to the names of the pitches of the piano keyboard, asked "What is between the keys?" The teacher responded with one word, "Nothing".
3. Actually, the designation of the light spectrum into seven distinct colors resulted from observing rainbows and glass prisms. Our system of pitch names is the result of a gradual evolution over a 1,000-year period.
4. We hear all the frequencies of the sound spectrum when we hear a jet engine at close range. Incidently, the acoustical term is "white noise".
5. ed., op. cit., p. 125.
6. The light frequencies have been adjusted to correspond more closely to our equal-tempered pitch scale.
7. Roland Hunt, Fragrant and Radiant Healing Symphony (London. H.G. White Publishers, 1937). We are given no information on the author, his sources or evidence for his claims.
9. Ibid., p. 40.
10. Ibid., p. 45.
11. The reader is advised to review the Chapter on the physical manifestation of sound.
12. Dane Rudhyar, *The Magic of Tone and the Art of Music* (Boulder, CO., Shambhala Books, 1982), p. 8.
13. William David, *The Harmonies of Sound, Color and Vibration* (Marina del Ray, CA, DeVorss, 1980). This recent book gives yet another interpretation of the correspondences of color and pitch: Middle "C" - Red, "D" - Green, "E" - Yellow, "F" - Purple Violet, "G" - Orange, "A" - Indigo, "B" - Blue. The author does not explain the origin of there correspondences.